DR. DORSETT D SMITH

Almost a *Christian*

A REBUKE TO LUKE-WARM CHRISTIANITY

"The Almost Christian is an effort to challenge lukewarm Almost Christians to repentance by exposing the error in the liberal postmodern church. The Book teaches historic biblical Christianity as taught by the Reformers. Each chapter is suitable for discussion in a small group bible study."

INK START MEDIA
265 Eastchester Dr Ste 133 #102
High Point NC 27262

Almost a Christian

A REBUKE TO LUKE-WARM CHRISTIANITY

REVISED EDITION
2023

DR. DORSETT D SMITH

Dedicated to my reformed brothers. My teaching has been influenced and inspired by those that have gone before me, particularly by the Puritan Saints, Calvin, Luther, Jonathan Edwards, John Flavel, and John Bunyan. I thank R.C. Sproul, Michael Horton, Brian Hoekstra, John Piper, and my Christian brothers and sisters for their prayers, example, and encouragement.

Table of Contents

Preface..v

Chapter 1 1
   "Almost a Christian" Discovered

Chapter 2 28
   Original Sin

Chapter 3 41
   What about the Blood?
   Covenant Theology

Chapter 4 54
   Legalism and Self-Righteousness

Chapter 5 64
   Biblical Conversion

Chapter 6 73
   Repentance

Chapter 7 86
   Pride

Chapter 8 92
   Entitlement Mentality

Chapter 9 99
   Bondservice and Submission

Chapter 10 105
   Postmodernism and Personal Freedom

Chapter 11 111
   Confession and Contrition

Chapter 12 118
   The Holy Spirit

Chapter 13 131
   The Holy Spirit as Revealer of Mystery

Chapter 14 141
   The Holy Spirit as Healer

Chapter 15 178
The Root of Bitterness

Chapter 16 . . . . **183**
What is a Spiritual Archetype?

Chapter 17 193
Gifts of the Spirit

Chapter 18 202
Listen and Obey

Chapter19 208
True and False Compassion

Chapter 20 224
Judgement versus Discernment

Chapter 21 230
Love of God

Chapter 22 237
Suffering and Persecution

Chapter 23 250
The Afterlife

Chapter 24 273
Situational Eschatology

Chapter 25 300
Christian Liberty

Chapter 26 305
Worship

Chapter 27 322
The Fear of God

Chapter 28 333
Christian Idolatry

Chapter 29 341
Conclusion

Chapter 30 343
Further Reading

Preface

This book is an uncompromising attempt to call the "Almost a Christian" to repentance and expose error. Biblical truth is absolute truth and offends postmodernists, who reject absolutes. The Christian claim that we have the only truth is non-negotiable and under heavy assault in Western culture. Many of my important comments have been shaped by those great saints who have gone before me, and I reference them in the text. Some readers may want further exegesis of certain passages and proof texts. Others may question why I have focused only on certain theological issues because of the length of the book precludes more extensive discussion. I have made the difficult choice to focus on the important current issues that my men's Bible leadership study struggles with rather than speaking to other important theological issues. I am more interested in making people think and challenging them, rather than having them agree with me on every theological issue. The biblical and prophetic call to Jeremiah and God's leadership remains: *"To root out and pull down, to destroy and to throw down, to build and plant"* (Jer 1:10).

Each chapter has been used as a resource for discussion in our Bible study. **The chapters are not necessarily to be read sequentially but present a series of important issues in the post-modern culture of today. This book is a call for the church to reexamine its foundations.**

I have tried to provide scriptural references for every important statement. I will let the reader struggle with God and not me about the truth statements of the Word of God. Like many scholars, my gift often is to complicate rather than simplify; for this I apologize to the reader. I am a fallen sinner saved by grace and fully recognize that my theology is imperfect but continually improving. I am deeply grateful to others for their spiritual insights, and this book contains very little that is original with me. I hopefully remain teachable and correctable and appreciative of comments and corrections from my readers. I have been taught and teach others to "*chew and swallow the good food and spit out the bones.*" I hope and pray that this book will be a blessing to everyone.

Dorsett D. Smith MD

Chapter 1

"Almost a Christian" Discovered

"Almost thou persuadest me to be a Christian." (Acts 26:28)

King Agrippa was almost successfully persuaded and convinced by Paul to place his faith in Jesus. The cost to King Agrippa would have been the possible loss of his secular kingdom followed by disgrace and death. Many are "almost a Christian," but their faith will fail when tested by fire.

What does this mean for those who call themselves Christian? Many are almost Christians like the five virgins in the parable of the ten virgins given by Jesus in Matthew 25:1–13. The ten virgins walked together, all expecting to meet the groom (typology of Jesus), and in a metaphorical way, they were members of the same church. Yet five virgins who did not have enough oil in their lamps were not members of the true church of Christ. Evidently, they had zeal without knowledge, yet all hoped in Christ.

Every church is a mixture, and God is separating a people for Himself. The tares and wheat grow together only to be separated at the call for the marriage supper of the lamb (Matthew 13:24–30). This does not mean that the disciple of Christ is to ignore those who pretend to be of Christ. God chooses those who are His, but we are to exhort those who think they are Christians but are not. We have a responsibility to bring the call for faith, repentance, conviction, and contrition for sin, and the remedy through the cross of Christ to produce true disciples. Some begin their Christian experience as hypocrites later to be converted.

1

We live in twenty-first century America where the gospel has been confused with mere religion or "if that's your thing, then that is okay with me, but I have my own gospel." The good news has been redefined by modernists. **Postmodern man has no fixed objective standard of right or wrong. Man has become a law unto himself. His life choices are arbitrary, and he cannot understand God's absolute standard without the conviction of the Holy Spirit. Salvation has always been a work of the Holy Spirit and has never been based on a better argument or the work of the flesh.** Francis Schaeffer was a twentieth-century prophet and a keen discerner of postmodern society. He commented that:

> The central problem of our age is not liberalism or modernism, nor the old Roman Catholicism or the new Roman Catholicism, nor the threat of communism, nor even the threat of rationalism and the monolithic consensus which surrounds us, nor I would add today, postmodernism or materialistic consumerism or visceral sensualism or whatever. All these are dangerous but not the primary threat. **The real problem is this: the church of the Lord Jesus Christ, individually or corporately, tending to do the *Lord's work in the power of the flesh rather than of the Spirit.*** The central problem is always in the midst of the people of God, not in the circumstances surrounding them." (Francis A. Schaeffer, *No Little People* Wheaton, 2003, page 66)

While I have the greatest respect for Schaeffer, I differ a little with Schaeffer in that I think **the problem with Western Christianity is also the failure to preach, live, or model the complete gospel that is focused on the wrath of God and the hopelessness of undeserving humanity without the redemptive work of Jesus on the cross.** The purpose of this book is to summarize the basic essentials of the Good News of Jesus Christ, which will be discussed in more details in the following chapters.

What is happening to church life in America today?

> Megachurches are attracting disenfranchised Americans. Approximately 7% of churches are megachurches and attract about 17% of churchgoers. About 80% are transfers from other churches. Approximately 46% attend small churches of 100 or less and 37% attend churches from 100 to 500 churchgoers. (www.Barna.com)

Approximately 4,000 churches close every year. Os Guinness writes the unchurched are really "semi-churched or refugees from three groups: legalistic fundamentalism, watered-down liberalism, and over ritualistic traditionalism." Contemporary megachurch pastors offer entertainment, anonymity, and often a feel-good message that avoids personal cost and prevents a deeper understanding of threatening theological issues such as election, the inspiration of Scripture, obedience, grace, God's wrath, holiness, justice, and sovereignty, and most of all, the cost of discipleship.

The product of most churches has been feel-good and self-satisfied "Almost Christians," who are lost <u>and</u> don't know it! A 2018 survey conducted by the Cultural Research Center at Arizona Christian University finds that American adults today increasingly adopt a "salvation-can-be-earned" perspective. A plurality of adults (48 percent) believes that if a person is generally good, or does enough good things during their life, they will "earn" a place in heaven. Only one-third of adults (35 percent) disagree.

A majority of Americans who describe themselves as Christian (52 percent) also accept a "works-oriented" means to God's acceptance—even those associated with churches whose official doctrine says eternal salvation comes only from embracing Jesus Christ as savior. Almost half of all adults associated with Pentecostal (46 percent), main-line Protestant (44 percent), and evangelical (41 percent) churches, as well as nearly two-thirds of Catholics (70 percent), hold that view.

While about 65 percent of American adults describe themselves as Christians, only about half (54 percent) believe they will experience heaven after they die. Only one-third of adults (33 percent) believe they will go to heaven solely because of confessing their sins and embracing Jesus as their savior. Another one-in-five expecting to experience heaven are counting on earning their way in or because they embrace universalism (i.e., that God will let all people into heaven).

Among those with other views, 15 percent said they don't know what will happen after they die; 13 percent said there is no life after death; 8 percent expect to be reincarnated; and another 8 percent believe they will go to a place of purification prior to entering heaven. A mere 2 percent believe they will go to hell.

Based on age groups, just 20 percent of people aged 18 to 29 believe that when they die, they will go to heaven only because they have confessed their sins and have accepted Jesus as their savior; 30 percent of those 30 to 49 and 40 percent of adults 50 and older hold that belief. Women were more likely than men (36 percent versus 30 percent, respectively), and those who have conservative political views were much more likely to hold that belief (52 percent) than were political moderates (28 percent) or liberals (16 percent). More than one-third of whites and blacks (35 percent each) also held this view compared to only one quarter of Hispanics (25 percent).

According to another 2018 Pew Research Center report, most Christian adults who self-identified as Christians also hold New Age beliefs characterized by reincarnation, astrology, psychics, and the presence of spiritual energy in animistic objects like mountains and trees. Overall, roughly 6 in 10 American evangelicals and 70% of Roman Catholics believe in one of these New Age beliefs. Instead of replacing traditional religious doctrines, New Age beliefs are blended in with them (syncretism).

Perhaps part of the problem of nominal Christians is a misunderstanding of the word "belief"! Modern man's understanding is that belief is intellectual assent. Christian belief is thought to be acceptance of a set of core beliefs such as the virgin birth, death and resurrection of Christ, the Trinity, the return of Christ for His saints, and the truth and inerrancy of Scripture. **The acceptance of core beliefs of Christianity as true does not make you a Christian! Sound doctrine is extremely important but doesn't save us. Our doctrine doesn't save us from pride, humility, presumption, arrogance and living for ourselves. Christ saves us through the death of self to a new life by the Holy Spirit. Many hope in educational regeneration, others in baptismal regeneration, others in a type of decisional regeneration. If you never have had a radical change in your nature, values, and attitudes resulting in a love of God and His word, as well as personal holiness, you probably are not saved.** The vast majority of people who claim to be Christians have been deceived by the Western culture that has confused intellectual acceptance of core values without the true faith to that of a born-again redeemed Christian. True Christianity is costly because obedience to God's law puts a true Christian at odds with Western moral values on marriage, homosexuality, abortion, cohabitation, etc. Few are willing to take up the cross and face rejection and persecution by their peers unless they have been regenerated or born again by the Holy Spirit. **Youth today want a gospel that is self-affirming, not self-denying.** (Matt 16:24)

> *"Examine yourselves whether ye be in the faith, prove your own selves, etc."*
>
> —(2Corinthians 13:5 KJV)

> *"A true revival means nothing less than a revolution, casting out the spirit of worldliness and selfishness, and making God and His love triumph in the heart and life."*
>
> —Andrew Murray

"Strengthening the souls of the disciples, encouraging them to continue in the faith, and saying that through many tribulations we must enter the kingdom of God."

—(Acts 14:22)

The English word *believe* is not a biblical word but only a poor substitute for the original Greek and Hebrew word meanings. When reading Scripture, the English word believe is used in many translations of the original Greek for the Greek word *pistis*, such as in Acts 16:31. *"Believe (pisteuo) in the Lord Jesus, and you will be saved."* **It is better to think of the original Greek usage of noun *pistis* or verb *pisteuo* meaning to have faith, to trust Him and to totally surrender to Him versus the English meaning of the word belief meaning to have intellectual understanding or cognitive knowledge. Intellectual acceptance is not the same as true biblical faith**.

"You believe that God is one; you do well. Even the demons believe— and shudder!" (James 2:19) The Greek verb *pisteuein* or the noun *pistis* means to have faith in, to trust in, hope in, and to be entirely surrendered to Jesus as Lord. True faith is desperate faith and a costly faith which requires the believer to give up all, repent, and follow Him. (Matt10:38,16:24-29,19:21; Luke 9:24-27,14:27) **Millions of "almost Christians" believe intellectually and profess Christ but do not possess saving faith which requires not only propositional faith or cognitive faith but God-given supernatural spiritual faith with complete surrender to the risen Christ. We are justified before God by not only what we know but who we know!** We must be born again by the Holy Spirit. True faith is relational not intellectual.

In the Old Testament, the Hebrew verb translated as belief means, for the most part, 'to be true; to be true' or 'be trustworthy' (*aman*). Lying behind this is the root meaning 'solid,' 'firm.' This sense of 'to be true' is intensified in the passive form of the verb so that one can speak of a person

as 'trustworthy' or 'reliable.' The causative form of the verb suggests the acceptance of someone as trustworthy or dependable. Thus, one accepts God as trustworthy and believes his word (Deut. 9:23) and his promises, as is the case with Abraham in Gen. 15:1-6: "*And he believed the Lord; and he reckoned it to him as righteousness.*" It has been argued that it is the use of the verb in the causative form that encompasses the most personal relationship of faith between God and the believer. (Deut. 7:6-7: *"the Lord your God has chosen you to be a people for his own possession")* and his loving-kindness is demonstrated by the many blessings they have received. This covenant relationship presupposes a mutuality of obligation: Deut. 7:9: "*Know therefore that the Lord your God is God, the faithful God who keeps covenant and steadfast love with those who love him and keep his commandments.*" Israel's response of faith is possible only because of God's prior and continued faithfulness. Isa. 43:10: "*You are my witnesses,' says the Lord, 'and my servant whom I have chosen, that you may know and believe and understand that I am He.'*" Notice God is the one that does the choosing. Knowledge is not used here in a speculative sense; the reference is to the knowledge of God's fidelity and loving-kindness experienced personally and in history.[1]

I often use the example of a man who fell over the edge of the Grand Canyon. As he was falling, he reached out and grabbed a branch of a small sampling that was extending out of the canyon wall. His only hope of escaping death was to hang onto the small branch. This is a desperate place where there has to be a complete trust in that small branch to keep him alive until help comes. Faith requires that a man places entire hope and trust in God alone for his salvation. This is a radical faith that doesn't trust in man or in one's own works, or in one's own righteousness, but only in God alone based on His righteousness and His love. This is called by many as "Lordship salvation."

1   Achtemeier, P. J., Harper & Row and Society of Biblical Literature. (1985). In <u>Harper's Bible dictionary</u> (1st ed., p. 299). San Francisco: Harper & Row.

It is important to separate Gospel and Law. <u>The Gospel</u> is about telling of God's redemption of man and deliverance from an evil world of death and decay by the blood sacrifice of God's son, Jesus Christ. The Gospel is about grace not works, or about receiving more than doing. We are saved by receiving the completed work of Christ on the cross for our sins with thanksgiving and then placing our trust (faith) in Christ's redeeming work for us.

<u>The Law</u> requires works, doing things for God to earn our salvation. Works build up self. Some only want a religion that they earn and can be proud of their own self-aggrandizing works. Salvation is about what Christ has already done for us by shedding His blood on the cross to purchase our salvation; not what we have done for Him or could ever do for Him, which is Law or works. The call of Christ is to die to self and have no hope in our good deeds. Our hope is to be in Christ alone and His finished work on the cross. True faith will always be followed by spirit-led works. (See James 2:14-26)

The object of saving faith is the whole revealed Word of God. Faith accepts and believes it as the very truth most sure. But the special act of faith which unites to Christ has as its object the person and the work of the Lord Jesus Christ (John 7:38; Acts 16:31). This is the specific act of faith by which a sinner is justified before God (Rom. 3:22, 25; Gal. 2:16; Phil. 3:9; John 3:16–36; Acts 10:43; 16:31). In this act of faith, the believer appropriates and rests on <u>Christ alone as Mediator</u> in all his offices. The oft quoted verse from Hebrews, *"Now faith is the assurance of things hoped for, the conviction of things not seen"* (11:1), and in chapter 12 verse 2 the author of Hebrews reminds us that our faith is given to us and perfected by the work of the Holy Spirit: *"looking to Jesus, the founder and perfecter of our faith, who for the joy that was set before him endured the cross, despising the shame, and is seated at the right hand of the throne of God."*

We have lost our way and are confused about the message of the gospel as well as the messenger. Perhaps, it's best to begin our discussion in defining what a Christian is. America is in crisis and rapidly becoming post-Christian like Scotland, where approximately 2–3 percent of the population is Christian (barna.org). To be a Christian, one must not only intellectually believe certain doctrinal things but also know God personally and relationally as well as intellectually and in a manner that involves religious experience and entails moral commitment. **It means to be *born again* or to be transformed by the Holy Spirit to be a new creature in Christ. Saving faith is entirely a work of the Holy Spirit.**

To be a Christian is to have "saving faith" that God, who stands at the beginning and is at the end of all things. Faith is given by grace and is holy, righteous, transcendent, and the creator of all things. All men are born sinners without hope of knowing God except by the grace of God. God has been, from eternity, seeking a people for Himself that will give all glory to Him. He sent His sinless Son to become human flesh, suffer death and humiliation, and rise bodily from the dead to atone for man's sins. He saved all men from the consequences of human sin, while knowing that only some would receive His free gift of salvation (2 Pet 3:9; 1 Tim 2:4). To trust in Scripture is to understand that Jesus has given to us as an authoritative exact representation of God the Father, not revealing Him in essentially the same kind of way as any other genuine prophet. Rather, it is to believe that in the active person of Jesus, who was more than a prophet, but the sinless Son of God who died on the cross, was resurrected from the dead and is the redeemer of His elect. He died for our sins, and therefore, **apart from Jesus, there is no hope for man.** The fatherhood of God would be essentially different had He not give His son for propitiation or atonement of humanity.

In other words, Christians deny that we can separate the being or nature of God from the history and person of Christ, through His work on the cross and His resurrection; and it is to affirm the basic meaning of the doctrines of the virgin birth, divine incarnation, crucifixion, resurrection, ascension, atoning work on the cross, and of the work of the Holy Spirit. It is Christ who now sits at the right hand of the Father and rules and reigns forever. Furthermore, we separate the distinct transcendent nature of the trinitarian God, the creator and sustainer of the universe, from ourselves as mere mortal men. **The object of saving faith is Jesus Christ as depicted in the whole revealed Word of God.** Faith accepts and believes Scripture as the very truth most sure. But the special act of faith which unites us to Christ has as its object the person and the work of the Lord Jesus Christ (John 7:38; Acts 16:31). This is the specific act of faith by which a sinner is justified before God (Rom. 3:22, 25; Gal. 2:16; Phil. 3:9; John 3:16–36; Acts 10:43; 16:31). In this act of faith, the believer appropriates and rests on Christ alone who forever intercedes for us as mediator before God our Father. (1 Kings 9:3; Pss. 34:15; 65:2; Matt. 7:11; Romans 8:26-27;1 John 5:15).

Religion by itself, without Christ as center, as revealed by the Holy Spirit, is an illusion in name and form and can neither comfort nor save. Man thinks because he knows about God that he knows God. God can only be known "*extra nos*" or outside of the mind, through the gift of the Holy Spirit. That statement sounds anti-intellectual, but we know Christ in our hearts while our heads can deceive us. The head seeks truth, and the heart seeks goodness and a meaningful relationship. Salvation is relational, not intellectual. Blaise Pascal, 17th century French philosopher and mathematician and one of the world's great intellectuals, wrote in his classic apologetic work *Pensées,* that: "*the heart has its reasons for which reason knows nothing . . . . **It is the heart which perceives God and not the reason.**"* Intuitive knowledge is not always explainable in rational terms, but if we have no witness of God in our hearts similar to that emotional witness with people we love, then we don't know Him (Exod 29:46; Lev 26:12; John 14:21; Rev 21:3)! Many critics call Christians stupid, ignorant, and foolish because they seem too emotional and not rational. Since we are fallible creatures, our emotions sometimes misperceive their objects; moral arguments that appeal to emotions are often met with the objection that emotions cannot possibly serve as evidence for the existence of objective proof of God since emotions can be deceived and manipulated. Reason alone can go only so far. I could have carefully reasoned intellectually about a relationship with my wife, but eventually I had to experience that relationship emotionally. To know God is to also know Him also rationally and emotionally just as we experience His wonder in creation (Psalm 19:1).

Biblical faith is the product of a miraculous regeneration (being born again) of the inner man's sinful heart, produced by the Holy Spirit, that opens the heart to true faith, given by grace, and not man's efforts or intellectual achievement. When we say man is saved by grace, we mean that saving faith is impossible, because of man's original sin nature, without the work of the Holy Spirit. Man's moral inability to save himself is overcome by the enabling power of the Holy Spirit. It is God's sovereign monergistic initiative that only saves man. **He chooses us; we do not choose Him** but gladly receive His gift of salvation (John 6:37, 6:44, 6:63; 6:65; 10:28; 15:16).

God is transcendent or outside of man. Modern Western man is hoping to find the god within or an immanent god but finds only the god of self-creation, who is like a genie in a bottle or rabbit's foot who only needs to be rubbed the right way to bring gifts of promotion, health, healed relationships, and wealth. This pagan *"rabbit's foot religion"* taps into man's greed and deepest needs for praise of men, recognition, fame, power, and fortune.

The favorite Scripture used by "*name it and claim it*" hyper-faith teachers is Luke 11:9–10: "*So I say to you, ask, and it will be given to you; seek, and you will find; knock, and it will be opened to you. For everyone who asks, receives; and he who seeks, finds; and to him who knocks, it will be opened.*" Proof texting or taking Scripture out of context ignores the call of Christ to give up *all*:

> **"If anyone wishes to come after Me, he must deny himself, and take up his cross and follow Me.** *For whoever wishes to save his life will lose it; but whoever loses his life for My sake will find it. For what will it profit a man if he gains the whole world and forfeits his soul? Or what will a man give in exchange for his soul?*"
>
> —(Matt 16:24–26)

> "*Life is wasted if we do not grasp the glory of the cross, cherish it for the treasure that it is, and cleave to it as the highest price of every pleasure and the deepest comfort in every pain. What was once foolishness to us-a crucified God-must become our wisdom and our power and our only boast in this world.*"
>
> —John Piper

Once we have died to self and are living for Christ, the things of this world lose their allure. Our desires change from worldly passions to asking God those things that build His Kingdom and His Glory, not our own kingdom.

The word **SALVATION** is usually misunderstood and thought by many to mean only the protection from the wrath of God, physical danger, moral distress, etc. (Ex 15:2; Ps 116:6) and a free ticket to heaven and eternal bliss. (Eph 2:8; Rom 5:21) **The question always has been what are we saved from? It is not only the wrath of God but the dominion of sin** (Rom 1:8, 3:9, 5:9) **Biblical salvation also means being saved from Self as well as the world, the flesh, and the devil**. (1 John 2:15-17, 5:19)

We think we can remain world- and self-centered and still go to heaven! True salvation frees us from the habits of sin that enslave us and self-centeredness. (Eph 4-17-24; I Thes 4:3-8; Titus 2:11-3:6) Salvation brings the promise of spiritual wholeness and peace. Our focus becomes outward rather than inward.

> *Salvation is thought easy, because of a mistake about faith: "Oh, say they, if a man does but believe, then heaven is his, Christ is his: as to him that believes not condemnation belongs." Now all natural men think it's very easy to believe. What to trust Christ with all thy heart? How ready is every unregenerate man to say, he does it? To presume is easy, to be secure and self-flattering is easy: but out of that same true sense of sin and deep humiliation for it, truly to rely on God's grace: this the godly heart finds not to be done without many conflicts in spiritual agony; faith therefore made the work of God spirit, and it is that which the devil does most oppose, because that does the most to withstand him.* (Spiritual Refining, The Anatomy of True and False Conversion, Anthony Burgess, International Outreach Inc., Ames, Iowa, 1652,1996 p133)

Scripture reminds us that "*broad is the way that leads to destruction, and narrow and hard is the way that leads to life and **few will find it.**"* (Matt 7:13-14)

The bait of Satan has always been that you can "have it all" because God loves you. **This is a deceptive entitlement message that if we worship God and obey His commandments, then God owes us blessings**. This was the same temptation to Jesus in Luke 4:5–6 when Satan took Jesus to a high mountain and offered Him all the kingdoms of this world if He would worship him. Again, this is the same message preached to the Western church that God wants to bless us and give us health and wealth. This is half of the gospel. The whole gospel message is that God wants to slay us! **The gospel**

message is to come and die to self, give up all, and follow me (Matt 16:24–25, 19:22; Mark 8:35–39; Luke 9:23–25). **If God loves us, He will discipline us as children** (Hebrews 12:2–12). We live in a fallen, wicked world, and like the Apostle Paul, we will face persecution, troubles, and trials that our loving God allows for the purpose of molding us in His image.

Postmodern man desires his independence and is looking to get from God rather than give to God. He chooses what he wants to believe and judges Scripture through the lens of his postmodern culture of situational ethics and multiculturalism. **Postmodern man's truth is largely subjective, and he avoids terms like absolute truth and the coming judgment of sinners**. It is largely "feelism," or emotionally based, and elevates the subjective over the objective in such things as Scripture, creeds, and confessions. He desires to be spiritual but not religious. His faith is in himself and "finding the spirit within himself" and not in God. The postmodern world has lost its center, and man wants to be as God. Man has become the center and now judges the religious world and Scripture from his own secular cultural perspective. Public opinion has become the referee of truth. Christian pundits have remarked that "God made man in His image, and man has been trying to return the favor ever since."

God is the true center and meaning of all things. Scripture judges the world and its culture and therefore is hated by the world. The true Christian sees the world through the lens of Scripture, not postmodern culture, and mores. **Modern Christian scholarship attempts to make the hard truths of Scripture more palatable and less offensive.** The truths of God offend and will always do so as exemplified in contemporary views of marriage, homosexuality, women's rights, abortion, euthanasia, the death penalty, and many other moral questions. Jesus told us in John 17:17 that: *"The spirit of truth, whom the world cannot receive, because it neither sees Him nor knows Him."* Understanding Scripture comes through knowing the Author of Scripture as revealed by the Holy Spirit. (I John 2:27)

"No one can have true intellectual knowledge of God unless he first has faith in accordingly, he's morally in tune with God. (Cornelius Van Til)

The postmodern worldview is multicultural and pantheistic, and many theologians, in an effort to simplify, have called the postmodern pantheistic camp "*One-ism*" meaning everything is of one essence or that any or all spirituality leads to one type of all-encompassing supernatural salvation. There is no need of Christ since man is his own god. God's law is rejected, and man becomes the lawgiver and finds right and wrong in the self. (Romans 1:18-32) Ultimately *Oneism* is about the self-worship and finding meaning and purpose for self. It is pagan syncretism and a new all-inclusive atheism that rejects Christianity. Eastern religions call this Nirvana, or Brahman. Others call this the "Omega Point" or some type of transhumanism or singularity in that all is divine (paganism). It is a form of deism where the spiritual powers of the universe are nonjudgmental and not involved in the regular affairs of men. There has been a converging of diverse different religions such as Catholicism, Islam, Judaism, and Eastern religions by the current Catholic Pope who has stated that all religions lead to the same god and all men can become gods! (Mormonism teaches this.) This is more than heresy; it is apostasy! It is also uncritical moral religious pluralism. (Peter Jones, **One or Two**, Main Entry Ed, Escondido CA, 2015)

Christianity is characterized by *"Two-ism,"*: God and man. Where there would be a convergence between sinful man and a Holy God, where God is Lord and man is a submitted bond servant. (Greek *Dulos*) Right and wrong is found in God and His law rather than the self. Our God is beyond ourselves, self-existent, self-sufficient, transcendent, immutable, omniscient, majestic, omnipotent, trustworthy, holy, wise, everlasting, incapable of evil, and is our Lawgiver and Judge. Yet He is personable and relational. He is a completely different being. He is a holy God of love and truth, is jealous for His children, and has burning anger or wrath against unrighteousness and ungodliness. He is unsearchable and knows all things and has foreknowledge of all things. He is full of glory and honor. His greatness and character are beyond man's comprehension. Jesus, "who being in the very nature of God, did not consider equality with God something to be grasped" (Philippians 2:6). Jesus Christ came as an example of the love of God for His creation and the promise of redemption for those who would trust in Jesus by faith.

Scripture tells us that Jesus and the Father are One in the trinitarian sense (Deut 6:4; John 14:7) and are entirely different from us fallen men. In Jesus, "The fullness of deity dwells bodily"; yet Paul reminds us "For now we see in a mirror, dimly, but then face to face. Now I know in part, but then I shall know just as I also am known." (1 Cor 13:12) The greatness, glory, honor, and holiness of God can only be seen dimly but will be known fully when Christ returns for His Church. Sinful man cannot approach our holy God except through the sacrificial work of His Son Jesus Christ through His Holy Spirit. "Two-ism" means our Father God, who is distinctly different from man, and His unique salvation is distinct from all other religions. There is only one way to a holy God, which is on His terms, as opposed to the many ways of "One-ism." One-ism believes that man is basically good, without the curse of original sin, and equal to God, and therefore God can be approached on man's own terms (Pelagianism)!

"In the past, the difficulty in accepting Christianity was its second point salvation. Everyone in pre-modern societies knew sin was real, andmany doubted their salvation. Today it's the exact opposite: everybody is saved, but there's no sin to be saved from. Thus, what originally came into the world as "good news" strikes the modern Man as bad news, as guilt ridden, moralistic, and judgmental. For the modern man is no longer *"convinced of sin, of righteousness, and of judgment."* (John 16:8) (Peter Kreeft, <u>Christianity for Modern Pagans: Pascal's Pensees Edited, Outlined, and Explained,</u> Ignatius Press 1993, p26)

I am a Christian scholar, who thinks good scholarship is essential for good exegesis. However, all of our intellectual knowledge and scholarship cannot understand the transcendent nature of God. Too many well-meaning Christians try to explain God to an unregenerate culture and, in the process, compromise the Gospel message of the transcendent God of "pick up your cross and follow me!" **The Bible message is that understanding follows saving faith**. This was Christ's message to Nicodemus (John 3:1–12). Nicodemus was a leader of the Jews, righteous according to the law, as well as a Bible scholar like many theologians of today, yet unconverted. He knew about the coming messiah but was not sure if Jesus was the Son of God. Nicodemus was not born again but curious about Jesus. **We don't understand to believe, but when we believe, we begin to understand. Augustine declared "believe that you may understand."**

Anselm, Archbishop of Canterbury's (1093-1109AD) definition of theology (the study of and understanding of God) was *Credo ut intelligam* **("I believe in order that I may understand").** We accept Christ first and then by the illumination of the Holy Spirit begin an intellectual journey of understanding God. This is why Jesus said to Nicodemus that to understand the things of God you must be **"born again."** The Holy Spirit must first regenerate or make us "born again" in order for us to see the Kingdom of God. "Truly, truly, I say to you, unless one is born again, he cannot see the kingdom of God" (John 3:3). Jesus came to renew our minds, not just change them.

"And do not be conformed to this world but be transformed (to be remodeled or changed into another form) by the renewing (renew of thought and will) of your mind, so that you may prove what the will of God is, that which is good and acceptable and perfect."

—Romans 12:2 AMP)

The postmodern is infatuated with the novel, the latest news, and the latest fad. Biblical truth is also old truth and never changes. Biblical scholarship is about discovering the old truth, not in finding newer revelations in Scripture. Francis Turretin said: "For since each of the oldest things is most true, no better stamp can be given especially in sacred argument than that something has more novelty. Old is best here and that which goes back to earliest antiquity." (*Institutes of Elenctic Theology*, by Francis Turretin)

Kierkegaard with great insight comments:

> **"The matter is quite simple. The Bible is very easy to understand. But we Christians are a bunch of scheming swindlers. We pretend to be unable to understand it because we know very well that the minute, we understand we are obliged to act accordingly**. Take any words in the New Testament and forget everything except pledging yourself to act accordingly. My God, you will say, if I do that my whole life will be ruined. How would I ever get on in the world? Herein lies the real place of Christian scholarship. (Liberal) Christian scholarship is the Church's prodigious invention to defend itself against the Bible, to ensure that we can continue to be good Christians without the Bible coming too close. Oh, priceless scholarship, what would we do without you? Dreadful it is to fall into the hands of the living God. Yes, it is even dreadful to be alone with the New Testament."

The things that need most to be pressed on men's attention are those mighty works of the Holy Spirit, inward repentance, inward faith, inward hope, inward hatred of sin, inward fear of the Lord, and inward love of God's law. *When we say to men to take comfort in their baptism or Church membership, it is not merely a horrible mistake, but cruel and misleading*. Popularity obtained by pandering to the senses or the sentiment of our hearers as well as making false promises is not worth anything. Many churches today draw crowds with sensational theater, music, performances, and false promises of help and wholeness. Many confuse an emotional experience with the touch of the Holy Spirit. Worshippers, who are not content with the Bible, the cross of Christ, simple prayers and simple praise, are worshippers of little value. The popular paradigm of present-day Christianity focuses on getting people to make a "decision for Christ," as if one decision is all that we need to make as opposed to making a daily decision to submit and obey Him.

Salvation can be "**EVENT CHRISTIANITY**" or "**PROCESS CHRISTIANITY**". Event Christians rely on an experience such as coming forward at a crusade or church service to receive Christ as savior, but not Lord. Unfortunately, most "Event Christians" place their hope in an experience that fades with time and does not result in a permanent ongoing transformative life. They may feel comfort that they have "fire insurance." The focus remains on self or what God can do for me. There is no willingness to suffer for Christ or face persecution. The major evangelical thrust is what author Larry Crabb calls **COMFORT CHRISTIANITY**. Christian marketers encourage Christians to settle for believing that God's good news is that accepting Christ means believing that he or she will go to heaven without further obedience to God's commandments and a constantly growing relationship with Christ. Their message is simple; God loves you and wants to bless you! It is a free gift so why not take it! There is no mention of the cost of discipleship. The hope is that now that they are "Christian" everything will work out through faith and prayer and that they will live a happy prosperous satisfied life! Often when trouble comes, they become angry with God.

You can only be "Born Again" once! "**Process Christianity**" is an ongoing growing dynamic relationship with the Trinity characterized by a thirst for more of God and His word as well as love for people. Most of all it results in repentance and a changed life. This Process Christian has an unsatiable desire for God and His word as well as fellowship with the saints. The "process Christian" doesn't see himself as complete but in ongoing process with an ever-growing relationship with his savior. He is characterized by brokenness, fruitfulness, humility, generosity, and contrition. He is willing to suffer and face persecution for Christ since self is no longer on the throne. He is "being saved daily," rather than trusting in a past one time profession of faith. He is being sanctified.

Many people have been misled by **Event Christianity**. Many evangelists call people to come forward to "Receive Christ" at an evangelical crusade or church service believing then they would be Christians since "they had accepted Christ." However, information from the Billy Graham Evangelistic Association suggests that less than 10% of those coming forward at a revival crusade attend church one month after the crusade and a very small percent attend church one year later. What is wrong? **The answer is complicated and largely is due to the intellectualism of the Western church where head belief or intellectual assent is separated from heart belief. We are saved by a change in heart by the Holy Spirit rather than a head change or intellectual acceptance based on a good argument.** Sublimely people understand that there is a cost to Christianity, but men unrealistically hope for salvation from God's wrath and Hell without facing the rejection of men and family and death to the self-life. (Matt 10:34-39) The test of obedience, and a radically changed life of submission and sacrifice is too great a price for many.

John Bunyan's allegorical narrative <u>Pilgrims Progress</u> (1678) best incapsulates the tortuous and difficult walk of the Almost Christian through various temptations such as Vanity Fair, battles, trials, giants, and despair. For more than 200 years it was the best-selling Christian book outside of the bible. It is rarely read by western christians today. **Conversion is too often presented in the modern era as a one-time event rather than a lifetime of growing with Christ with, ups and downs, joys and sorrows, and the call of death to self, and repentance from sin.**

*"Enter by the narrow gate. For the gate is wide and the way is easy that leads to destruction, and those who enter by it are many. For the gate is narrow and the way is hard that leads to life, and **those who find it are few**"* (Matthew 7:13-14)

The evangelist commonly calls on people to choose God not recognizing that God choses His own people. **We don't choose Him He chooses us.**

"For you are a people holy to the Lord your God. The Lord your God has chosen you to be a people for his treasured possession, out of all the peoples who are on the face of the earth. It was not because you were more in number than any other people that the Lord set his love on you and chose you, for you were the fewest of all peoples, but it is because the Lord loves you and is keeping the oath that he swore to your fathers, that the Lord has brought you out with a mighty hand and redeemed you from the house of slavery, from the hand of Pharaoh king of Egypt. Know therefore that the Lord your God is God, the faithful God who keeps covenant and steadfast love with those who love him and keep his commandments, to a thousand generations." (Deut 7:6-9)

Peter affirms, (I Peter 2:9-10) a hopeless sinner can never choose God because of his sin nature is opposed to God. God must choose him. Luther reminds us that "our person, nature, and entire existence are corrupted through Adam's fall. Therefore, not a single work can be good in us, until our nature and personal being are changed and renewed. The tree is not good; therefore, the fruits are evil."[2] **We are saved by God's sovereign grace alone, not by our own works.** (Eph 2:4-10)

Salvation can only be understood contextually in the hopelessness of man captive to sin. (Rom 3:10-20) We would rather preach the Good News rather than the Bad News that man is lost and sinners

---

2   Luther, M. (1999). <u>Luther's works, vol. 52: Sermons II.</u> (J. J. Pelikan, H. C. Oswald, & H. T. Lehmann, Eds.) (Vol. 52, p. 151). Philadelphia: Fortress Press.

will spend eternity in Hell. We all live to please ourselves not others and think that we are basically good. If we don't see ourselves as sinners, then we don't need a savior! The message of the gospel is that man is not good and cannot save himself by "Accepting Jesus" or be comforted by believing the bible. We forget that demons believe or accept Jesus and tremble, (James 2:19) Saving faith is radically different from simple belief and acceptance. Who are we to think we can accept Jesus as the Lord of lords, the King of kings, and the Creator of all things? **Our hope should be as hopeless sinners that He (God) can accept us not that we accept Him! True biblical faith is supernatural faith, that is a gift from God, that changes man to be a new creation in Christ. (2 Cor 5:17) It means that we live not for ourselves but for Him.** (2 Cor 5:14-15)

> John MacArthur comments: 'There are no summons to repentance, no warning of judgment, no call for brokenness, no expectation of a contrite heart, and no reason for deep sorrow over sin. It is a message of easy salvation, a call for hasty decision, often accompanied by false promises of health, happiness, and material blessing. This is not the gospel according to Jesus." John MacArthur, *The Gospel According to Jesus* (p. 209)

Faith involves not only an intellectual element, an emotional element, and a volitional element. The word *faith* means to trust in, believe in, to have confidence in, to rely on, and submit to the one who you have faith in! **Ultimately, true faith means a complete surrender to God, which results in obedience and a constancy and firmness that is unshakable.** Faith understands that Christianity is full of mysteries which are beyond human comprehension or unprovable by science. Faith is super relational and can only be comprehended by the heart, not the mind, radically changed by the Holy Spirit. Faith arises from the depth of the human heart.

"Now faith is the assurance of things hoped for, the <u>conviction of things not seen</u>. *For by it the people of old received their commendation. By faith we understand that the universe was created by the word of God, so that what is seen was not made out of things that are visible.* (Hebrews 11:1-3)

Christ's kingdom is a condition of the heart. Those who believe will desire to obey God even though their obedience is imperfect. Man cannot help himself because of his sin nature. What man cannot do for himself; God through the work of Christ provides as grace to the lost sinner. (John 3:5, 6:44, 6:63, 6:65)

Grace is the kindness shown to someone who does not deserve it, cannot earn it, and could never repay it. Grace also is an empowerment by the Holy Spirit that works in us to illuminate God's love for us shown through Christ's sacrifice on the cross and to please God through works led by and performed only by the Holy Spirit for *"we know that a person is not justified by works of the law but through faith in Jesus Christ, so we also have believed in Christ Jesus, in order to be justified by faith in Christ and not by works of the law, because by works of the law no one will be justified."* (Gal 2:16)

The simplicity of the gospel continues to confuse many. The basic elements of the gospel are summarized in Hebrews 6 as follows:

1. Repentance
2. Faith
3. Baptism
4. Laying on of hands to receive the Holy Spirit
5. The promise of resurrection from the dead
6. The promise of eternal judgment

"Therefore, let us go on and get past the elementary stage in the teachings and doctrine of Christ (the Messiah), advancing steadily toward the completeness and perfection that belong to spiritual maturity. Let us not again be laying

the foundation of repentance and abandonment of dead works (dead formalism) and of the faith [by which you turned] to God, with teachings about washings [Baptism], the laying on of hands, the resurrection from the dead, and eternal judgment and punishment. [These are all matters of which you should have been fully aware long, long ago.]" (Hebrews 6:1–3 AMP)

Peter on the day of Pentecost called on the Jews to "*repent and be baptized*" (Acts 2:38), and "those who accepted and welcomed his message were baptized. (Acts 2:41). Notice all were baptized on the same day that they received Christ. This rarely occurs in the Western church but is a common practice in developing nations. The call to the church in Hebrews 6:1 is to mature and move on from the basics. This isn't going to happen until the Western church practices the basics.

Faith involves not only an intellectual element, an emotional element, and a volitional element. The word *faith* means to trust in, believe in, to have confidence in, to rely on, and submit to the one who you have faith in! **Ultimately, true faith means a complete surrender to God, which results in obedience and a constancy and firmness that is unshakable.** Faith understands that Christianity is full of mysteries which are beyond human comprehension or unprovable by science. Faith is super relational and can only be comprehended by the heart, not the mind, radically changed by the Holy Spirit. Faith arises from the depth of the human heart. (*Now faith is the assurance of things hoped for, the* <u>conviction of things not seen</u>. *For by it the people of old received their commendation. By faith we understand that the universe was created by the word of God, so that what is seen was not made out of things that are visible.* (Hebrews 11:1-3) Christ's kingdom is a condition of the heart. Those who believe will desire to obey God even though their obedience is imperfect.

Man cannot help himself because of his sin nature. What man cannot do for himself, God through the work of Christ provides as grace to the lost sinner. Grace is the kindness shown to someone who does not deserve it, cannot earn it, and could never repay it. Grace also is an empowerment that works in us to illuminate God's love for us shown through Christ's sacrifice on the cross and to please God through works led by and performed only by the Holy Spirit for *"we know that a person is not justified by works of the law but through faith in Jesus Christ, so we also have believed in Christ Jesus, in order to be justified by faith in Christ and not by works of the law, because by works of the law no one will be justified."* (Gal 2:16)

"Unless we preach Jesus rather than a set of "morals of the story" or timeless principles or good advice, people will never truly understand, love, or obey the Word of God." —Tim Keller, *Preaching: Communicating Faith in an Age of Skepticism.*

> "The nature of Christ's salvation is woefully misrepresented by the present-day evangelist. He announces a Savior from hell rather than a Savior from sin. And that is why so many are fatally deceived, for there are multitudes who wish to escape the Lake of fire who have no desire to be delivered from their carnality and worldliness." —A. W. Pink

> "Satan is not fighting churches; he is joining them. He does more harm by sowing tares than by pulling up wheat. He accomplishes more by imitation than by outright opposition."—Vance Havner

> "When I'm in the West, I see all the mighty church buildings and all the expensive equipment, plush carpets, and state-of-the-art sound systems. I can assure the Western church with absolute certainty that you don't need any more church buildings. Church buildings will never bring the revival you seek. The pursuit of more

possessions will never bring revival. Jesus truly stated, *"A man's life does not consist in the abundance of his possessions."*—Lk 12:15. The first thing needed for revival to return to your churches is the Word of the Lord. God's Word is missing. Sure, there are many preachers and thousands of tapes and videos of Bible teaching, but so little contains the sharp truth of God's Word. It's the truth that will set you free. Not only is knowledge of God's Word missing, but obedience to that Word. There's not much action taking place." (Chinese Pastor Yun, *The Heavenly Man*, page 296–297)

No wonder that the Chinese church prays that the American church would experience persecution. Their prayer is similar to Peter's: *"May the God of all grace, who called us to His eternal glory by Christ Jesus, after you have suffered a while, perfect, establish, strengthen, and settle you"* (1 Pet 5:10).

"There is a common worldly kind of Christianity in this day, which many have, and think they have enough. This cheap Christianity . . . offends nobody, requires no sacrifice, costs nothing, and is worth nothing!" (J.C Ryle)

"Unquestionably the world would like to change the church, but does the church still want to change the world, or is its only concern to change the church in light of the world? Something is rotten in the state of Evangelicalism, and all too often it is impossible to tell who is changing whom. "(Os Guinness, *Impossible People: Christian Courage and the Struggle for the Soul of Civilization*, IVP 2016)

"They profess to know God, but by their deeds they deny Him, being detestable and disobedient and worthless for any good deed." (Titus 1:16 NASB)

"One hundred religious persons knit into unity by careful organization do not make a church any more than 11 dead men make a football team." (A. W. Tozer)

"For the time has come for judgment to begin at the house of God; and if it begins with us first, what will be the end of those who do not obey the gospel of God? No. If the righteous one is scarcely saved. Where will the ungodly and the sinner appear? Therefore, let those who suffer according to the will of God commit their souls to Him in doing good, as to a faithful Creator." (I Peter 4:17–19, NKJV)

Remember that the distinction between an almost Christian and a true Christian is death to the self or old man. **We must die to be born again. The only real Christian is a dead Christian!**

"Let me learn by paradox that the way down is the way up, that to be low is to be high that the broken heart is the healed heart, that the contrite spirit is the rejoicing spirit, that the repenting soul is the victorious soul, that to have nothing is to possess all, that to bear the cross is to wear the crown, that to give is to receive, that the valley is the place of vision."

(The Valley of Vision, A Collection of Puritan Prayers and Devotions)

Chapter 2
Original Sin

It is the doctrine of *original sin* that distinguishes Christianity from all other religions. If there is no original sin, then there is no need of atonement, and Christ's sacrifice on the cross was useless. The fall of Adam and Eve (Gen 3) signals the human attempt to assert independence from God and His will. **The condition of radical corruption, or total depravity, is the fallen state known as *original sin.*** This means our hearts are totally depraved, desperately wicked, and eternally lost without hope except for the grace of God. It means there is no hope in self-reformation or any type of merit for good works again except for the unmerited grace of God. The doctrine of original sin does not refer just to the first sin committed by Adam and Eve, but to the *result* of that first sin on all mankind. We are all born sinners because we have inherited the sin nature and the guilt of Adam. **The biblical concept of "sin" is not just about doing wrong, or more literally *missing the mark,* it is about loving self, more than loving God, and hence is about a broken covenant relationship with a Holy God who demands to place Himself first as Lord of All.** It is the motivations of the heart and our inherent sinful, unholy nature that separates us from a Holy God. Biblically, **we are totally depraved, meaning we are incapable of pleasing God by our own works.** That is a hard pill to swallow for most of us. We all think that there is some good in us, but God says no, there is *"none righteous"* (Rom 3:10–18; Psalm 10:1–11; 14:1–3).

God's righteous anger at sin, and the fact that holy justice required a perfect, sinless substitution on our behalf, is often omitted in the incomplete gospel preached by many. Only the blood sacrifice of a sinless holy man, Jesus Christ, could alone atone for our sin. The current teaching of many that "man is good" ignores the depth of original sin and produces **Christless pseudo-Christianity. If man is good, then Christ died in vain, and the cross was unnecessary. The biblical view of man is that he is miserable, pitiable, corrupt, prideful, arrogant, and bankrupt, and in a state of guilt, imminent danger, and condemnation before God.** Psalm 14:3 reminds us:

> And Jesus answered them, *"Those who are well have no need of a physician, but those who are sick. [32] I have not come to call the righteous but sinners to repentance."* [3]

> *"They have all turned aside, together they have become corrupt; There is no one who does good, not even one."* Luke 4:31-32

Because man is in enmity with God, he will have no title to heaven and faces eternal destruction in hell. Paul argues for sin's universality: *"for all have sinned and fall short of the glory of God"* (Rom 3:23). Later in the same discourse, Paul reiterates this point: *"Therefore, just as through one man sin entered into the world, and death through sin, and so death spread to all men, because all sinned"* (Rom 5:12), and *"whatever is not from faith is sin"* (Romans 14:23). This is a very unpleasant message of original sin is largely avoided by many church leaders. **This message of eternal damnation was not avoided by Jesus who spoke more about hell than heaven.**

The first doctrine that must be confessed and ever on the lips of a true Christian is that he is a sinner deserving of hell but saved by grace or the unmerited favor of God (Eph 2:8–9). Unless he sees himself as a sinner and unworthy, he is largely unteachable and unreachable. Paul in his prison epistle of 1 Timothy reminds us:

> *I obtained mercy for the reason that in me, as the foremost*

3   *The Holy Bible: English Standard Version* (Lk 5:31–32). (2016). Crossway Bibles.

[of sinners], Jesus Christ might show forth and display all His perfect long-suffering and patience for an example to [encourage] those who would thereafter believe on Him for [the gaining of] eternal life." (1 Tim 1:16 AMP)

The truth of man's predicament must be balanced with God's graciousness to sinners and Jesus's ultimate love payment on the cross for sinners.

Timothy Keller reminds us: "You're more wicked than you ever believed but at the same time more loved and accepted than you dared to hope." (Tim Keller, *Jesus the King: Understanding the Life and Death of the Son of God*)

John Calvin reminds us: "Christ came *"To save sinners."* Indeed, Jesus said: "I have not come to call the righteous but sinners to repentance" (Luke 5:32; 1 Tim 1:15).

Luther said: **"The recognition of sin is the beginning of salvation**. The words *sin* and *sinners* are emphatic, for they who acknowledge that it is the office of Christ to save, have difficulty in admitting this thought that such a salvation belongs to "sinners." Our mind is always impelled to look at our worthiness; and as soon as our unworthiness is seen, our confidence sinks. Accordingly, the more anyone is oppressed by his sins, let him the more courageously give himself to Christ, relying on this doctrine, that He came to bring salvation not to the righteous but to "sinners."

Titus succinctly summarizes the essence of the gospel.

"But when the kindness of God our Savior and His love for mankind appeared, He saved us, not on the basis of deeds which we have done in righteousness, but according to His mercy, by the washing of regeneration and renewing by the Holy Spirit, whom He poured out upon us richly through

Jesus Christ our Savior, so that being justified by His grace (Unmerited Favor and power for transformation) we would be made heirs according to the hope of eternal life." (Titus 3:4–7 explanation added)

Pelagius was a fourth century (380-410 AD) Christian monk who assumed that *"moral responsibility always carries with it moral ability."* Pelagius thought it would be unjust of God to require his creatures to do what they are unable to do in their own power. He reasoned if God requires moral perfection, then mankind must be able to achieve perfection. The deeper issue is the inference that God would be unfair—if man is treated as a robot unable to make his own moral choices. Pelagius had a distorted view of God's justice as well as man's total depravity. He did not believe that man inherited Adam's sin and therefore could choose God based on his own free will. In reality, we forget that we deserve justice and the eternal damnation of God as hopeless sinners, and we don't deserve the mercy and grace of God shown to us through our only redeemer Jesus Christ. Though grace *facilitates* our quest for moral perfection, grace is also *necessary* for us to reach it because of our sin-corrupted souls. **Many theologians define grace as** *"unmerited favor,"* **but it is so much more. Grace is the** *"enabling empowerment of the Holy Spirit."* Augustine opposed Pelagius and argued that man lacks the human ability to choose God because of his corrupted sinful human nature. This offends many who pridefully want to exert their free choice because they do not believe in original sin and therefore feel free to choose whom they will serve. They believe in a universal redemption with sufficient grace that allows all men independently to respond to God's offer of salvation. If this were true, man would take glory for himself and congratulate himself for his choice! Johnathan Edwards wrote about original sin and concluded that reason could never explain how all men are born sinners through Adam's sin. We must rely on scripture in Romans chapter 5:12-21 to explain original sin.

Therefore, just as sin came into the world through one man, and death through sin, and so death spread to all men because all sinned— [13] *for sin indeed was in the world before the law was given, but sin is not counted where there is no law.* [14] *Yet death reigned from Adam to Moses, even over those whose sinning was not like the transgression of Adam, who was a type of the one who was to come.*

[15] *But the free gift is not like the trespass. For if many died through one man's trespass, much more have the grace of God and the free gift by the grace of that one-man Jesus Christ abounded for many.* [16] *And the free gift is not like the result of that one man's sin. For the judgment following one trespass brought condemnation, but the free gift following many trespasses brought justification.* [17] *For if, because of one man's trespass, death reigned through that one man, much more will those who receive the abundance of grace and the free gift of righteousness reign in life through the one-man Jesus Christ.*

[18] *Therefore, as one trespass led to condemnation for all men, so one act of righteousness leads to justification and life for all men.* [19] ***For as by the one man's disobedience the many were made sinners, so by the one man's obedience the many will be made righteous****.* [20] *Now the law came in to increase the trespass, but where sin increased, grace abounded all the more,* [21] *so that, as sin reigned in death, grace also might reign through righteousness leading to eternal life through Jesus Christ our Lord.* [4]

However, the Bible is clear. Human actions are divinely determined without excluding the exercise of human freedom in those actions. Men can make decisions for reasons, which to themselves seem reasonable and free from any external coercion, yet unknowingly, they are fulfilling the sovereign will of God! How this happens is a mystery. **The reformers argued that salvation was a sovereign monergistic work of the Holy Spirit**

4   *The Holy Bible: English Standard Version* (Ro 5:12–21). (2016). Crossway Bibles.

based on God's foreknowledge and election. Many struggle with election because of the implication that God is not fair, in that He chooses some but not others. (Eph 1:4–5) Who will argue with a sovereign God and instruct the Almighty?

R.C. Sproul points out that **"the very essence of grace is that it is undeserved. God always reserves the right to have mercy upon whom he will have mercy. God may owe people justice, but never mercy."** God is not under obligation to save anybody. If he chooses to save some, that in no way obligates him to save the rest. Again, the Bible insists that it is God's divine prerogative to have mercy upon whom he will have mercy. God is never obligated to be merciful to sinners. "The Potter chooses what he will make with His clay—some vessels for honor and some for dishonor!" Isaiah tells us "You turn things around! Shall the potter be considered as equal with the clay, that what is made would say to its maker, 'He did not make me'; Or what is formed say to him who formed it, 'He has no understanding'?" (Isa 29:16).

> *"Woe to the one who quarrels with his Maker—An earthenware vessel among the vessels of earth! Will the clay say to the potter, 'What are you doing?' Or the thing you are making says, 'He has no hands?'. . .It is I who made the earth, and created man upon it. I stretched out the heavens with My hands and I ordained all their hosts."*
>
> (Isa 45:9–12)

Election is a wonderful manifestation of God's love in that He has chosen some helpless, undeserving sinners to faith and then has promised to keep them from falling until the final judgment. God keeps all glory to Himself because He is the author and keeper of our salvation. How wonderful is our God!

God's grace not only facilitates our efforts to obey God, but because of our fallen nature, grace empowerment is absolutely necessary and is a free gift from God. Before the fall, the requirement for moral perfection was already present in Adam. The fall did not change the requirement, but it did change us. What was once a moral possibility for Adam in the garden before the fall became a moral impossibility after the fall because of inherited original sin. Man's reason often leads to heresy and deception. We need God's Word, not only for our reason to be, but as our guide to all truth. Any hope that man places in himself must meet the cross. It is at the cross that man must lay down his intellect in exchange for the mind of Christ, the Word of God, by the empowerment of the Holy Spirit (2 Cor 5:21).

Since the second great awakening and Charles Finney, Robert Sandeman, and many others, there has been a post-reformation misunderstanding of grace. This is called by some theologians "free grace" as opposed to "sovereign grace." Etienne Gilson commented in his book *The Spirit of Medieval Philosophy*:

> "For the first time, with the Reformation, there appeared this conception of a grace that saves a man without changing them, or a justice that redeems corrupted nature without restoring it, of a Christ who pardons the sinner for self-inflicted wounds but does not heal them."

True, saving faith is heart faith, not intellectual acceptance, acknowledgement, or simple belief. The reformers understood that man cannot change himself. The hope of all converted men is the work of the Holy Spirit who imputes righteousness to us and sanctifies us through our faith. The root problem again is misunderstanding the sinful nature of man and the wonderful redemptive work on the cross that changes us, because Christ is in us and we become the Temple of the Holy Spirit (1 Cor 3:16). The root error in the

Arminian Doctrine of Free Grace is the failure to understand that man's part in his salvation of repentance and faith are the fruits and effect of God's grace and are not the essential works supplied by the sinner himself. **True faith and repentance are the evidence not the cause of regeneration.** True faith is about complete abandonment in Christ as our *only hope of sanctification.* We are to present ourselves as a living sacrifice to God.

> "*I beseech you therefore, brethren, by the mercies of God, that you present your bodies a living sacrifice, holy, acceptable to God, which is your reasonable service. And do not be conformed to this world, but be transformed by the renewing of your mind, that you may prove what is that good and acceptable and perfect will of God.*" (Romans 12:1–2)

The Christian man is a redeemed sinner in process like the Apostle Paul, constantly being changed by the work of the Holy Spirit. The true believer is not only saved but is always in the process of sanctification—saved and continually being saved (Phil 2:12).

Man is radically diseased, and man needs a radical cure (Matt 9:13; Luke 15:7; 19:10). Remember Jesus told His disciples: "*But go and learn what this means: 'I desire mercy and not sacrifice.' For I did not come to call the righteous, but sinners, to repentance.*" The ignorance of the extent of the fall and of the whole doctrine of original sin is one grand reason why many can neither understand, appreciate, nor receive true Christianity.

Peter did not tell people just to "believe and be saved." Nor did he ask them to merely make a decision, to cast a vote for Jesus. No, he told them to repent first and then be baptized in obedience to Christ! What gospel did Paul preach to the pagan Essenes on Mars Hill? He told them very directly, "*God now command all men everywhere to repent*" (Acts 17:30).

35

There are three important "cannots" in Scripture that describe the hopelessness of man to save himself:

1. *Man cannot see* God or save himself unless he is born again (John 3:3).
2. *Man cannot understand* God until he has been given a new nature for God (1 Cor 1:18, 23; 2:14).
3. *Man cannot come* to God until he be first effectually called by the Holy Spirit (John 6:38, 44–45, 65; 10:26–29).

Fortunately, what man cannot do God can do, through the redeeming work of Christ. Our hope is in the mercy of God and not in ourselves or our own goodness.

1. *Man can confess his sin,* bow his knee, and ask for true repentance. (Mark 1:15; Rom 3:10; Psalm 51).
2. *Man can be contrite* and come to the Lord as an undeserving beggar. (Isaiah 57:15; 51:17; 66:2; Psalm 34:18; 2 Tim 2:11).
3. *Man can hope and call on the mercy of God* and his loving kindness and forgiveness to be saved. (Psalm 51; Isa 6:5; Acts 17:27; Col 1:27; Heb 6:19; Psalm 39:7; Luke 7:29; Rom 9:11).
4. *Man can submit to God's authority and sovereignty and surrender.* (Rom 1:5; 1 Cor 7:15; 2 Cor 10:6; Deut 6:1–9; Isa 45:23; 1 John 2:3–6; 1 Peter 4:17).
5. *Man can and must repent* (Matt 4:17; Mark 1:14–15; 6:12; Acts 2:36–30; 13:23–24; 2 Pet 3:9).
6. *Man can and must be crucified with Christ that he might live unto God.* (Matt 10:38; Gal 2:19–20; 2 Tim 2:11; Rom 7:4–6; 2 Cor 4:12; 5:14–15, 1 Peter 4:1; Rev 12:11). My hope is entirely in the cross of Christ and nothing else. Now we must take up His cross, leave all, and follow Him.

Scripture is abundantly clear that our human condition is hopeless. Man cannot save himself. He is facing eternal destruction in the fires of hell. Often men realize that Jesus promised that if men hated Him, they would hate his disciples as well (John 15:20). We would often prefer the praise of men rather than the praise of God. We fear men more than we fear God. Perfect love casts out fear (1 John 4:18). If we love God, we will not love the world or the praise of men (1 John 2:15). We must give up all to be followers of Christ (Matt 10:24–39; 16:24–26). **Remember that good people** *(those that trust in their own goodness or good works)* **go to hell and sinners** *(those who place no hope in themselves or works but trust in Christ alone, by faith alone)* **go to heaven.**

> "A disciple is not above his teacher, nor a slave above his master. It is enough for the disciple that he become like his teacher, and the slave like his master. If they have called the head of the house Beelzebul, how much more will they malign the members of his household! Therefore, do not fear them, for there is nothing concealed that will not be revealed, or hidden that will not be known. What I tell you in the darkness, speak in the light; and what you hear whispered in your ear, proclaim upon the housetops. Do not fear those who kill the body but are unable to kill the soul; but rather fear Him who is able to destroy both soul and body in hell. Are not two sparrows sold for a cent? And yet not one of them will fall to the ground apart from your Father, but the very hairs of your head are all numbered. So do not fear; you are more valuable than many sparrows. Therefore, everyone who confesses Me before men, I will also confess him before My Father who is in heaven. But whoever denies Me before men, I will also deny him before My Father who is in heaven. Do not think that I came to bring peace on the earth; I did not come to bring peace, but a sword. For I came to SET A MAN AGAINST HIS FATHER, AND A DAUGHTER AGAINST HER MOTHER,

AND A DAUGHTER-IN-LAW AGAINST HER MOTHER-IN-LAW; and
A MAN'S ENEMIES WILL BE THE MEMBERS OF HIS HOUSEHOLD.
He who loves father or mother more than Me is not worthy
of Me; and he who loves son or daughter more than Me is
not worthy of Me. And he who does not take his cross and
follow after Me is not worthy of Me. **He who has found**
his life will lose it, and he who has lost his life for My
sake will find it." (Matt 10:24–39 NASB)

"For we who live are always delivered to death for Jesus' sake,
that the life of Jesus also may be manifested in our mortal flesh.
So, death is working in us, but life in you." (2 Cor 4:11–12)

The "flesh" is too bad to be cleansed; it must be crucified.
(Watchman Nee)

"Any concept of grace that makes us feel more comfortable
sinning is not biblical grace. God's grace never encourages us to
live in sin, on the contrary, it empowers us to say no to sin and
yes to truth." (Randy Alcorn)

You may say, "God doesn't hate anybody. God is love." No, my
friend. You need to understand something. Jesus Christ, the
prophets, and the apostles taught this: apart from the grace of
God revealed in Jesus Christ our Lord the only thing left for you
is the wrath, the fierce anger of God because of your rebellion
and your sin. (Paul Washer)

"The nature of Christ's salvation is woefully
misrepresented by the present-day evangelist. **He**
announces a Savior from hell rather than a Savior
from sin. And that is why so many are fatally deceived,
for there are multitudes who wish to escape the Lake
of Fire who have no desire to be delivered from their
carnality and worldliness." —Arthur W. Pink

"Suffer me to beseech you, or rather to give you warning, not to rest satisfied with a form of godliness, denying the power thereof. ***There can be no true religion, till there be a discovery of your lost state by nature and practice, and an unfeigned acceptance of Christ Jesus, as he is offered in the gospel.*** Unhappy are they who either despise his mercy or are ashamed of his cross! Believe it, there is no salvation in any other. There is no other name under heaven given amongst men by which we must be saved." (John Witherspoon, then President of Princeton, Sermon given July 4, 1776, emphasis added)

As Christ has a gospel, Satan has a gospel too; the latter being a clever counterfeit of the former. So closely does the gospel of Satan resemble the truth that it multiplies the unsaved that are deceived by it. The nature of Christ's salvation is woefully misrepresented by the present-day evangelist. He announces a savior from hell rather than a Savior from sin. And that is why so **many are fatally deceived, for there are multitudes who wish to escape the lake of fire who have no desire to be delivered from their carnality and worldliness.** (A.W. Pink) **I'm convinced that the popular evangelistic message of our age actually lures people into this deception. It promises a wonderful comfortable plan for everyone's life. It obliterates the offense of the cross.** (1 Cor 2:23, Gal 5:11) Though it presents Christ as the way, the truth, and the life, it says nothing of a small gate or the narrow way. Its subject is the love of God, but there's no mention of God's wrath. This is a people who are deprived not depraved. The false message is full of love and understanding, but there's no mention of a Holy God who hates sin. There are no summons to repentance, no warning of judgment, no call for brokenness, no expectation of a contrite heart, and no reason for deep sorrow over sin. It is a message of easy salvation, a call for hasty decision, often accompanied by false promises of health, happiness, and material blessing. This is not the gospel according to Jesus." John MacArthur, *The Gospel According to Jesus* (p. 209)

"Eternity to the godly is a day that has no sunset; eternity to the wicked is a night that has no sunrise."

—Thomas Watson

"To the church, a revival means humiliation, a bitter knowledge of unworthiness and an open and humiliating confession of sin on the part of her ministers and people. It is not the easy and glorious thing many think it to be... it accuses them of sin, it tells them they are dead, it calls them to awake, to renounce the world and to follow Christ."

—James Burns, 'Revival, Their Laws and Leaders'.

A pilgrim divine reflected upon his sin and prayed:

"Grant that I may always weep to the praise of the mercy found, and tell to others as long as I live,
  that thou art a sin pardoning God,
  taking up the blasphemer and the ungodly,
  and washing them from their deepest stain."

Chapter 3

What about the Blood?
Covenant Theology

"For the life of the flesh is in the blood, and I have given it for you on the altar to make atonement for your souls, for it is the blood that makes atonement by the life*."* (Lev 17:11)

Why is blood important in scripture? The Bible mentions frequently about the blood of bulls and sheep as well as men, but most of all the precious blood of Christ. The story of redemption history was illustrated through the great covenants made with Adam, Noah, Abraham, Moses, Israel, and David. What was so special about the blood of Jesus and the New Covenant? To understand Christ's work on the cross the reader needs to understand biblical covenant.

"Therefore, brethren, since we have confidence to enter the holy place by the blood of Jesus, by a new and living way which He inaugurated for us through the veil, that is, His flesh." Hebrews 10:19)

The biblical word Covenant or Hebrew *Berith* is derived from a root which means "to cut," and hence a covenant is a "cutting," with reference to the cutting or dividing of animals into two parts, and the contracting parties passing between them, in making a covenant (Gen. 15; Jer. 34:18, 19). The Greek "διαθήκη, *diatheke*" is a sacred kinship bond between two parties with sanctions ratified by swearing an oath. **An inadequate rendering of the Greek word diatheke as "testament" rather than "covenant" by earlier biblical translators has obscured the theological meaning of the**

41

division of salvation history and the biblical canon into the old and new testaments rather than more properly into old and new covenants. *Testamentum* is a Latin word for covenant which is probably the source of much confusion caused by the writers of the authorized 1611 version of the King James Bible.

Covenant making was a widespread custom throughout the ancient Near East and Graeco-Roman culture, serving as a means to forge sociopolitical bonds between individuals or groups. The idea of covenant follows the ancient near east suzerain vassal pattern. It required how a lesser poor person or vassal to make a blood oath to the greater power such as a king or suzerain for protection and prosperity. An oath was taken that required the shedding of blood as a visible sign of the certain death of the oath breaker. God's covenants are prominent in every period of salvation history. Divine covenants reveal the saving plan of God for establishing communion with Israel and the nations, ultimately fulfilled by the death and resurrection of Christ.

Ancient covenants were solemnized through certain accompanying rituals, such as the swearing of an oath (e.g., by Abraham's steward Eliezer; Gen. 24:2–3, 9, 41), a shared meal (as between Abimelech and Isaac; 26:28–30), or the exchanging of clothes (as between David and Jonathan; 1 Sam. 18:4). A common ancient Near Eastern custom was the cutting of sacrificial animals into pieces, as mentioned in the account of God's covenant with Abraham (Gen. 15:9–21; cf. Jer. 34:18–20). After the animals were cut lengthwise and the pieces of meat placed opposite one another, the participants walked between the pieces, perhaps symbolizing that whoever would break the covenant would be "cut" like the animals (the standard idiom meaning to make a covenant. The Heb. *kāraṭ bᵉrîṭ* "cut a covenant," may derive from this custom. The word covenant is used nearly 300 times in the Old Testament and about 30 times in the New Testament.

Covenant language is more prominent in the Old Testament, which reflects its futuristic character as "a story in search of an ending." The language of divine kinship (e.g., "father," "son") emerges in the New Testament, because Christ's fulfillment of the Old Covenant forges familial bonds of divine communion with all humanity. The covenant ceremony at Josh. 24, which contains these basic elements: the **preamble**, presenting the participants (vv. 1–2); 1) **historical prologue** describing the previous relations of God and Israel (vv. 2–13); **stipulations** (v. 14); list of 2) **witnesses** (v. 22; cf. v. 27)**; 3) sanctions—curses and blessings** (vv. 19–20, 25); 4) **provision for deposit of the covenant document and its periodic reading** (v. 26); and the 5) **oaths** (vv. 15, 21) and often a **common meal** (I Cor 11:23-26). It has been suggested that additional stipulations are contained in the legislation represented by the Book of the Covenant (Exod. 20:22–23:33). Numerous examples of curses and blessings can be attested such as in Deuteronomy chapters 28-30.

A central factor in the Judeo-Christian transition is God's covenant with his people, presented as always initiated by God himself, first with Adam (Gen 1:28, 2:15) then Noah (Gen. 9:8–17), then with Abram (Gen. 15; 17), and later with Abraham's descendants, the Israelites of the Exodus (Exod. 19–24), (Deuteronomy 4-7) and finally a new covenant of grace (Jeremiah 31:31-34).

The understanding covenant is central to understanding the redemptive-historical central framework of the Bible. It is understanding the biblical concept of covenant that holds the Bible together and explains various parts of the Bible in relation to the whole. Our relationship with God is by nature covenantal. It is covenant that brings together all the diverse themes to scripture. Covenants are about relationships between a greater power (suzerain) such as a prince or king to a lesser people. It requires equal commitments from one to the other. It is a picture of God's covenantal dealings with history. It is about law and grace.

It is about blessing and cursing. When Jesus wanted to explain the significance of his death to his disciples, he expounded the doctrine of the covenants (Matt 26; Mark 14; Luke 22; 1Cor 11). When God wanted to assure Abraham of the certainty of his word of promise, he made a covenant (Gen 12; 15; 17). Life is connected with blood; blood becomes the supreme offering to God. In the ratification of the covenant (Ex 24), Moses poured half the sacrificial blood on the altar; after reading the covenant to the people and receiving their affirmative response, he sprinkled the rest of the blood on them and said, *"This is the blood of the covenant that the Lord has made with you in accordance with all these words"* (Ex 24:8). Sprinkling blood on both the altar and the people bound God and the Israelites together in covenant relationship.

The essence of covenant is to be found in a particular kind of relationship between persons. Mutual obligations characterize that kind of relationship. Thus, a covenant relationship is not merely a mutual acquaintance but a commitment to responsibility, obedience, and action such as in a marriage covenant. A key word in Scripture to describe that commitment is "faithfulness," acted out in a context of abiding friendship.

A covenant agreement between two parties that specifies requirements for at least one party and includes blessing and curses for obedience or failure (Deuteronomy 28). The Old Testament required circumcision and animal sacrifice. Baptism is the New Testament replacement of circumcision. In baptism an individual is temporally submerged beneath the water to symbolizing death to the old man who is now raised up as a new creature in Christ. **In the Old Testament circumcision was the outward sign of entrance into a covenant community. In the New Testament baptism is the entrance into a new covenant of grace and God's promises to His covenant people.**

God's design for man begins with a covenant of works between Adam as the federal head and representative of the human race. Eternal life was promised to Adam if he would obey God's commandments. God said to Adam *"Be fruitful and multiply and fill the earth and subdue it and have dominion over the fish of the sea and over the birds of the heavens and over every living thing that moves on the earth."* (Genesis 1:28) "The Lord God took the man and put him in the garden of Eden to work it and keep it. [16] And the Lord God commanded the man, saying, *"You may surely eat of every tree of the garden, [17] but of the tree of the knowledge of good and evil you shall not eat, for in the day that you eat of it you shall surely die."* (Genesis 2:15-16) God promised death if Adam disobeyed. Adam's disobedience and death which had resulted in sin and death in all mankind (<u>Rom 5:12–21</u>; <u>1Cor 15:21–22</u>). When Adam disobeyed; God promised a future Redeemer who would save mankind. (Genesis 3:15)

> *I will put enmity between you and the woman, and between your offspring and her offspring; he shall bruise your head, and you shall bruise his heel.*

This promise of law and grace was administered through various other promises and ordinances such as religious rites and circumcision. All biblical covenants are blood covenants. Abel's sacrifice of the shedding of blood of his sheep was accepted by God but his brother Cain was rejected. Animal sacrifice or circumcision satisfied the oaths of covenant that disobedience to the stipulations (Law) required the death by the shedding of blood by the oath breaker. The new covenant sign was the shedding of Jesus blood on the cross to seal the covenant of grace is later celebrated by taking communion or the Eucharist by the drinking of Christ's blood and eating of his flesh. The new covenant was ratified at the Last Supper (Luke 22:20) with the institution of the Eucharist, when the disciples share a sacrificial meal with Jesus like the one Moses and the elders of Israel shared with God at

Sinai (Exod 24:11). Indeed, Jesus' solemn declaration, *"This is my blood of the covenant"* (Matt 26:28), echoes the words of Moses while sprinkling the blood of the sacrificial animals to ratify the covenant at Mount Sinai (Exod 24:8). Thus, the Eucharist represents Christ's blood sacrifice and the family meal of the new covenant (Luke 22:14–29; 1 Cor 10:16–17; 11:23–25). God hasn't changed and under the New Covenant. God continues to command repentance, faith, and obedience. He gives us the Holy Spirit to enable us to obey Him and maintain our relationship with Him by His new covenant of grace.

> *Therefore, remember that at one time you Gentiles in the flesh, called "the uncircumcision" by what is called the circumcision, which is made in the flesh by hands—* [12] *remember that you were at that time separated from Christ, alienated from the commonwealth of Israel and strangers to the covenants of promise, having no hope and without God in the world.* [13] *But now in Christ Jesus you who once were far off have been brought near by the blood of Christ.* [14] *For he himself is our peace, who has made us both one and has broken down in his flesh the dividing wall of hostility* [15] *by abolishing the law of commandments expressed in ordinances, that he might create in himself one new man in place of the two, so making peace,* [16] *and might reconcile us both to God in one body through the cross, thereby killing the hostility.* Eph 2:11-16

> *"Whoever, therefore, eats the bread or drinks the cup of the Lord in an unworthy manner will be guilty concerning the body and blood of the Lord.* [28] *Let a person examine himself, then, and so eat of the bread and drink of the cup.* [29] *For anyone who eats and drinks without discerning the body eats and drinks judgment on himself.* "I Cor 11:23-29

In entering a covenant, Jehovah was solemnly called on to witness the transaction (Gen. 31:50), and hence it was called a "covenant of the Lord" (1 Sam. 20:8). The passover exemplifies the protection of the blood of the lamb followed by the covenant meal. (Exodus 12:13)

> *"The blood shall be a sign for you, on the houses where you are. And when I see the blood, I will pass over you, and no plague will befall you to destroy you, when I strike the land of Egypt".*

Joshua renewed God's covenant with Moses and Israel by the shedding of blood by requiring circumcision of all men of Israel before taking the land. (Josh 5:2) Circumcision was followed by the passover meal. (Josh 5:10)

The marriage compact is called "the covenant of God" (Prov. 2:17), because the marriage was made in God's name and is sanctified by the shedding of blood through sexual intercourse on the marriage night and is followed by the covenant meal. This is repeated when Christ comes for his Church or Bride by the shedding of His own blood and fulfills the New Covenant. This is followed by the marriage supper of the lamb. (Rev 19:7)

> *Let us rejoice and exult*
> *and give him the glory,*
> *for the marriage supper of the Lamb has come,*
> *and his Bride has made herself ready.*

Wicked men are spoken of as acting as if they had made a "covenant with death" not to destroy them, or with hell not to devour them (Isa. 28:15, 18). The covenant theme in the OT, implicit in the garden of Eden, is developed from Noah to Abraham and reaches its first climax in the covenant formed between God and Israel at Mt Sinai.

The word covenant is used with reference to God's revelation of himself in the way of promise or of favour to men. Thus, God's promise to Noah after the Flood is called a covenant (Gen. 9; Jer. 33:20, "*my covenant*").

> Then God said to Noah and to his sons with him, [9] "*Behold,* **I establish my covenant** *with you and your offspring after you,* [10] *and with every living creature that is with you, the birds, the livestock, and every beast of the earth with you, as many as came out of the ark; it is for every beast of the earth.* [11] *I establish my covenant with you, that never again shall all flesh be cut off by the waters of the flood, and never again shall there be a flood to destroy the earth."* [12] *And God said, "This is the sign of the covenant that I make between me and you and every living creature that is with you, for all future generations.*[5] Genesis 9:8-12

The covenant that God makes with Noah embraces the whole human race *in common* or is called common grace that ensures the *preservation* of the natural and social order versus special grace which is exclusive to a holy elect people that are distinguished from the rest of the human race. Louis Berkhof explains, "There is no objection to this terminology ["covenant of nature or common grace"], provided it does not convey the impression that this [Noahic] covenant is dissociated altogether from the covenant of grace." Given the fact that the covenant of grace is redemptive, Palmer Robertson is completely correct when he writes, "The covenant with Noah emphasizes the close interrelation of the creative and redemptive covenants." It is important to recall that the flood is a type of baptism according to (I Peter 3:20-21). Can the Noahic covenant, then, be stripped of all redemptive aspects?

5   *The Holy Bible: English Standard Version* (Ge 9:8–12). (2016). Crossway Bibles.

We have an account of God's covenant with Abraham (Gen. 17, comp. Lev. 26:42) When Abram was ninety-nine years old the LORD appeared to Abram and said to him,

> "*I am God Almighty; walk before me, and be blameless,* ² *that I may make my covenant between me and you and may multiply you greatly."* ³ *Then Abram fell on his face. And God said to him,* ⁴ *"Behold, my covenant is with you, and you shall be the father of a multitude of nations.* ⁵ *No longer shall your name be called Abram, but your name shall be Abraham, for I have made you the father of a multitude of nations.* ⁶ *I will make you exceedingly fruitful, and I will make you into nations, and kings shall come from you.* ⁷ *And* **I will establish my covenant** *between me and you and your offspring after you throughout their generations for an everlasting covenant, to be God to you and to your offspring after you.* ⁸ *And I will give to you and to your offspring after you the land of your sojournings, all the land of Canaan, for an everlasting possession, and I will be their God."* And God said to Abraham*: "As for you, you shall keep my covenant, you and your offspring after you throughout their generations.* ¹⁰ ***This is my covenant***, *which you shall keep, between me and you and your offspring after you: Every male among you shall be circumcised.* ¹¹ *You shall be circumcised in the flesh of your foreskins, and it shall be a sign of the covenant between me and you.* ¹² *He who is eight days old among you shall be circumcised. Every male throughout your generations, whether born in your house or bought with your money from any foreigner who is not of your offspring,* ¹³ *both he who is born in your house and he who is bought with your money, shall surely be circumcised. So shall my covenant be in your flesh an everlasting covenant.* ¹⁴ ***Any uncircumcised male who is not circumcised in the flesh of his foreskin shall be cut off from his people; he has broken my covenant.***" Genesis 17:1-14

And God said to Moses: *Thus, you shall say to the house of Jacob, and tell the people of Israel: 'You yourselves have seen what I did to the Egyptians, and how I bore you on eagles' wings and brought you to myself. Now therefore, if you will indeed obey my voice and keep my covenant, you shall be my treasured possession among all peoples, for all the earth is mine; and you shall be to me a kingdom of priests and a holy nation.' These are the words that you shall speak to the people of Israel."* Exodus 19:3-6

Abraham helps us to understand how to live in the two kingdoms: "Abraham and his descendants were "sojourners" and "strangers" (Gen. 12:10; 15:13; 20:1; 21:34; 23:4; Heb. 11:13), precisely what Christians today are called to be (1 Pet. 2:11). As participants in the Noahic covenant, they joined in cultural activities with their pagan neighbors in the common kingdom. As participants in the Abrahamic covenant, they were simultaneously citizens of the redemptive kingdom, remaining radically separate from their neighbors in their religious commitment as they trusted in the true God for justification (Gen. 15:6) and eternal life (Heb. 11:13–16)"

There is a covenant of the priesthood (Num. 25:12, 13; Deut. 33:9; Neh. 13:29), and of the covenant of Sinai (Ex. 34:27, 28; Lev. 26:15), which was afterwards renewed at different times in the history of Israel (Deut. 29; Josh. 24; 2 Chr. 15; 23; 29; 34; Ezra 10; Neh. 9). In conformity with human custom, God's covenant is said to be confirmed with an oath (Deut. 4:31; Ps. 89:3), and to be accompanied by a sign (Gen. 9; 17). Hence the covenant is called God's "counsel," "oath," "promise" (Ps. 89:3, 4; 105:8–11; Heb. 6:13–20; Luke 1:68–75). God's covenant consists wholly in the bestowal of blessing (Isa. 59:21; Jer. 31:33, 34). The term covenant is also used to designate the regular succession of day and night (Jer. 33:20), the Sabbath (Ex. 31:16), circumcision (Gen. 17:9, 10), and in general any ordinance of God (Jer. 34:13, 14). A "covenant of salt" signifies an everlasting covenant, in the sealing or ratifying of which salt, as an emblem of perpetuity, is used (Num. 18:19; Lev. 2:13; 2 Chr. 13:5).

Finally, just before the destruction of Jerusalem God promises a new covenant of grace:

> "Behold, the days are coming, declares the LORD, when **I will make a new covenant** with the house of Israel and the house of Judah, [32] not like the covenant that I made with their fathers on the day when I took them by the hand to bring them out of the land of Egypt, my covenant that they broke, though I was their husband, declares the LORD. [33] For this is the covenant that I will make with the house of Israel after those days, declares the LORD: I will put my law within them, and I will write it on their hearts. And I will be their God, and they shall be my people." Jer 31:31-33

Covenants may be divided into two categories: a **Covenant of Works or Law (OT) or a Covenant of Grace** (NT). The covenant of works is the law under which Adam was placed at creation. In this covenant, (1.) The contracting parties were (a) God the moral Governor, and (b) Adam, a free moral agent, and representative of all his natural posterity (Rom. 5:12–19). (2.) The promise was "eternal life" (Matt. 19:16, 17; Gal. 3:12). (3.) The condition was perfect obedience to the law, the test in this case being abstaining from eating the fruit of the "tree of knowledge," etc. (4.) The penalty was death (Gen. 2:16, 17). This covenant is abrogated under the gospel, in as much as Christ has fulfilled all its conditions on behalf of his people and dispenses to them all its blessings. In Heb. 8:6; 9:15; 12:24, where this title is given to Christ, the language used ("new," "better") has reference to the fact that while Christ was from the beginning the sacerdotal mediator of the covenant, the "one mediator" (1 Tim. 2:5), he is now visibly disclosed or revealed as the true mediator, and as the immediate administrator of the new covenant. Christ, the surety of, mentioned in Heb. 7:22, where the word rendered "testament" means the new or Christian dispensation of the covenant as contrasted with the old or Mosaic dispensation. He is surety as priest, in that he discharges all the obligations of his people under the broken covenant of works; and as King, in that he dispenses all its blessings to his people. Hebrews teaches that Jesus is the covenant mediator (Greek, *mesites*) of the New Covenant, who—through his atoning death—actually provided the basis of forgiveness of sins represented in the sacrificial system of the Old Covenant (Heb 9:11–10:10). Paul, too, teaches that Jesus accomplished the prophecy of the New Covenant in his death (1Cor 11:25–26), and therefore Paul saw himself as a minister of the New Covenant (2 Cor 3:6).

The covenant of grace has been the same under all dispensations. From the very beginning (Gen 3:15) of the world's history the plan of salvation has been always the same having the same promise, the same Saviour, the same condition, the same salvation. Of this one covenant of grace there have been various dispensations. These are sometimes reckoned as four: (1.) The dispensation or revelation of the covenant in God's dealings with men from Adam to Abraham. (2.) From Abraham to Moses, when there was a clearer and fuller revelation than in the first period. (3.) From Moses to Christ. This is the period of the Mosaic covenant or economy. Finally, at a low point in covenant history the Bible introduces the prophet Jeremiah's prophecy of a "new covenant" in Israel's future. Jer 31:31. Jeremiah's prophecy eventually found fulfillment in the person and work of Jesus Christ. (4.) The gospel dispensation, which is not temporary and preparatory like those that went before, but permanent and final. It will last till the resurrection and the final judgment.

> *"But if we walk in the light, as he is in the light, we have fellowship with one another, and the **blood of Jesus his Son cleanses us from all sin**."* (I John 1:7)

God's covenant requires perfect obedience to his law. The law breaker faces eternal damnation if he cannot totally obey the stipulations of the covenant which is acting like an unbreakable contract. If he obeys the law or stipulations, he is promised eternal life, if he disobeys the law eternal death. A basic understanding of covenant theology is necessary to understand Christ's work on the cross for us. He was the only perfectly obedient unspotted human without sin who could satisfy God's demands of a sinless blood sacrifice for payment of man's sin and normal man's inability to obey the covenant stipulations of the law since all men are sinners. (Romans 5:12, Psalm 14) This is the wonderful story of redemption which cannot be understood without a basic understanding of covenant. Praise the Lord! Christ paid for my sin on the cross to satisfy God's covenant requirements of a sinless blood sacrifice to pay for all of man's sin and disobedience. I am now free from the penalty of the law by the shedding of Christ's blood on the cross and I chose to obey Christ because I love Him and want to serve Him as motivated by the Holy Spirit. Paul reminds us In Ephesians 2: 1-10:

*And you were dead in the trespasses and sins [2] in which you once walked, following the course of this world, following the prince of the power of the air, the spirit that is now at work in the sons of disobedience— [3] among whom we all once lived in the passions of our flesh, carrying out the desires of the body and the mind, and were by nature children of wrath, like the rest of mankind. [4] But God, being rich in mercy, because of the great love with which he loved us, [5] even when we were dead in our trespasses, made us alive together with Christ—by grace you have been saved— [6] and raised us up with him and seated us with him in the heavenly places in Christ Jesus, [7] so that in the coming ages he might show the immeasurable riches of his grace in kindness toward us in Christ Jesus. [8] **For by grace you have been saved through faith. And this is not your own doing; it is the gift of God,** [9] **not a result of works, so that no one may boast**. [10] For we are his workmanship, created in Christ Jesus for good works, which God prepared beforehand, that we should walk in them.[6]*

> *"Worthy, are you to take the scroll*
> *and to open its seals, for you were slain, and*
> ***by your blood you ransomed people for God***
> *from every tribe and language and people and nation,*
> *and you have made them a kingdom and priests to our God,*
> *and they shall reign on the earth."* (Rev 5:9-10)

6   *The Holy Bible: English Standard Version* (Eph 2:1–10). (2016). Crossway Bibles.

Chapter 4

Legalism and Self-Righteousness

Certainly, one of the greatest enemies of the Gospel of Christ is the grand delusion of *self-righteousness, or legalism,* or being like the *Pharisees.* Matthew 5:20 says, "For I say to you that unless your righteousness surpasses *that* of the scribes and Pharisees, you will not enter the kingdom of heaven." Many "almost Christians" are self-satisfied with themselves because they "choose" or made a decision for Christ when they simply have chosen to join the pharisaical, religious church party of "almost Christians." Satan's deception is to trick man into thinking he is basically good and only needs to get better. ***Salvation by good deeds is the grand delusion of all man-made religions.***

God calls us to be holy, but legalism is related to a misunderstanding of our position in Christ. Paul told the Corinthians: *"All things are lawful for me, but all things are not helpful. All things are lawful for me, but I will not be brought under the power of any"* (1 Cor 6:12). Can we do whatever we please? Heavens, no! Paul goes on to explain:

> Do you not know that your bodies are members of Christ? Shall I then take the members of Christ and make them members of a harlot? Certainly not! Or do *you not know that he who is joined to a harlot is one body with her? For "the two," he says, "shall become one flesh." But he who is joined to the Lord is one spirit with Him. Flee sexual immorality. Every sin that a man does is outside the body,*

54

but he who commits sexual immorality sins against his own body. Or do you not know that your body is the temple of the Holy Spirit who is in you, whom you have from God, and you are not your own? For you were bought at a price; therefore, glorify God in your body and in your spirit, which are God's. (1 Cor 6:15–20)

Holiness is based on the fact we were bought (we are now God's possession) for the price paid on the cross to be a living *temple of the Holy Spirit* (1 Cor 3:17, 6:19). Christ now lives in us, and whoever commits sexual immorality sins against Christ, who now dwells within him. **Personal holiness is not about fleeing from the world to live in a monastery. It is about respecting God's property since you are a temple of the Holy Spirit**. Holiness begins from within a man by the work of the Holy Spirit, not from without. "*We are complete in Him.*" (Col 2:10–23), and Christ in us is the hope for progressive holiness. He has set us free from the elementary principles of this world and "*the appearance of wisdom in self-made religion and self-abasement and severe treatment of the body but are of no value against fleshly indulgence*" (Col 2:23).

For many non-Christians as well as Christians, overt legalism is repugnant. The disciplined life consisting of attending church several times a week, dressing conservatively, home schooling, observing certain dietary laws, rejecting non-biblical entertainment such as playing cards, dancing, movies, and television seems too legalistic. The Pharisees prided themselves in attempting to observe not only the Ten Commandments but also the civil, dietary, and ceremonial laws totaling 611 laws mentioned in the Torah as well as other rules of behavior that were added later. The Pharisees, or "separate ones" in Hebrew, became "the interpreters," referring to their unique interpretations of biblical law. Josephus, a Jewish historian of the first century who wrote for non-Jews in Greek, calls the Pharisees a "choice of life and a philosophy." The Pharisees were zealous observers of the Old Testament law and especially concerned with ritual purity, tithing, food, and the correct observance of Sabbath and the public appearance of righteousness. As respects *touching*, prohibitions and distinctions no less minute were insisted on. "Do not handle, do not taste, do not touch" (Col 2:21)! To anyone familiar with these religious regulations, the apostle's words of rebuke of pharisaic legalism are poignant.

> "*When He had disarmed the rulers and authorities, He made a public display of them, having triumphed over them through Him. Therefore no one is to act as your judge in regard to food or drink or in respect to a festival or a new moon or a Sabbath day—things which are a mere shadow of what is to come; but the substance belongs to Christ. Let no one keep defrauding you of your prize by delighting in self-abasement and the worship of the angels, taking his stand on visions he has seen, inflated without cause by his fleshly mind.*" (Col. 2:15–18)

The Pharisees claimed to love God but rejected Jesus and became His main opponents. The sect of the Pharisee became an extra-biblical system of religion where man was justified by works rather than faith. The apostle Paul, however, was raised a Pharisee and continued to regard himself as a Pharisee in the sense of being obedient to the Jewish civil, ceremonial, and legal law in order to reach the Jews for Christ, even after he became a missionary for Christ (Phil. 3:5).

The Gospel of Matthew presents the Pharisees as personifications of evil, as people incapable of speaking or thinking anything good (Matt 9:4; 12:34, 39, 45; 16:4; 22:18; 23:15). This quality identifies them closely with Satan, the evil one (13:19, 38–39). Throughout the Gospel, they are identified with epithets that characterize them as offspring of the devil rather than as children of God: "brood of vipers" (3:7; 12:34; 23:33) and "child of hell" (23:15). The meaning of such identification becomes clear in a parable Jesus tells. The world is like a field in which God has placed potentially good people, and the devil has planted evil people among them (13:24–30, 36–43). Jesus explicitly identifies the Pharisees as being among those "plants that the heavenly Father did not plant"; they are not God's people, and they will be uprooted in time (15:13).

> *And He also told this parable to some people who trusted in themselves that they were righteous and viewed others with contempt: "Two men went up into the temple to pray, one a Pharisee and the other a tax collector. "The Pharisee stood and was praying this to himself: 'God, I thank You that I am not like other people: swindlers, unjust, adulterers, or even like this tax collector. 'I fast twice a week; I pay tithes of all that I get.' "But the tax collector, standing some distance away, was even unwilling to lift up his eyes to heaven, but was beating his breast, saying, 'God, be merciful to me, the sinner!' "I tell you; this man went to his house justified rather than the other; for everyone who exalts himself will be humbled, but he who humbles himself will be exalted.* (Luke 18:9–14)

In his prayer, the Pharisee drew attention to himself by boasting to God (and anyone listening) how self-important he was. He was, if you will, a braggart. He also was an intolerant bigot because he loathed the poor, despised, lower-class publican. And we notice two things about him. First, he seemingly lived a good life in order to inform the world that he was good in and of himself. Evidently, there is no mention of any community leaders who heard his confession, denying that he was a "good" person. He talked about what he offered to God and humanity ("see what I give?") while needing nothing in return. He had it all and was an unabashed narcissist filled with pride. He had works of righteousness. The point of this parable of Jesus is to condemn self-righteousness; that is why He led off His parable with this introduction: "*He also told this parable to some people who trusted in themselves that they were righteous, and viewed others with contempt.*"

The tax collector prayed in an opposite way from the Pharisee. Where the Pharisee stood tall before God, the tax collector could not even raise his eyes to heaven. Instead, he beat himself on the breast and begged God to have mercy on him. He drew God's loving and compassionate attention by telling God that he was a sinner in need of God's grace. The Pharisee, who had regarded *everyone but himself as a sinner*, was compared with the publican who regarded *everyone else as righteous* compared with himself, "the sinner." He came with empty hands, in need of God's mercy. He needed it all. This parable underscores two points about how we are to approach God: humility and confession of our sin with a repentant heart.

The parable of the Good Samaritan in Luke 10:30-37 also casts light on such comparisons as between "the righteous" elder brother and the pardoned prodigal, or the ninety-nine that "need no repentance" and the lost treasure that was found. Finally, this: "Except your righteousness shall exceed the righteousness of the Scribes and Pharisees, ye shall in no case enter into the Kingdom of heaven" (Matt 5:20). And so, the parable ends with the general principle, so often enunciated: "*For every one that exalteth himself shall be abased; and he that humbleth himself shall be exalted*" (Luke 18:14 KJV).

Natural man would rather earn his place in heaven by works rather than receive the free gift of salvation offered by Jesus. The natural man is suspicious of any offer that claims to be free and may belittle evangelicals who claim salvation is a free gift from God. He prefers offers that require progressive work on his part. He may be more attracted to Mormonism or Catholicism or other religions where the individual earns his salvation. Men enjoy and are attracted to a challenge and often desire to work out their own salvation.

One of the great mistakes of modern evangelism has been the dumbing down of the call to salvation to making a simple decision for Christ! The great challenge is to *"give up all and follow me"* (Matt 10:38; 16:24–25; Luke 9:23–24). **In actuality, the true offer of salvation to the seeker is not free at all but costs the recipient his life!!**

It is an exchange between man and God where a man loses his life and everything important to him in exchange for a completely new life in Christ (2 Cor 5:17). Martin Luther called it **"The Great Exchange." At the cross, man's sins are exchanged for Christ's righteousness** (2 Cor 5:21). That is radical Christianity. **Unfortunately, many evangelists are merchandising the blessings of Christ and the promise of heaven without requiring complete surrender of the seeker. This is a false, cross-less Christianity**. A works-based approach to Christian religion fosters self-righteousness, legalism, pride, and arrogance. Many men think that they are basically good and will be accepted by God because they are good people. They are not unlike the Jewish Pharisees in the New Testament. Unfortunately, few understand the irony that **hell is full of good people—yes some of the very best people, religious people, pastors, theologians who have never repented. Heaven is actually full of only repentant sinners! We are not saved by religion but saved by a trusting relationship with Christ by faith. *Only repentant sinners saved by grace alone go to heaven. The self-righteous who trust in themselves, and their good works go to hell!*** If we don't think of ourselves as sinners, we are surely deceived.

> *"If we say that we have no sin, we are deceiving ourselves and the truth is not in us. If we confess our sins, He is faithful and righteous to forgive us our sins and to cleanse us from all unrighteousness. If we say that we have not sinned, we make Him a liar and His word is not in us"* (1 John 1:8–10).

Paul and Peter commented about those who profess Christianity but were false prophets (1 Tim 6:3–5; 2 Tim 2:16–19; 2 Pet 2:1–22). Many know the truth but *"who perish, because they did not receive the love of the truth, that they might be saved"* (2 Thess 2:10 NKJV).

We begin by approaching God with an understanding of who He is, and then we are to approach God with an understanding of who we are. We are sinners at the core—poor and frail in our abilities. We need God. **We don't need to convince God of how good we are, rather God sees how good we are not. We cannot depend on our righteous works, social status, wealth, church attendance, church office, or other men's good opinion of our character. Self-righteous people forget that we can never please a Holy God by any non-spiritually inspired righteous work.** God is the author of all good works, and it is God working through His Holy Spirit that produces any and all works acceptable to Him. We boast in God's marvelous mercy that He chooses to use sinners to be vessels of His goodness to a fallen world. If we want God to hear our prayers, we must learn to approach God as a hopeless undeserving sinner, not a self-righteous Pharisee. Paul, the transformed Pharisee, said of himself:

"It is a trustworthy statement, deserving full acceptance, that Christ Jesus came into the world to save sinners, among whom I am foremost of all." (1 Tim 1:15) It is God *"who has saved us and called us with a holy calling, not according to our works, but according to His own purpose and grace which was granted us in Christ Jesus from all eternity"* (2 Tim 1:9).

I am a confessed Pharisee. I can identify with the self-righteous Pharisee since I am guilty of being a "Christian bigot." I have been repulsed by the hypocrisy of many religious people by thinking that I was superior to these hypocrites while not seeing the passion and heart of many who sincerely want to please God. The Pharisees were ardent, sincere, "almost a Christian," religious people no different than many of us. Jesus mourned for Jerusalem and those who rejected Him, and we also should mourn for the lost. We constantly need to remember that *"thereby but for the grace and mercy of God go I."*

It is so easy to justify ourselves to God by being a good person whom God must love because He has so gifted us materially and seemingly spiritually. **Christianity is undeserved, and no one can explain why God chooses some undeserving sinners and not others as His children**. Thus, I know that God came to save sinners of which I am one, justified by the grace and mercy of God alone and without any religious works. Paul admonishes the Galatians:

> *"You foolish Galatians, who has bewitched you, before whose eyes Jesus Christ was publicly portrayed as crucified? This is the only thing I want to find out from you: did you receive the Spirit by the works of the Law, or by hearing with faith? Are you so foolish? Having begun by the Spirit, are you now being perfected by the flesh?"* (Galatians 3:1–3)

Those "almost a Christian" seekers need to be released from carrying the heavy burden of useless works.

> *"Come to Me, all who are weary and heavy-laden, and I will give you rest. Take My yoke upon you and learn from Me, for I am gentle and humble in heart, and YOU WILL FIND REST FOR YOUR SOULS. For My yoke is easy and My burden is light."* (Matthew 11:28–30)

Jesus offers freedom from useless works toward a peace beyond understanding.

Going to church doesn't make you a Christian any more than going to the garage makes you a car. (Laurence J. Peter)

An unholy church! It is useless to the world, and of no esteem among men. It is an abomination, hell´s laughter, heaven´s abhorrence. The worst evils which have ever come upon the world have been brought upon her by an unholy church. (C. H. Spurgeon)

I think our doctrine has been forgotten, assumed, ignored, and even misshapen and distorted by the habits and rituals of daily life in a narcissistic culture. . . . Religion, spirituality, and moral earnestness—what Paul called "the appearance of godliness but denying its power" (2 Tim 3:5)—can continue to thrive in our environment precisely because they avoid the scandal of Christ. (Michael Horton)

Certainly, one of the great problems in today's churches is a man-pleasing spirit. We are not to fear men but to fear God. If we love our Lord and fear Him, we will not fear man. John tells us:

"Love has been perfected among us in this: that we may have boldness in the Day of Judgment; because as He is, so are we in this world. There is no fear in love; but perfect love casts out fear, because fear involves torment. But he who fears has not been made perfect in love. We love Him because He first loved us." (1 John 4: 17–19 NKJV)

Religious hypocrites suffer from crippling disease: a chronic fear of man. It is an utterly debilitating condition that undermines obedience and faith. How often we too are stricken with it—whether we are hypocrites for not! We are intimidated by man. How many moves of God are cut short by a man fearing spirit? "But what will people say?" The fear of man is a snare (Prov 29:25); it is so easy to be caught up in it. King Saul had a commission from the Lord, but he was afraid of the people and so he gave in to them. (I Sam 15:24). He had one eye on God and the other eye on man. Because he was double-minded and unstable at heart, he lost both the flock and God's favor. He forfeited the kingship to another. God wanted a man after his own heart.

"Too many leaders are pursuing the crowd when they're supposed to be following the cloud. They are experts in bringing in the people but novices in bringing down the power. Rather than cultivating

faith, their courting favor. **They want to be in tune with the sheep, but they have gotten out of harmony with the Shepherd.** And He knows what is good for the flock. Doing things His way is life. The pastor who walks in His footsteps will truly serve the sheep... **Our gospel message has been doubly defective. We have injured our hearers in two ways. We have failed to tell them that the old life must end; and we have failed to show them new life in Him."** (Michael L. Brown, *The Rude Awakening, How Saved Are We?* Destiny Image Publishers, 1990)

Thousands are deceived into supposing that they have "accepted Christ" as their "personal Savior", who have not first received Him as Lord." A.W. Pink

Chapter 5
Biblical Conversion

What is biblical conversion, or how can a man be saved from eternity in hell? The heart of man is deceitful, and we think we can approach God on our own terms. There has always been a group of people who believe in the name of Jesus. Yet Jesus, in his day, could not commit himself to them because He knew all men and that many would never believe (John 2:23–25). Language is important. **The word *conversion* means not just a change of mind about Christ but also a life change in the heart, resulting in a changed life and behavior resulting from an infusion of God's grace** (James 1:22; 2:14). Many evangelists have asked people to accept the Lord and to ask Jesus into their hearts. **The words "accept the Lord" are an affront to God.** Who are we as sinners to come and stand before a Holy God, the creator of all things, and say "I accept you as Lord and Savior!" (Psalm 8:1–4)?

The call just to accept Jesus rejects the message of the cross and demonstrates the arrogance of some men. God is the Lord of the universe and creator of all things; He does not need man's approval or acceptance. But man needs God's approval and acceptance or faces eternal judgment. A man who knows his own sin recognizes that he humbly can only call upon a Holy God's great mercy to receive him, a sinner, and to submit to His sovereign righteous judgments and commandments. ***God accepts us, we don't accept Him.*** No man is converted by force of argument but by the convicting work of the Holy Spirit. Our God is sovereign, and none of us deserve His offer to receive salvation—not of works but by the free gift of saving faith through Christ's propitiatory work on the cross.

> *"For all have sinned and fall short of the glory of God, being justified freely by His grace through the redemption that is in Christ Jesus, whom God set forth as a propitiation (atonement) by His blood, through faith, to demonstrate His righteousness, because in His forbearance God had passed over the sins that were previously committed, to demonstrate at the present time His righteousness, that He might be just and the justifier of the one who has faith in Jesus."* (Rom 3:22–26)

The thought that, somehow, we can choose God implies that the gift of salvation is freely given to anyone who just asks Jesus into his or her heart. Man doesn't choose God. God chooses His children. *"God has mercy on whom He chooses to have mercy, and He hardens whom He chooses to harden"* (Rom 9:18). **The reformers said that Christ's sacrifice on the cross was *sufficient* to save everyone but *efficient* to save only some, His elect. Man lacks the power and ability to overcome his sinful fallen nature.** Many feel that the work of conversion is accomplished through a rational argument. Americans are very pragmatic and rational and struggle with God's sovereignty. Saving faith is not intellectually obtained by a rational argument but is a gift from God. Sometimes, it seems God is just not fair, for we are not recognizing that if God would give man what he deserves, then none would be saved. **The word *fair* is not in Scripture and is an insult to a sovereign God.** God saves some by the work of grace through the Holy Spirit that changes man's heart and mind and draws him to the Lord. **To believe that man must give permission to the Holy Spirit for salvation is to steal glory from God and to make salvation a work of man.**

Salvation is a monergistic work of God. This means that our faith is a sovereign gift of God that glorifies God alone and is independent of human action. Man cannot save himself! Our position as sinners is to surrender to the call, to give up all, to die to self, and to follow Christ (Matt 16:24–25). Romans 1:17 says, *"The just shall live by faith."*

This inspired Luther to declare **"faith alone saves, not the works of man."** John Calvin and Luther understood that man is saved by grace through faith alone in Christ alone. The reformers' emphasis was that saving faith is the work of the Holy Spirit through the gift of God's grace alone. It is God's grace through Christ's redemptive work on the cross that saves.

Faith in the work of the cross justifies, or makes us right with God, through the great exchange on the cross where Christ took our unrighteousness in exchange for his holy, unblemished righteousness. *"For He made Him who knew no sin to be sin for us, that we might become the righteousness of God in Him"* (2 Cor 5:21). Our faith is based on relational knowledge of the triune God through Scripture and history and rests squarely on the promises and character of God. We believers are *reckoned* righteous once and forever at the cross. There is a work of grace that also is making us righteous called sanctification. Being made righteous (justified) and sanctified are part of the same action of the Holy Spirit. The only difference is that being made righteous is a one-time event while being made holy (sanctification) is a lifelong process. It is the work of grace that slowly and progressively makes us more like Christ so that we can lead a moral life. The grace of God equips us, as well as calls us, to good works, particularly hope, holiness, and love.

A true conversion experience is characterized by meekness, modesty, and self-diffidence rather than a spirit of pride and arrogance and self-righteousness (James 4:6). True faith produces righteous living by the changes of the inner man by the Holy Spirit (James 2:14–19) but not meritorious works of the flesh that attempt to earn favor with God. Good works are the good fruit from a good tree grounded in Christ (John 1:12; 2 Cor 5:17). John Calvin wrote in his *Institutes of the Christian Religion* (Vol 2:98):

We dream not of faith which is devoid of good works, nor the justification which can exist without them. How would you then obtain justification in Christ? You must previously possess Christ. But you cannot possess him without being made partaker of His sanctification: for Christ cannot be divided. . . . thus, it appears how true it is that *we are justified not without and yet not by works.* **This means that the justification by faith in Christ (Rom 1:17) is unearned and a gift from God. Saving faith will produce works of the spirit not of the flesh.** (James 2:18).

Matthew Henry in his *Commentary on the Whole Bible* wrote:

We are too apt to rest in a bare confession of faith, and to think that this will save us; it is a cheap and easy religion to say, we believe in the articles of the Christian faith; but it is a grand illusion to imagine that this is enough to bring us to heaven. Those works which evidence true faith must be works of self-denial, and such as God himself commands. The most plausible profession of faith, without works is dead. We must not think that either, without the other, will justify and save us. This is the grace of God where and we stand and we should stand to it.

The question for many generations has been: is this teaching about a covenant of works in righteousness or a covenant of grace? Most reformers agreed that the fruit of repentance can be used as evidence of saving faith, and our assurance must be objective and external to us, with the exception of the internal witness of the Holy Spirit. There always will be seekers who believe in a covenant of works and seek to prove their salvation by their works. However, **saving faith changes a person both inwardly, as well as outwardly**. True faith will be fruitful in good, unselfish works that bring glory to God and not men. Those with saving faith are new creatures who undergo a progressive metamorphosis because of the grace of God and work of the Holy Spirit, like when a worm changes into a butterfly (2 Cor 5:17). I know I am saved, that I am being saved, and that one day I will be complete in Christ. My justification is entirely by grace alone through faith alone. In other words, all of my salvation (100%) is due to God's graciousness, and none is due to my effort (0%) or anything good in me. The faith I have is an undeserved unearned gift from God.

Finally, after nearly 500 years of church debate, the Catholic and Lutheran churches have come to the appearance of an agreement of the basic common understanding of salvation. The agreement looks good on paper, but the definitions of words such as grace, justification, and salvation are actually quite different between Catholics and Protestants. Protestants understand justification as a singular act in which God declares an unrighteous individual righteous at one time (2 Cor 5:21; Eph 2:8; Phil 1:29; Acts 16:14). Catholics distinguish between initial justification at baptism and permanent justification accomplished by a continuous lifetime of good works (James 2:14–26; Gal 5:19–21; Matt 19:17). Basically, the Catholic Church has been making increasing overtures to Protestants by saying we agree on the essentials of the faith, so why can't we be one big happy family? For Catholics, justification is by works and faith. For Protestants it is by faith alone without works. We don't agree on the essentials, including the authority of Scripture. These distinctives have not changed since the Council of Trent (1545–1567). However, more recently, there has been a great effort to find doctrinal agreement between Catholics and Protestants, particularly on the doctrine of justification.

> "We confess together that all persons depend completely on the saving grace of God for their salvation. The freedom they possess in relation to persons and the things of this world is no freedom in relation to salvation, for

as sinners they stand under God's judgment and are incapable of turning by themselves to God to seek deliverance, of meriting their justification before God, or of attaining salvation by their own abilities. *Justification takes place solely by God's grace.* Because Catholics and Lutherans confess this together, it is true to say." (*Joint Declaration on the Doctrine of Justification* by the Lutheran World Federation and the Catholic Church 1999)

Postmodern multiculturalism deemphasizes theological distinctives. The definitions of words, such as justification, are critical. True biblical orthodox Christianity is being increasingly marginalized as hypercritical, out of date, prejudicial, and unyielding to "new" ideas.

Not only has there been a misunderstanding of justification and there has been a misunderstanding of biblical confession. The historical context of the word *confession*, which in the Greek can mean to "make a statement, in the legal sense or to bear witness or to make solemn statements of faith, or to confess something in faith," or "to express openly one's allegiance to a proposition or person—to profess, to confess, confession." Romans 10:9–10, 13 is where Paul writes:

> *"If you confess with your mouth the Lord Jesus and believe in your heart that God has raised him from the dead you will be saved for with a heart one believes to righteousness and with the mouth is made to salvation. . . . For whoever calls upon the name of the Lord shall be saved."* (Romans 10:9-10)

Paul was speaking to the Jews in 10:3–6, who were ignorant of God's righteousness and were seeking to establish their own righteousness. They had not submitted to the righteousness of God and did not understand the righteousness of faith. Proper biblical scholarship always requires interpretation of Scripture according to the context and genre of the times and in the original language. Scripture interprets scripture.

In ancient Roman times, the understanding of confession was to stand at the gate of the city before the elders and confess your faith to either Christ or Caesar. One only had to say in Greek "**Kaiser Kurios**," which means Caesar is Lord, or to lose one's head or face crucifixion by confessing the Christian God, who was (and is) superior to all other gods and King over all kings—and that all power was given to Christ. This was seen as rebellion against the Roman government by denying Caesar as King of kings. For the average pagan Roman, this confession was trivial since Romans had many gods, and it was a simple matter to add Caesar to the panoply of pagan gods. The Christian message has always been "**Christos Kurios**" or Jesus, the Christ, is Lord and the *only one true God and King and ruler of all mankind*.

To confess Jesus as Lord has always meant rebellion against the world system and worldly rulers. True faith will be tested, as it is costly as opposed to cheap grace and cheap faith.

"If the world hates you, you know that it hated me before it hated you. If you were of the world, the world would love its own. Yet because you're not of this world, but I chose you out of this world, therefore the world hates you" (John 15:18–19). Jesus reminded the disciples in John 16:2, *"They will make you outcasts from the synagogue, but an hour is coming for everyone who kills you to think that he is offering service to God."*

The true confession of Christ to the marketplace indicates that salvation has already occurred, and the professor of faith is willing to pay the price of possible death for his confession. **The message of the gospel has always been to *come and die daily* and receive new life in Christ** (Luke 9:23)**. Only dead men can receive new life in Christ**. In other words, t**he only good Christian is a dead Christian**. It was an outward confession of a changed heart and life. Peter (Luke 22:32) could not confess Christ on the night of Christ's betrayal, but once he received the Holy Spirit after Christ's resurrection, he was extremely bold when he stood up to the Council and the High Priest in Acts chapter four and said, *"And there is* *salvation in no one else; for there is no other name under heaven that has been given among men by which we must be saved"* (Acts 4:5–13). **The missing message in today's evangelism is the cost of discipleship, the cross, and the exclusivism of God's sovereign call. The false gospel is about acceptance of God's grace in salvation without a corresponding call to die to self, repent of sin, or live a life of obedience to the Lord.**

The German theologian and Christian martyr Dietrich Bonhoeffer's famous call to a return to biblical Christianity was:

> **"*Cheap grace* is preaching forgiveness without requiring repentance, baptism without church discipline, Communion without confession... Cheap grace is grace without discipleship, grace without the cross, grace without Jesus Christ, living and incarnate... *Costly grace* is the gospel which must be sought again and again, the gift which must be asked for, the door at which a man must know...It is costly because it costs man his life, and it is grace because it gives man the only true life. "The biblical message places emphasis on agreement or acceptance of the historical facts about Jesus and the promises of Scripture.

The biblical message has always been about *receiving and submitting to Jesus* and the cross, rather than *accepting* the Lord.

> Paris Reidhead said, "And so it had gotten down to the place where salvation was nothing more than the assent to a scheme or a formula." Religion is hanging around the cross; Christianity is getting on the cross. (Steve Hill)

> The "flesh" is too bad to be cleansed; it must be crucified. (Watchman Nee)

> A whole new generation of Christians has come up believing that it is possible to 'accept' Christ without forsaking the world. (A. W. Tozer)

"For more than 60 years the Christian church has gone around the world telling people to "pray this little prayer after me" in order to be "saved" or converted. Some call it "Asking Jesus into your heart" or "Giving your heart to the Lord," or praying the "Sinner's prayer." But would it surprise you to learn that such a thing is found NOWHERE in the entire Bible? Is there ever a time when an apostle or evangelist in the New Testament leads someone in such a "salvation prayer"—or anything like it? No—never." (Andrew Strom)

God is not Fair

God is not fair.
Some are born tall, some short
Some are born without arms or legs
Some are slow mentally, some brilliant
Some are ugly, some beautiful
Some are black, some yellow
Some are red, some white
Some are born in poverty, some to riches
God is not fair.
If I were to receive God's justice, where would I be?
If I were to stand before God's judgement seat
Would he remind me that He requires spiritual righteousness?
God is not fair
What would happen to me if God was fair?
God sent His only son to die a horrible death on the cross for me.
God is not fair.
It was so unfair that Jesus who led a perfect life had to die for my sin
God is not fair.
If God was fair, I would never see heaven, the sinner that I am.
God is not fair
Because God is not fair, I can receive the undeserved cleansing
blood of Jesus
I thank God that He is not fair!

(Dorsett D Smith MD)

Chapter 6

Repentance

God is the giver of all good things, and the fullness of all power is found in God. The "almost a Christian" believes that if he accepts the basic theological and religious tenets of the Christian faith, he is receiving the Holy Spirit. A true Christian receives the gift of God's salvation as an undeserving beggar based on the unmerited favor shown by a loving God. He is repentant. The true Christian places his hope in God's election and the promise that what God starts He will finish (John. 7:39; 20:22; Acts 1:8; 2:38; Rev. 8:15; 1 Cor. 2:12).

The words commonly used, such as "ask Jesus in your heart," "give your heart to the Lord," or "accept Jesus as Lord and Savior" are not found in the Bible. **The biblical call to repent, receive, believe, and be baptized** was made by Peter chapter 2:37–38 of the book of Acts: *"Repent, I let everyone of you be baptized in the name of Jesus Christ for the remission of sins; and you shall receive the gift of the Holy Spirit."* Mark quotes Jesus as saying *"the time is fulfilled and the kingdom of God is at hand. Repent and believe in the gospel."* (Mark 1:15) Luke finishes his Gospel with *"the Great Commission" that repentance and remission of sins should be preached in His name to all nations, beginning at Jerusalem"* (Luke 24:47).

Some men ask: if we are justified by faith alone, why is repentance necessary? Repentance is inextricably connected to salvation by faith because God does not allow a converted man to continue in sin. The new birth, regeneration, or "born-again" experience results in a changed heart and a spirit of repentance. If there is no repentance, then there never was a changed heart or true salvation by saving faith. *A changed heart always results in changed behavior and a call to repentance.* The call to repent is universal to all that believe.

The Israelites are without exception a sinful people, all of them needing the salvation, which Jesus brings (Mt 1:21; Lk 1:77). In demonstration of God's grace, Jesus proclaims his gospel to the entire nation (Mt 4:23; 9:35; 15:24; Lk 4:43; 9:6; 20:1). From the most respectable to the least, all are summoned to submit to God's rule, all are invited to come and partake freely of the banquet he has spread (Lk 14:16–24). But the gift of salvation must be received if it is to be experienced (Mk 10:15). And while it is indeed a gift which costs nothing, it is also a priceless treasure for which a wise person will freely sacrifice everything else (Mt 13:44–46; a sacrifice exceeded only by the cost of rejecting the gospel: Mt 11:20–24; Mk 8:34–39; Lk 14:24, 33). **"Repent and believe in the gospel,"** commands Jesus (Mk 1:15). **Notice that repentance is stressed as a condition of salvation (Mk. 1:15; 6:12; Lk. 24:47) Many Christian theologians believe that the condition of salvation is by faith alone (Romans 3:28, 5:1) and that repentance will follow saving faith. The reformers believed that repentance precedes conversion and is a regenerative work of the Holy Spirit. Which is it?**

The self-righteous and the self-sufficient must be jolted out of their false sense of security and humbly recognize their need of God (Lk 6:24–26). Only then will Jesus's message to the poor be seen as gospel. An announcement of liberation (4:18–19) is good news only to people who are enslaved and know they are. The command applies also to the destitute and the afflicted. Those among them who bemoan their lot without repenting of their sin must learn that it is being personally related to God as subject to sovereign and as child to father which makes one "blessed" (Mt 5:3–10). But something further is needed for the response to be complete: **a person cannot believe Jesus's gospel without a commitment to the trinitarian personhood of God. (11:28; 18:6; cf. John 3:16).** Even those who are already "poor in spirit," in the sense defined earlier, are not really "blessed" until they acknowledge the truth of Jesus's claims (Mt 11:6) and commit themselves to a life of obedience on his terms (7:21–27). This prepares us for the next point.

Repent, for the kingdom of heaven is at hand (Matt. 3:2; Matt. 4:17); I have not come to call the righteous, but sinners to repentance (Luke 5:32); repent and believe the gospel (Mark 1:15); they preached that men should repent (Mark 6:12); repentance and forgiveness should be preached (Luke 24:47); there is joy before the angels of God over one sinner who repents (Luke 15:10); repent and turn to God (Acts 3:19); he commands all people everywhere to repent (Acts 17:30); testifying of repentance toward God and faith in our Lord Jesus Christ (Acts 20:21); they must turn to God in repentance (Acts 26:20); repentance from dead works (Heb. 6:1).

True repentance is a gift from God. God gives repentance to Israel (Acts 5:31); God has granted to the Gentiles repentance unto life (Acts 11:18); God may grant them repentance (2 Tim. 2:25); God's kindness leads you to repentance (Rom. 2:4); he wants all to come to repentance (2 Pet. 3:9). Signs of Repentance: I repent in dust and ashes (Job 42:6); a baptism of repentance (Matt. 3:11; Mark 1:4; Luke 3:3; Acts 13:24; Acts 19:4); repent and be baptized (Acts 2:38); when God saw their deeds, how they turned from their wicked way (Jonah 3:10); your fathers repented (Zech. 1:6); Godly sorrow produces repentance without regret leading to salvation (2 Cor. 7:10); when they turn from their sin (1 Kgs. 8:35); bring forth fruit fitting repentance (Matt. 3:8; Luke 3:8); perform deeds fitting repentance (Acts 26:20); if the miracles had been done, they would have repented in sackcloth and ashes (Luke 10:13); Tyre and Sidon would have repented long ago (Matt. 11:21); Nineveh repented at the preaching of Jonah (Matt. 12:41); Godly sorrow produces repentance (2 Cor. 7:9–10).

Truly, these times of ignorance God overlooked, but now commands *all men everywhere to repent* because he has appointed a day on which he will judge the world in righteousness by the Man whom he has ordained. He has given assurance of this to all by raising Him from the dead. (Acts 17:30–31; 26:20; Luke 24:47)

Leonard Ravenhill stated: **"Get rid of this bunkum about the 'carnal Christian.' Forget it! If you're carnal, you're not saved, or you never have truly repented."**

Repentance is much more than a changed mind but is a turn from self to be Christ-centered rather than self-centered. Man's problem is worship of self, and the only solution is to be Christ-centered, and not self-centered, by the work of the cross in our lives. Pop psychology promotes self-love in the context that you can't love others unless you love yourself. **The message of Christianity is that Christ came to slay the self and not save it; Repent!** What we can't do for ourselves, Jesus did on the cross. This sanctifying work is a continuous lifelong process.

> **R**epentance begins with **R**ecognition of an offense against God, then Godly **R**emorse or **R**egret and proceeds through **R**enunciation of the sin and **R**eversal by **R**eliance on God and then **R**estitution wherever possible.

The Westminster Confession Question 76 defines repentances as follows:

> **"Repentance unto life is a saving grace wrought in the heart of a sinner by the Spirit and word of God,** whereby, out of the sight and sense, not only of the danger, but also of the filthiness and odiousness of his sins, and upon the apprehension of God's mercy in Christ to such as are penitent, he so grieves for and hates his sins, **as that he turns from them all to God**, purposing and endeavouring constantly to walk with him in all the ways of new obedience."

The call for repentance on the part of man in the Old Testament (OT) is a call for him to return, or turn around, from the direction he was going. The Hebrew שׁוּב (šûb) means to "*(re)turn* or to turn around" and points man to his creaturely (and covenant) dependence on God. This Hebrew word for repentance, šûb, is the twelfth most frequently used verb in the OT, appearing just over 1050 times. It appears most often in Jeremiah (111 times) followed by Psalms (seventy-one times), Genesis (sixty-eight times), Ezekiel (sixty-two times), 1 Kings (sixty-two times), 2 Chronicles (sixty-one times), 2 Kings (fifty-five times), and Isaiah (fifty-one times). Such calls to turn around or repent are particularly frequent in the pre-exilic prophets. Amos 4:6–11 makes it clear that the evil that God intended as a consequence of Israel's sin is not malicious or vindictive but, rather, is intended to bring Israel to repentance. He who commits evil finds further evil willed by God. But he who repents of his evil often finds a God who repents of *his* evil. Thus, says the Lord of hosts, **"'Return to Me,' declares the Lord of hosts, '*that I may return to you,*' says the Lord of hosts"** (Zech 1:3). The Bible is rich in idioms describing man's responsibility in the process of repentance. Such phrases would include the following: "incline your heart unto the Lord your God" (Josh 24:23), "circumcise yourselves to the Lord" (Jer 4:4), "wash your heart from wickedness" (Jer 4:14), "break up your fallow ground" (Hos 10:12), and so forth. All these expressions of man's penitential activity, however, are subsumed and summarized by this one verb šûb. For better than any other verb it combines in itself the two requisites of repentance: to turn from evil and to turn to the good. One of the most eloquent pleas for repentance comes in Hosea 6:1–3 and 14:1–2—a plea alternating with hope and despair (3:5; 5:4; 7:10), with 11:1–11 that is particularly poignant. Equally moving are the hopes of Isaiah expressed in the name of his son, Shearjashub ("*a remnant shall return,*" 7:3; see also 10:21; 30:15; 19:22) and the pleadings of Jeremiah (3:1–4:4; 8:4–7; 14:1–22; 15:15–21), both mingled with foreboding and despair (Is. 6:10; 9:13; Jer 13:23). Other powerful expressions are Deut. 30:1–10; 1 Kings. 8:33–40, 46–53; 2 Chron. 7:14; Isa 55:6–7; Ezk. 18:21–24, 30–32; 33:11–16; Joel 2:12–14. See also particularly 1 Sam. 7:3; 2 Ki. 17:13; 2 Chron. 15:4; 30:6–9; Neh. 1:9; Ps. 78:34; Ezk. 14:6; Dan. 9:3; Zech. 1:3; Mal. 3:7. The classic example of national repentance was that led by Josiah (2 Kings. 22–23; 2 Chron. 34–35).

In the NT, the Greek word translated "repent" is *metanoia* (μετάνοια) is used about 60 times, which usually means "to change one's mind," and so also "to regret, feel remorse" (*i.e.,* over the view previously held). This note of remorse is present in the parable of the tax collector (Lk. 18:13), probably in Mt. 21:29, 32; 27:3 and Lk. 17:4 ('I am sorry'), and most explicitly in 2 Cor. 7:8–10. But the NT usage is much more influenced by the OT; šûb as ***repentance, not just as a feeling sorry or changing one's mind, is a turning around, a complete alteration of the basic motivation and direction of one's life.*** This is why the best translation for it is often 'to convert,' that is, 'to turn around' (conversion) or the Greek word *epistrepho* as used in Luke 22:32 displaying a complete turnaround.

It also helps to explain why John the Baptist demanded baptism as an expression of this repentance, not just for obvious "sinners," but for "righteous" Jews as well—baptism as a decisive act of turning from the old way of life and a throwing oneself on the mercy of the Coming One (Mt. 3:2, 11; Mk. 1:4; Lk. 3:3, 8; Acts 13:24; 19:4). Jesus's call for repentance receives explicit mention in Mk. (1:15, 6:12) and Mt. (4:17;11:20, 12:41), but is emphasized by Lk. (5:32; 10:13; 11:32; 13:3, 5; 15:7, 10; 16:30; 17:3, 24:47). Other sayings and incidents in all three Gospels, however, express very clearly the character of the repentance, which Jesus's whole ministry demanded. Its radical nature, as a complete turning around and return, is emphasized by the parable of the Prodigal Son (Lk. 15:11–24). Its unconditional character appears from the parable of the Pharisee and tax collector—repentance means acknowledging that no one has a possible claim upon God and submitting oneself without excuse or attempted justification to God's mercy (Lk. 18:13). The "turn around" in previous values and lifestyle is highlighted by the encounter with the rich young man (Mk. 10:17–22) and Zacchaeus (Lk. 19:8). Above all, Mt. 18:3 makes it clear that to convert is to become like a child, that is, to acknowledge one's immaturity before God, one's inability to live life apart from God, and to accept one's total dependence on God. *There can be no forgiveness of sin without repentance.*

The call for repentance (and promises of forgiveness) features regularly in Luke's record of the preaching of the first Christians (Acts 2:38; 3:19; 8:22; 17:30; 20:21; 26:20)**. Here in Luke 22:32, the Greek word for repentance is replaced by *epistrepho*** (ἐπιστρέφω): to return (to turn around, change, or return; can also be translated to be converted; Acts 3:19; 9:35; 11:21; 14:15; 15:19; 26:18, 20; 28:27), where it means more a turning away (from sin) and a turning from self to God, the creator of all things, or conversion (see particularly Acts 3:19; 26:20), though each by itself the verb can embrace both senses (as in Acts 11:18; 1 Thess. 1:9).

It is clear from Acts 5:31 and 11:18 that no difficulty was felt in **describing repentance both as God's gift and as man's responsibility**. At the same time, Isaiah 6:9–10 is cited several times as an explanation of men's failure to convert (Mt. 13:14ff., Mk. 4:12; Jn. 12:40; Acts 28:26f.).

The writer to the Hebrews also indicates the importance of initial repentance (6:1), but whereas he questions the possibility of a second repentance (6:4–6; 12:17), others are even more emphatic in their belief that *Christians* can and need to repent continually. (2 Cor. 7:9, 12:21; Jas. 5:19ff., 1 Jn. 1:5–2:2; Rev. 2:5, 16, 21, 3:3, 19).

Western man believes that his salvation is based on accepting the basic theological and religious tenets of the Christian faith. This is very different from the biblical call of repentance, faith, and baptism. It is the reception of the Holy Spirit that distinguishes Christians from the world and religion, and it is the reception of the Holy Spirit that determines whether a man is Christian or not (Acts 8:16–17, 10:47, 19:2). Jesus promised the gift of the Holy Spirit to his disciples and said it was better for him to leave because the Holy Spirit would guide them and teach them all things (John 14–16). God must regenerate our souls and then draw us to receive the gift of conversion through faith in Jesus and the work of the Holy Spirit. *Man, simply cannot save himself without the help of the Holy Spirit.* Paul emphasizes in Galatians chapter 3 that those who have faith are the true sons of Abraham. He goes on to say that "the just shall live by faith." He rebukes the Galatian men and asks the question *"did you receive the Spirit by works of the law or by the hearing of faith? Are you so foolish? Having begun in the spirit are you now being made perfect but the flesh"* (Gal 3:2–3)?

Paul is saying, *"Everywhere I've been, I've preached repentance and a turn to God, performing deeds in keeping with their repentance."* A genuine repentance proves itself by its actions. (Acts 26:20). These passages make clear to us that the apostolic church preached unabashedly the same gospel John and Jesus preached: *"Repent for the remission of your sins"* (Mark 1:4, 15)!

Many Armenian or "Free Grace" (as opposed to "Sovereign Grace") Christians believe that man must repent to be saved based on his own free will, or that man must volitionally contribute to his salvation through repentance. Scripture emphasizes that **repentance is the product of saving faith**, and man cannot earn his salvation or become repentant without the regenerative power of God through the enabling gift of the Holy Spirit. Man contributes nothing to his salvation. **Man cannot produce faith and repentance without the grace of God.** This produces tension, and man asks: why does God demand something that we can't do without the grace of God?

Repentance is a call to turn from our sinful selves and turn to God by confessing our sin and crying out to God for regeneration by the Holy Spirit. Faith and repentance are the evidence of a true work of the regenerative power of the Holy Spirit. The call to repentance is a call to the saving faith that produces repentance. *Jesus came to slay the self, not to*

save it*.* It is a call to turn from our old self-life to a new life in Christ. Faith and repentance are evidence of the true work of regenerative power of the Holy Spirit. Faith and repentance are two sides of the same coin and cannot be separated. The call to repentance is also a call to the saving faith that produces repentance (Acts 20:21).

> "How can someone who's going his own way go God's way? How can a person who's utterly committed to sin, the flesh, and the devil, and be utterly committed to Jesus Christ and righteousness? ***It is necessary to turn from in order to turn to. Repentance and faith are different sides of the same turning.* In repentance we turn from sin; in Faith we turn to Jesus Christ our righteousness.**" (*Repentance: The First Word of the Gospel* by Richard Owen Roberts, Crossway Books, 2002, p. 69).

> "Repentance unto life is a saving grace, wrought in the heart of a sinner by the Spirit and word of God, whereby, out of the sight and sense, not only of the danger, but also of the filthiness and odiousness of his sins, and upon the apprehension of God's mercy in Christ to such as are penitent, he so grieves for and hates his sins, as that he turns from them all to God, purposing and endeavouring constantly to walk with him in all the ways of new obedience." Westminster Confession of Faith *question 76.*

> "The man whose little sermon is 'repent' sets himself against his age, and will for the time being, be battered mercilessly by the age whose moral tone he challenges. There is but one end for such a man—'off with his head!' You had better not try to preach repentance until you have pledged your head to heaven." (Joseph Parker)

"Some people do not like to hear much of repentance; but I think it is so necessary that if I should die in the pulpit, I would desire to die preaching repentance." (Matthew Henry)

"Your intentions to repentance, and the neglect of that soul-saving duty, will rise up in judgment against you. Repentance carries with it a Divine rhetoric and persuades Christ to forgive multitudes of sins committed against him. Say not with thyself, To-morrow I will repent; for it is thy duty to do it daily." (John Bunyan)

"Let no man ever persuade you that any religion deserves to be called the Gospel, and which repentance toward God, has not a most prominent place. A Gospel indeed! That is no Gospel, in which repentance is not a principal thing. A Gospel! It is the Gospel of man, but not of God. A Gospel! It comes from the earth, and not from heaven. The Gospel! It is not a Gospel at all; it is rank, antinomianism, and nothing else." (J C Ryle)

In 1899, when William Booth, founder of the Salvation Army, was asked about the chief dangers confronting the church going into the twentieth century, he said that his main concerns were that the twentieth-century church would have **"*Religion without the Holy Spirit, Christianity without Christ, forgiveness without repentance, salvation without regeneration, politics without God, and heaven without hell.*"**

In summary true repentance is as follows:

REPENTANCE

TRUE	FALSE
GODLY SORROW II COR 7:9-10	SORROW FOR SELF AND PAST
FOR SINS	SORROW FOR GETTING CAUGHT
SEES SELF AS PROBLEM LUKE 5:32	SEES BEHAVIOR AS PROBLEM
POWER OF SIN (No self-control)	PENALTY OF SIN (Consequences)
A HEART BROKEN FOR SIN AND	A HEART CONVICTED BY SIN
FROM SIN MARK 2:17 (HATES SIN)	LUKE 3:3 (DOESN'T HATE SIN)
WILLING TO BE CHANGED BY GOD	WILLING TO CHANGE MY MIND
CHOOSES TO SIN NO MORE HEB 6:1	SORROW FOR SINS HEB 6:6
BASED ON FAITH IN GOD'S ABILITY	BASED ON LAW, LEADS TO WORKS
GRACE, GRACE ALONE ACTS 20:21	II TIM 2:25
RELIANCE ON GOD'S STRENGTH	RELIANCE ON STRENGTH OF SELF
POWER WITHOUT ROM 2:4	POWER WITHIN HEB 12:17
CHANGED HEART II COR 7:11	CHANGED MIND (AFRAID OF CONSEQUENCES)
CAUSES CHANGED LIVING ACTS 26:20	CHANGED IDEAS LUKE 3:8 (partial reformation)
LEADS TO FOCUS ON GOD	SELF REFORMATION IS SELF
AND OTHERS MATT 3:8	CENTERED, HOPELESS ACTS 26:17
PROOF IS CHANGED LIFE	ACTIONS MAY CHANGE WITHOUT MATT 3:2-12 CHANGE IN ATTITUDE, INNER MAN
ALL MEN (SINNERS) NEED TO	NEEDED BY OTHERS, NOT ME
MATT 13:1-5	HYPOCRITICAL CONCEALMENT OF SIN
CONTINUAL PROCESS I PETER 3:9	ONE TIME EVENT (still under sin's power)
PRODUCES GOD'S RIGHTEOUSNESS	PRODUCES SELF RIGHTEOUSNESS
NO FORGIVENESS WITHOUT IT	FORGIVENESS AND REPENTANCE
ACTS 5:31,11:18)	ARE SEEN AS SEPARATE ISSUES. LUKE 24:47
WORK OF GRACE ALONE	MAN'S WORK (EPHESIANS 2:8-9
(GALATIANS 1:6-9)	LEGALISM
MAKES COMPREHENSIVE	NO TRUE RESTITUTION
RESTITUTION (LUKE 19:8-10)	(EXODUS 22:6,12, LEV 5:16)

Restitution is a biblical concept closely related to the idea of **Restoration.** Unfortunately, it is not given much attention by many Bible teachers. If I were to rob a bank and then be captured by the police. I am sure I would **Regret** my mistake and have a <u>change of mind</u> (Greek *metanoia*) about my bad choices. I am sure I would have regret and worldly **Remorse** about my bad choices. This may mean that I have not truly repented and recognized my sin against God, I also need to **Renounce** my sin and sin nature and **Return** to God. Once I develop Godly **Remorse,** I will desire to make restitution. **Restitution** means that not only will I return the money I stole but will seek forgiveness and **Reconciliation** with all those affected by my sin. **Restoration** indicates replacement for whatever was taken, destroyed or emotionally and physically injured. **Restitution** means repayment over and above the actual loss, analogous to what is today called 'punitive' damages (e.g., Exod. 22:1–15; Lev. 6:1–7; Num. 5:5–7). For example, the ancient law found in Exod. 22:1, 4 clearly stipulates that anyone who steals an ox or a sheep must pay restitution to the owner of the animal(s). If the thief kills or sells the ox, he is required to pay restitution of five oxen; if he kills or sells the sheep, he is required to pay restitution of four sheep (cf. also 2 Sam. 12:6). If, however, the animal has not been harmed and is found safe in the possession of the thief, the culprit is required to pay double. Interestingly enough, if the thief has no means to pay this fine, he is to be sold as payment for his theft. In most of the New Testament writings, the word group used to designate the idea of restitution or restoration has a rather different meaning, namely, that of **Restoring in the sense of Reestablishing relationship with God and man or Return from self-serving sin to serving God.** (Matt. 17:11; Mark 9:12; Acts 1:6; 3:21) or even healing (Matt. 12:13; Mark 3:5; Luke 6:10; Mark 8:25)

Repentance is inseparable from Joy. David Wilkerson reminds us:

> "Most Christians never associate joy with repentance, but repentance is actually the mother of all joy in Jesus. Without it, there can be no joy. When David disobeyed, he lost the joy of the Lord, and it could only be restored by true repentance. So, he prayed, *"Wash me thoroughly from my iniquity, and cleanse me from my sin. For I acknowledge my transgressions, and my sin is always before me"* (Psalm 51:2-3).

David also prayed to regain what he had lost: *"Restore to me the joy of Your salvation"* (51:12).

It is impossible to maintain the joy of the Lord if sin is present in one's life. We must increasingly separate ourselves from the world around us. How can the Holy Spirit pour out joy on a people who continue to indulge in adultery, addictions, and materialism, living like those who do not follow Christ?

Only the joy of the Lord supplies us with true strength. We can talk all we want about our long walk with Christ, but if we aren't allowing the Holy Spirit to maintain the joy of the Lord in our hearts—if we aren't continually hungering for his Word—then we are losing our fire, and we won't be ready for what comes upon the world in these last days.

How do we maintain the joy of the Lord? We do it the same way we obtained His joy in the beginning.

First, we love, honor, and hunger excitedly for God's Word. Second, we continually walk in repentance. Third, we separate ourselves from all worldly influences.

This is how a Holy Spirit-infused person or church maintains "Jesus joy": rejoicing always, full of gladness.

In Summary, remember the seven Rs of repentance:

1. **R**emorse
2. **R**enunciation
3. **R**eliance on God
4. **R**eversal
5. **R**estitution
6. **R**econciliation
7. Submission to God's **R**ule

"Repentance is more than just sorrow for the past; repentance is a change of mind and heart, a new life of denying self and serving the Savior as king in self's place." (J.I. Packer)

Chapter 7
Pride

The basic issue with all of us is our pride, of which Paul spoke in the letter to the Galatians. It was pride that motivated the Galatians to think that salvation was by works. Pride is the desire of men and women either to serve themselves or to protect their place at the center of their existence. Pride was the first sin and the foundation of sin and lust (Ezek 28:1–19). It is self-love or idolatry of self that needs the killing of pride by the cross. A Christian, of course, would never say that he deserved salvation and perhaps never thinks it. **But the difficulty every Christian has is being and remaining genuinely amazed and heartbroken at God's grace to him or her without thinking that somehow God's grace was deserved or earned.** These thoughts are evidence of the pride that still fills our hearts. Jonathan Edwards reminds us that "**pride is God's most stubborn enemy**! There is no sin so much like the devil as pride. It is a secret and subtle sin and appears in a great many shapes which are undetected and unsuspected." Pride deceives us that we are somehow worthy of God's redemption and sacrifice on the cross!

We think so well of ourselves; it is very hard to think that God should not think good of us as well. The lie of our culture is man's need of a sense of self-worth because of low self-esteem. **The work of the cross is to show man that he is an absolutely unworthy sinner with no hope without the grace of God.** No man had lower self-esteem than the Apostle Paul, who called himself the "chief of sinners" (1 Tim 1:15). He was transparent and humble and spoke faithfully for God because the self was crucified with Christ.

"And when I came to you, brethren, I did not come with superiority of speech or of wisdom, proclaiming to you the testimony of God. For I determined to know nothing among you except Jesus Christ, and Him crucified. I was with you in weakness and in fear and in much trembling, and my message and my preaching were not in persuasive words of wisdom, but in demonstration of the Spirit and of power, so that your faith would not rest on the wisdom of men, but on the power of God." (1 Cor 2:1–5)

"We are fools for Christ's sake, but you are wise in Christ! We are weak, but you are strong! You are distinguished, but we are dishonored! To the present hour we both hunger and thirst, and we are poorly clothed, and beaten, and homeless. And we labor, working with our own hands. Being reviled, we bless; being persecuted, we endure; being defamed, we entreat. We have been made as the filth of the world, the offscouring of all things until now." (1 Cor 4:10–13)

Jesus reminds us that He chose us, and we did not choose Him. *"You did not choose me, but I chose you* and appointed you that you should go make sure you should remain"* (John 15:16). ***"No one can come to Me unless it has been granted to him by My Father"*** (John 6:65); *"My sheep hear my voice,* and I know them, and they follow me. And *I give them eternal life,* and they shall never perish; neither shalt anyone snatch them out of my hand"* (John 10:27–29). Since God is the author of our salvation according to His predetermined plan, we do not choose Him, but He chooses us.

"Just as he chose us in him before the foundation of the world, that we should be holy and without blame before him in love, having predestined us to adoption as sons by Jesus Christ to himself according to the good pleasure of his will." (Ephesians 1:4–5)

"For by Grace you have been saved through faith: and that not of yourselves, it is a gift of God" (Eph 2:8). There is no good answer why God has chosen some but not others. God knows who are His sheep, and they will respond to the call of the good Shepherd when He calls.

> "I am the good shepherd; and I know my sheep, and am known by my own. . . . And other sheep I have which are not of this fold: they also will I bring, and *they will hear my voice*, and there will be one flock and one shepherd."
> (John 10:14, 16)

The call of Christ usually comes from hearing the word of God spoken through men.

> "How then shall they call on him and who may have not believed? And how shall they believe in him who may have not heard? And how shall they hear without a preacher? How shall they preach unless they are sent? . . . . So, faith comes by hearing, and hearing by the word of God."
> (Rom 10:14-15, 17)

The mantra of postmodern society is "Free Choice." Some things never seem to change since this was the theology of Pelagius about free will in the fourth century AD. Pelagius believed there was no original sin, and therefore man was free to make his own moral choices. Many people reject the concept of the sovereignty of God and insist that if they can't choose God for themselves or by their own free will, they will reject a sovereign Christ. Men do not recognize the difference between their moral inability to make the ultimate moral choice of Jesus as Savior and Lord and their ability, freedom, or free will to make non-moral choices such as choosing secular things like clothing, food, friends, housing, transportation, schooling, and so forth. **God chooses us; we do not choose Him** (John 6:44, 65; 15:16).

Christianity requires the Christian to give up all and follow Christ (Matt 16:24–28). It has been estimated that only 10 percent of the Roman world was Christian prior to Emperor Constantine. Some historians have estimated that only 17 percent of Americans belonged to a church at the time of the American Revolution and 37 percent by the time of the Civil War; by 1980, 62 percent of Americans were members of a church (The Churching of America, 1776–2005 by Roger Finke and Rodney Stark, Rutgers University Press 2005). *The increase in church membership over the last 200 years seems to be inversely correlated with American morality!* What is the problem? The more personal wealth there was in America, the less true spirituality. Modernity blesses material abundance and equates prosperity with God's approval and blessing. Christianity has largely been replaced by religion. *The classic orthodox message of "come and die, give up all, and follow me" has been replaced by a consumer-driven message that you can have it all and still be a follower of Jesus if you simply accept a spiritual message of no cost and no cross.* Just believe in a message of easy grace: God loves you, and He forgives you without requiring repentance.

The average American does not see himself as inherently sinful and is more interested in buying "fire insurance" for the extremely cheap cost of simply "accepting Jesus" rather than true repentance, leaving all, dying to self, taking up his cross, and receiving a radically changed life (Matt 10:38–39; 16:24–28; Luke 9:24–27; 14:27) **The average American thinks of himself as being spiritual but not religious.** With the rise of the megachurch, there is emphasis on cheap grace, minimal biblical content, and little creedal affirmation. People attend church for many reasons, such as the need for amusement, fellowship, the enjoyment of drama and music, a confirming message, as well as a cure for loneliness, addictions, social and marriage problems— but most of all for the need of personal affirmation. **The postmodern church's mantra is that "Jesus loves everybody, and we don't**

judge anyone." Modernists are deists in that they believe God may exist but does not judge or intervene in the affairs of men. Gone is Christian orthodoxy and biblical truth about sin and judgment. Many churches today are consumer driven and largely therapeutic and teach a moralistic therapeutic deism, proudly claiming: "We are a hospital and are here to heal all your problems." The true gospel wounds, offends, and confronts sin and can cut a man to the quick and expose his sinful heart when spoken with the anointing of the Holy Spirit. It may even make his problems worse by exposing his destructive behavior.

Any Gospel, that doesn't offend the sinner and present the justice of God and the eternal damnation of sinners, is not the real gospel. **The postmodern gospel is heaven-focused versus the orthodox gospel, which is hell-focused on the eternal damnation of sinners and their need of a savior.**

We live in interesting times. These are the times of a great falling away in the Western world and simultaneously a time of great revival in the Second and Third worlds. Many Muslims are converting to Christianity. It is estimated that 40 percent of Muslim conversions are coming by dreams and visions of the Lord. Once a Muslim experiences a spiritual dream about Christ, he seeks to find an explanation by asking someone with a Bible. Once they find and hear the Word of God, they become Christians! Billions of Bibles in hundreds of different languages have been spread around the world in preparation of a great end-time harvest.

Remember the rich young ruler who asked the question, *"Good master, what good things shall I do that I might have eternal life?"* He claimed to have obeyed the commandments beginning as a youth being perfect in his obedience. And, yes, he was almost a Christian. The call of Jesus was to give up all and to sell what he had and then give it to the poor, so that he would have treasure in heaven. The gospel call was too radical for this young man (Matt 19:21–26).

We want God on our terms so we can keep our stuff and enjoy life. The gospel call to "pick up your cross and follow Me!" is too radical for most men. True faith is expensive. In fact, it costs you your life. You can't have a new life in Christ without losing the old life. The message of the gospel is no compromise. The only good Christians are dead Christians, or those who died to the old man in exchange for the new life in Christ.

And he who does not take up his cross and follow after me is not worthy of me. He who finds his life will lose it and he who loses his life for my sake will find it ." (Matt 10:38–39; 16:24–26; Mark 8:34–37; Luke 9:23–25; John 12:24–25).

"So, because you are lukewarm, and neither hot nor cold, I will spew you out of my mouth." (Rev. 3:16)

"A true faith in Jesus Christ will not suffer us to be idle. No, it is an active, lively, restless principle; it fills the heart, so that it cannot be easy till it is doing something for Jesus Christ." (George Whitefield)

"A world of nice people, content in their own niceness, looking no further, turned away from God, would be just as desperately in need of salvation as a miserable world— and might be even more difficult to save." (C. S. Lewis)

"Any concept of grace that makes us feel more comfortable sinning is not biblical grace. God's grace never encourages us to live in sin, on the contrary, it empowers us to say no to sin and yes to truth." (Randy Alcorn)

"I remind you that there are churches so completely out of the hands of God that if the Holy Spirit withdrew from them, they wouldn't find it out for many months." (A. W. Tozer)

"The knowledge of God is, in fact, a lifetime pursuit, not an instantaneous download." (David F. Wells)

Chapter 8
Entitlement Mentality

Lack of Gratitude and Thanksgiving: Today's Christianity is often contaminated by the "entitlement mentality" of the pew sitter. A classic early example of out-of-control self-centeredness is seen in the case of Diotrephes. He is mentioned in 3 John 9–10, where the Apostle says: *"I have written something to the church, but Diotrephes, who **likes to put himself first**, does not acknowledge our authority. . . . He is talking wicked nonsense against us. And not content with that, he refuses to welcome the brothers, and also stops those who want to and puts them out of the church."*

Diotrephes illustrates the truth that self-love is the mother of all heresies. Every false teaching and every rebellion against God's authority are ultimately rooted in a fleshly desire to have preeminence—in effect, to claim for oneself the glory that properly belongs to Christ. Every heretic the church has ever seen has tried to supplant God's truth and God's authority with his own overblown ego.

Indeed, self-centeredness itself is heretical because it is the very antithesis of everything Jesus taught or exemplified. And it produces seeds that give rise to every other heresy imaginable. It was an argument from the greater to the lesser. If the eternal Lord of glory was willing to take up a towel and wash His disciples' filthy feet, then there is no way those who claim to be His disciples should seek preeminence for themselves. Christ is our model, not Diotrephes. (John MacArthur, Table Talk, March 2012)

Proverbs describes what modern man calls narcissism or "scoffer," the biblical name for the self-absorbed, arrogant, haughty man who acts with arrogant pride. (Proverbs 21:24) The quintessential narcissist is Satan himself. The serpent's temptation to Adam and Eve in the garden was that *"they could be like God,"* which has always been the desire of Satan for himself and subsequently fallen man. Today's generation has certainly bit the apple!

> *"How you are fallen from heaven, O Day Star, son of Dawn! How you are cut down to the ground, you who laid the nations low! You said in your heart, 'I will ascend to heaven; above the stars of God I will set my throne on high; I will sit on the mount of assembly in the far reaches of the north; I will ascend above the heights of the clouds; I will make myself like the Most High."* (Isaiah 14:12-14) This is narcissism.

We now live in the "Me Generation." Many men now focus on self, autonomy, self-realization, disrespect of authority, and entitlement. The postmodern exhibits a lack of empathy and charity, and an increase in narcissism and laziness.

G. K. Chesterton once was asked to participate as a guest editorialist at a London Newspaper to the question *"What is wrong with the world?"* He responded, *"Dear Editors, I am!"* That was a very succinct answer to a complex question and points to our corrupt self-loving hearts. It is me, me, all about me. Augustine spoke of two cities. The earthly city was defined by love of self, extending to contempt of God. The heavenly city was defined by a love of God, extending to contempt of self.

Narcissism is an inflated sense of self. It was pointed out by Mortimer Adler in 1941 that American education was increasingly becoming "frothy and vapid." He properly placed the blame on American parenting and educators who want to protect children from pain and embarrassment. Children were to be protected from pain and suffering and low self-esteem.

Every child had to be successful and be showered with praise. The societal emphasis has become on an unrealistic self-esteem which results in an inflated ego. Schools and colleges use grade inflation to promote an unrealistic pseudo-sense of success and ability. When the child meets the real world, frustration and anger develop because they are not prepared for adulthood and honest self-examination. Young people may riot because of their frustration when they discover their actual limitations.

The issue for the postmodern seeker is "what God can do for me," rather than what I can do to surrender to God's authority and Word. We thank the celestial Santa Claus for the good things at the pagan holiday of Christmas. He brings, but not the bad. Our God brings both the good and what seems at the time to be bad. We completely misunderstand *"the Christmas Spirit."* We think of ourselves as good and deserving of gifts at Christmas. Let us examine the attributes given to Santa.

> *Santa Is Omniscient:* He knows how children behave throughout the year. The familiar song says, "He knows if we've been bad or good." Also he perfectly knows what children want for Christmas, even if the child does not have the opportunity to tell him personally.

> *Santa Is Omnipotent:* No storm is too great to hinder Santa from performing his annual miracle of delivering gifts throughout the world. He also denies the laws of nature by flying and by coming down the narrowest (and hottest) of chimneys. Nor should we forget his amazing ability to produce millions of gifts throughout the year. Is anything too hard for Santa? With Santa, all things are possible.

> *Santa Is Omnipresent:* To visit every home in the world in one evening requires nothing less than omnipresence. Every child in the world can wake up in the morning and say "Santa was present in my home." Prior to Christmas, Santa also appears at hundreds of street corners and shopping centers throughout the country at the same time.

Santa Is Faithful: You can always count on Santa. Santa never fails, and he never breaks his word. When Santa makes a promise, he keeps it. When he promises a child a gift, that child will never be disappointed. Children are fully persuaded that what Santa has promised, he is also able to perform. The child that believes in Santa will not be put to shame. He is totally dependable & trustworthy.

Santa Is Eternal: Santa, with his white beard and weather-beaten face, is the very essence of eternity. Year after year goes by, and Santa grows no older. Generations have come and gone, but Santa is still there. His life is endless, and Santa cannot die. To Santa belongs an unending life.

Santa Is Immutable: Yesterday, today, and forever, Santa is the same. He never seems to change. He is always happy. He is always jolly. He is always kind to children. In a changing world, you can always count on Santa being Santa.

Santa Is Love: Santa loves all the boys and girls in the world. And Santa is no respecter of persons. He loves them all—black and yellow, red and white.

Santa Is Righteous: All that Santa does is right. He makes no mistakes. Every child's stocking contains exactly the right thing.

Santa Is Good: Santa showers his blessings to all. Every good and perfect gift comes from Santa. He is the supreme Giver of Christmas. It is Santa who brings the best gift of all.

Santa Is Sovereign: On Christmas Eve, Santa is in complete control of the situation. Circumstances do not faze him (such as storms, chimney sizes, red-hot fireplaces, etc.) He is the king of Christmas.

Santa Is Coming: Santa is coming to town. You had better be ready. You better watch out. You better be good. He's coming. Are you prepared for his coming? Are you prepared when Santa comes to reward every boy and girl according to his work? Millions of boys and girls each year wait with expectation for the glorious appearance of the great Santa God. What a blessed hope for countless numbers of children. His reward is with him. What a comforting hope the boys and girls have as they prepare for his coming. During the night, he may come at any time. Even so, come Santa come.

Santa Is Worshipped: Santa is worshipped and loved by millions of children the world around. Children love him so much that all throughout the year they seek to please him so that when they see him they will not be ashamed. O come let us adore him.

Santa Has Helpers. These are not angels but elves, which are small, often mischievous creatures considered to have magical powers. These are demons.

Santa lives in the *North Pole*, which is the darkest place on the earth or the farthest place on earth from the sun (Son) or light. It is a frozen wasteland far different from the warmth and beauty brought by the sun or Son of God, the true reason for Christmas. (DDS 1980)

***Santa* is a name created by the transposition of the letters of the name *Satan*.**

Our natural expression of thanks is in response to blessings, protection, or love. Often, we thank the wrong person, exemplified by Santa. Satan wants glory for himself and to deflect the glory and thanksgiving rightly due to God. In the Judeo-Christian tradition, gratitude is not a tool used to manipulate the will of God. The

Christian knows that he deserves only judgment in hell, and the gift of redemption by Jesus Christ is totally undeserved. His thanksgiving is never coerced or fabricated in his mind; rather, his gratitude is a joyful commitment of one's personality in thanksgiving to God for the marvelous undeserved gift of redemption by Christ. We are to be thankful for all things, including suffering, sickness, and persecutions because we respect God's sovereignty. This means we are grateful for the good and the bad. ***The common lack of proper gratitude in the church today dishonors God mightily and suggests an unrepentant heart.*** Prayers of thanksgiving and praise are the foundation of a biblical Christian life! "In everything give thanks for this is the will of God in Christ Jesus for you" (1 Thess 5:18).

A general attitude of thanksgiving in both the trials and blessings of life distinguishes the Christian. Paul enjoins his churches to give thanks for all things, in all circumstances (Eph 5:20; 1 Thess 5:18), even in suffering (Rom 5:3–5; James 1:1–4), and to do everything in the name of Jesus out of a spirit of gratitude (Col 3:17). On the other hand, thanklessness marks godless and wicked men who suppress the truth about God (Rom 1:18–21).

In the New Testament, the vocabulary for thanksgiving and gratitude expands, and expressions increase. The Greek verb *eucharisteō* and the cognate noun *eucharistia* together appear about fifty-five times. Several other terms convey the idea, most commonly *charis* or gift (often with *echō:* I have). Thanksgiving is a motive for Christian life and conduct, a general attitude toward both the blessings and trials of life, a central component of prayer, and the context for the proper use of material things. The sacrament of communion, or the Eucharist, reminds us of Christ's sacrifice on the cross for us.

The Gospels introduce and the Epistles develop the concept that gratitude for God's deliverance in Christ characterizes the believer. When a sinful woman interrupted a dinner party to anoint Jesus with precious perfume, Jesus told his shocked host that her action sprang from gratitude for forgiveness (Luke 7:40–47). When Jesus healed ten lepers as they walked to the temple, he marveled aloud that only one, a Samaritan, returned to thank him (Luke 7:11–19). Paul agrees that believers should be thankful for every individual provision, and that gratitude for God's saving grace envelops the entire Christian life. Those whom God has brought from death to life should offer their bodies to him as instruments of righteousness (Rom 6:13). In view of God's mercies, knowing they were bought at a price, they should offer their bodies to God as living sacrifices in general and honor him with purity in particular (Rom 12:1; 1 Cor. 6:20). Those who have received an unshakeable kingdom from God should be thankful, worship God, and faithfully endure the hardships of persecution (Heb 12:28; note context).

In the New Testament, the object of thanksgiving is the love of God expressed in the redemptive work of Christ. The apostle Paul thanked God for that gift of grace (1 Cor 1:4; 2 Cor 9:15) and the ability to preach the gospel (2 Cor 2:14; 1 Tim 1:12). Paul thankfully participated in the spiritual gifts (1 Cor 14:18). Gratitude for love and faith among believers pervades his letters (Rom 6:17; Eph 1:15–16; Phil 1:3–5; Col 1:3–4; 1 Thess 1:2–3).

Because the expression of gratitude is tied so closely to the response of faith, Paul encouraged believers to give thanks in all things (Rom 14:6; 1 Thess 5:18). He commanded Christians to pray with thanksgiving (Phil 4:6; Col 4:2) in the name of Christ, who has made all thanksgiving possible (Eph 5:20). In his teaching on how to celebrate the Lord's Supper, Paul specified that Christians should give thanks, just as the Lord "had given thanks" (1 Cor 11:24). **It is an attitude of gratitude that characterizes true Christian faith and is the essence of the celebration of the Lord's Supper and the gift of salvation through Jesus's sacrifice on the cross. Ingratitude suggests the lack of a true salvation experience because of the lack of understanding and appreciation of the unmerited favor and grace from our God to an undeserving sinner.**

Chapter 9

Bondservice and Submission

"Yet it shall not be so amongst you: but whoever desires to become great amongst you let him be your servant. And whoever desires to be first amongst you let him be your slave. Just as the Son of Man did not come to be served but to serve and to give his life as a ransom for many."* (Matt 20:26–28)

> *If anyone would come after me, let him deny himself and take up his cross and follow me. For whoever would save his life will lose it, but whoever loses his life for my sake will find it. For what will it profit a man if he gains the whole world and forfeits his soul? Or what shall a man give in return for his soul? For the Son of Man is going to come with his angels in the glory of his Father, and then he will repay each person according to what he has done. Truly, I say to you, there are some standing here who will not taste death until they see the Son of Man coming in his kingdom.* (Matt 16:24-27)

The call of Christ is to be a bondservant. For too many the preaching of the cross is foolishness and the cost too great. Jesus reminds us, "these things I have spoken to you, that in me you may have peace. In the world you will have tribulation; but be of good cheer, I have overcome the world" (John 16:33).

The Christian bears the mark of God. He is called *voluntarily to be a bondservant* and to bear the piercing of his ear with the shedding of blood as in Exodus 21:2–6 and Deut 15:16–17: "I love my master, my wife, and my children; I will not go out free, then his master must bring him to the judges, and he will bring him to the door or the doorposts, and his master will pierce his ear with an awl, and he shall serve him forever." The Christian is also called to be a perpetual servant for life. It is the blood of Christ that sanctifies us and was used symbolically for the concentration of the High Priest:

> "Next he brought Aaron's sons forward, and Moses put some of the blood on their right earlobes, on their right thumbs, and on the big toes of their right feet, and Moses splashed the rest of the blood against the altar's sides. . .. As has been done today, the Lord has commanded to be done to make atonement." (Lev 8:24, 34)

Why did God require piercing of the ear? To incline the ear was to listen (2 Kings 19:16) or even to obey (Jer. 11:8). To give ear was to pay careful attention (Job 32:11). To turn the ears toward wisdom (Prov. 2:2) was to desire understanding, and the ear exercised judgment (Job 12:11) and understanding (13:1). Without the metaphorical piercing of the ear, the servant can't hear his Master. The pierced ear is also a mark of God's ownership, like circumcision. Every Christian is marked in some way by God as evidence of His ownership (Rom 4:11, 11:2).

In today's postmodern culture, the goal of man is personal autonomy or the ability to do whatever he pleases without being judged by social norms. There is no such thing as personal freedom or autonomy. We are bond slaves to either sin or to righteousness. Morally, the power which enslaves is sin (John 8:34), and liberty consists not simply in external freedom or in possession of the formal power of choice but in deliverance from the darkening of the mind, the tyranny of sinful lusts, and the enthrallment of the will, induced by a morally corrupt state. Only God has absolute freedom. He is not controlled from the outside. We are slaves to our sin nature or are bondservants of our Lord. Christ is our only hope.

A man may have much spiritual understanding of the things of God but still lack the will to obey God. ***Many men have light in their head but no heat in their heart.*** Some have knowledge but no zeal; others have zeal but no knowledge. It is knowledge and zeal for God that makes us true Christians. Knowledge can fill the head but may not touch the heart. The Pharisees had great knowledge of Scripture and followed the external duties of godliness, but Jesus called them "whited sepulchers" because they had no true spiritual understanding of the things of God or the person of His Son. The Pharisees pretended godliness by their conversation and external duties but denied the power of the Holy Spirit and resurrection life.

A man can be a scholar and professor of religion but yet unconverted. He may live a form of godless hypocrisy, taking himself to be wise but yet a fool. For many have confidence in their religion and good behavior but are not Christians. Jesus reminds us in the Sermon on the Mount that:

> *"Not everyone who says to me, Lord, Lord, shall enter the kingdom of heaven but he who does the will of my father in heaven. Many will say to me in that day and Lord, have we not prophesied in your name, cast out demons in your name, and done many wonders in your name? "And then I will declare to them I never knew you depart from me, you practice lawlessness."* (Matt 7:21–23)

Many will go to hell with the name of Christ in their mouths. Of course, the naysayers will say, "Didn't Jesus say that '*he who confesses me before him I will confess before my father in heaven?*' Doesn't this mean that if Christ confesses our names to His Father, then God our Father will never disown us?"

Most men are good Christians by the verdict of their own opinion, but we know that the law allows no man to be a witness in his own case (Deut 17:6). The heart of man is a great imposter and a cheat in the world, and God tells us in Jeremiah 17:9–10 that "*the heart is deceitful above all things.*" In today's culture, serious self-examination is not encouraged. Many men think they have fire insurance because they have "accepted" Jesus. Their faith is in their own faith or in their excellent character that demonstrates that they deserve to be in heaven, since they are better than most men. Jeremiah 17:5 reminds us that, "cursed is the man who trusts in man and makes his flesh his strength." The reader must be careful since our hearts are deceitful and vulnerable to the lies of the enemy. We must cry to God for discernment since we can be deceived by false miracles, healings, words of prophecy, and so forth as well as a false impression of our own "Christian" character and righteousness. Many "almost a Christian" men believe that saving faith does not require submission to both the Gospel and the Law; instead, they are a law unto themselves.

Part of being a bondservant is to *be submitted to authority*. When Moses came down from the mountain, he had two tablets of the law in his hands. Each tablet contained five laws. The fifth law on the first tablet is to *honor your mother and father.* Many Bible commentators have miscategorized the first four Commandments as being about honoring and loving God and the next six Commandments about honoring and loving your fellow man. This is not correct. To honor your mother and father is to honor and love the Lord, who appoints all authority over us, good and bad. All five laws on the first tablet are about our relationship to God, and the second five commandments are about loving our neighbor. The proper biblical understanding of the fifth commandment about honoring your mother and father is to honor all authority that God has placed in your life. This would include wives submitting to their husbands. Husbands submitting to their employers, public officials, police, and all authority that God places in their lives, as well as their parents.

If a man is not under authority, he's in rebellion against God, since God appoints all authority (Romans 13:1–7). God speaks in authority through His Word, the Scriptures. God has clearly spoken about sexual sins such as adultery, sex outside of marriage, homosexuality, and honesty, integrity, feeding the poor, taking care of widows, abortion, modest dress for women, helping those in prison, and so on; yet many selectively have chosen various Bible passages saying that those admonitions don't apply in today's culture!

A man cannot call himself a Christian, which means to be a servant of the Most High God, and not submit to God's appointed authority. When we disrespect authority, we are disrespecting God Himself, who placed all authority good and bad over man. Daniel (4:17, 23) reminds us that God appoints all authority including the most wicked of men. "That the Most High rules in the kingdom of men, gives it to whomever He will, and sets over it the lowest of men."

Paul reminds all men, women and children as well as bondservants to submit to their masters.

> *Wives, submit to your own husbands, as is fitting in the Lord. Husbands, love your wives and do not be bitter toward them. Children, obey your parents in all things, for this is well pleasing to the Lord. Fathers do not provoke your children, lest they become discouraged. Bondservants, obey in all things your masters according to the flesh, not with eyeservice, as men-pleasers, but in sincerity of heart, fearing God. And whatever you do, do it heartily, as to the Lord and not to me, knowing that from the Lord you will receive the reward of the inheritance; for you serve the Lord Christ.* (Col 3:18–24)

"Wives, likewise, be submissive to your own husbands, that even if some do not obey the word. For in this manner, in former times, the holy women who trusted in God also adorned themselves, being submissive to their own husbands" (1 Pet 3:1, 5)

"Therefore, submit yourselves to every ordinance of man for the Lord's sake, whether to the king as supreme, or to governors, as to those who are sent by him for the punishment of evildoers and for the praise of those who do good. For this is the will of God, that by doing good you may put to silence the ignorance of foolish men—**as free, yet not using liberty as a cloak for vice, but as bondservants of God. Honor all people. Love the brotherhood. Fear God. Honor the king.** " (1 Pet 2:13–17)

Chapter 10

Postmodernism and Personal Freedom

The American mantra is *Freedom*, which has resulted in a *postmodern* worldview. The American Revolution was about freedom from the authority of the King of England and, subsequently, all authority. Americans struggle with authority of any type, including God Himself. Alexis de Tocqueville, a French intellectual and aristocrat who came to America in 1835. (Alexis de Tocqueville, *Democracy in America*, edited by Richard D, Heffner, Signet Classic Printing 2001) He admired American courage, drive, and work ethic. He also understood that the American pioneer spirit was very practical and unbound by traditional Puritan theology. He warned America of the coming danger of egalitarianism that substituted the rule of law for the rule of the majority. American's love of freedom, equality, and individualism has brought conformity—ironically—the very opposite of individual freedom. De Tocqueville understood from his experiences in the French Revolution the tyranny of the majority, and when man turns inward, that truth becomes subjective. American pragmatism searched for simplicity and valued straight talk and isn't that "the pioneer spirit?" Nineteenth-century evangelists Charles Finney and Dwight L. Moody had a low view of the formal study of theology. Instead, they championed the common sense and dignity of the average man's ability and his personal intuition to understand the Bible. Their concept was that theology was thought to be an elitist occupation. This has resulted in a weak church, ignorant of biblical truth.

Long, theological confessions such as the Westminster Confession or Heidelberg Catechism are too deep and complex for postmoderns and have been largely ignored in favor of simple statements of faith of only a few sentences. The Apostles Creed is no longer repeated, taught, or understood in many "Bible churches," nor do they have clear statements on the essentials of biblical faith. The mantra is "just believe"—believe what? **Modern Christianity is characterized mainly by biblical ignorance and a "faith" not rooted in Scripture and sound biblical foundation. Postmoderns have faith in their own faith rather than true faith given by God** through regeneration or a "born-again" experience of the grace of God. **If the "almost a Christian" can't bow his knee and submit to all of Scripture and the law, which teaches that all men are hopeless lost sinners and cannot find God by righteous works and intellectual "acceptance" of God except by the grace of God, then he is not a Christian!**

The terms absolute truth, authority, infallibility, inerrancy, special revelation, and objective truths are pooh-poohed as being old-fashioned, rigid, Stone Age, and anti-intellectual to our postmodern culture. **For the postmodern man, truth is private; it is about finding truth in the inner self or enlightenment of the rational mind. Since it is about finding truth in the inner self, it is gnostic and essentially hedonistic. Man wants to find the knowledge of God within himself rather than from the God who is outside of himself.** Scripture is very public in that God publicly calls men to Himself. Christianity comes from outside of the self and is doctrinally shaped by Scripture, history, and the external work of the cross of Christ. *"If the foundations are destroyed, what can the righteous do"* (Psalm 11:3)?

The new terminology for postmodernism is inclusiveness, tolerance for other people's views, religious pluralism, multiculturalism, personal autonomy, and openness to new understanding of truth, since truth is continually evolving.

Truth is seen as relative; what is morally correct in one situation may not be appropriate in another. Morals are thought to constantly evolve when there is no external source of truth. **Truth is no longer absolute, nor is there any uniqueness to our biblical faith.** It is the concept of relative truth that is the foundation of liberal tolerance. Truth today is just personal and no longer universal and is seen only in terms of what it means to each person. Truth to the postmodern is what works. This is the pragmatism that allows mystical Eastern practices such as fortune telling, theosophy, divination, séances, visualization, contemplative prayer, centering prayer, palm reading, Zen, guided imagery, channeling, altered states of consciousness, hypnosis, necromancy, tarot cards, yoga, Reiki, witchcraft, astrology, soothsaying or clairvoyance, transcendental meditation, and so forth. If it works and is useful, it must be true. This is American "Christian" pragmatism! Extra-biblical practices such as theosophy believe that spiritual knowledge can be achieved through spiritual ecstasy, direct intuition, contemplative spirituality, or special revelation like ancient gnosticism. **Man wants to find God in himself or find the "higher self," and then he can be as God.** This is neo-orthodox, gnostic, new-age, as well as pagan in that it presents a new way of thinking based on Eastern occultism in evaluating truth. These occult practices are absolutely and unconditionally forbidden by God, yet there has largely been silence from church leaders, many of whom endorse contemplative prayer! There is absolutely no such thing as an empty or neutral mind! The mind will be filled with thoughts of God or thoughts from Satan.

Meditation and finding the inner self or "**contemplative spirituality**" has been reintroduced into the Western church by those who seek favor with God by introspective self-scrutiny. Proponents of Christian yoga and other meditation techniques forget that yoga can be dangerous because it involves "emptying the mind" or actually entering a place of mental passivity. Medically speaking, there is no such thing as an empty mind since the mind is always working until brain death. This act of mental passivity, such as occurs with hypnotism, could actually open the mind to welcome other kinds of spirits from the dark side. This is what often happens to those who become high on street drugs or become drunk from alcohol to a point of mental passivity, which allows demonic thoughts and spirits a foothold. We need to set our minds on God through Scripture, and He will show Himself to us. Satan is very subtle (Gen 3:1–7), and there is a very fine line between Eastern New Age meditation and Christian meditation. **Our effort to find God through meditation can be a subtle effort to find self and empower the self, rather than dying to self and knowing the cross.**

The Orthodox Church is seen as dogmatic, and the Postmoderns are anti-dogmatic. Today's humanists are religiously inclusive, and the Orthodox Church is seen as intolerant and exclusive. **Today's Christianity is "Christianity-Lite" (Jesus loves everybody)** or called "**The Emergent Church**" and "easy to believe" in that it doesn't conflict with contemporary lifestyles or truth claims. Biblical truth never changes. It is objective and not just subjective or about personal feelings. Truth is not to be displaced by emotional feelings or pragmatism!

Once truth becomes subjective, it divorces itself from the holiness of God and the behavioral requirements of God. Instead, the postmodern gospel is about self-help. Worship, rather than *worthship*, is largely about entertainment and feeling good about self. Sin is no longer about defiance of God's holiness but about not breaking societal norms.

Postmodernism is a pluralistic religious relativism, which emphasizes tolerance rather than absolute truth. Tolerance has replaced truth. *Their logic is self-defeating, oxymoronic, and makes no logical sense since it claims that the only absolute truth is that there is no absolute truth!* Different religions are considered largely cultural with competing truth claims; all of which have their cultural validity, but there is no single absolute truth or way to the true God. This is religious multiculturalism. Jesus offends the postmodern by His exclusivity. This is best exemplified in John 14:6 where Jesus says, *"I am the way, the truth and the life and no one comes to the Father but by me!"* This can be expanded to say absolutely that Jesus is the only way, the only truth, the only way to real life, and the only way to the Father. How radical!

Ecumenism, (religious inclusivism and pluralism in disguise) or the principle of promoting unity among Christian churches with other faiths, makes attempts for unity but often at the expense of foundational Christian truth. Pope Francis delivered this message during an audience with Lutheran pilgrims in the Paul VI Hall at the Vatican, Thursday, October 13, 2016. Like his predecessors, Francis has reached out to Protestants, Orthodox, and other Christians to heal Christianity's divisions. But unlike his predecessors, Francis has said theological differences should be put aside, so Christians can work together on issues of pressing social concern.

Claims that "we all worship the same God, so why can't we get along," are often from the enemy of truth and lead to a compromised Gospel in the name of unity and brotherly love. We don't worship the same God as other religions, such as Islam, Buddhism, and Hinduism, and there is no other God in heaven or earth but Christ Jesus. His foundational truth is not negotiable!

Postmoderns place their hope in man and the divine within; Christians place their hope in the triune God, the divine without, and the truth of Scripture (Psalm 118:8).

Pseudo-Christian Postmodernism subtly promotes fascism by encouraging intellectual elitism through empowering speech of political correctness, fairness, tolerance, personal autonomy, and multiculturalism or what could be called "Cultural Totalitarianism." Aggressive secularism leads to ideological tyranny. The elites have now been empowered as gods to decide what subjective truths, such as issues on the definition of marriage and homosexuality, bathroom choice, public evangelism, and so forth, will be enforced by politically correct truth police and government! **Any society, such as America with a history of a biblical foundation and godliness that now rejects the truth claims of God and makes men the arbitrator and definer of truth, will face the wrath and judgment of God! To reject His truth, since Jesus is the truth, is to reject God Himself (John 14:6).**

> "It is only by believing in God that we can criticize the Government. Once abolish the God, and the Government becomes God. The truth is that irreligion is the opium of the people. Wherever the people do not believe in something beyond the world, they will worship the world. But above all, they worship the strongest thing in the world." (G. K. Chesterton)

> "One who is himself a god needs no religion; he is divine in himself. He must not bow his head . . . The more man lives in his artificial man-made reality amongst man's structures and machinery, the more strongly he receives the impression that he is the creator of his own existence." (Emil Brunner)

> "But realize this, that in the last days difficult times will come. For men will be lovers of self, lovers of money, boastful, arrogant, revilers, disobedient to parents, ungrateful, unholy, unloving, irreconcilable, malicious gossips, without self-control, brutal, haters of good, treacherous, reckless, conceited, lovers of pleasure rather than lovers of God, holding to a form of godliness, although they have denied its power; Avoid such men as these." (2 Tim 3:1–5)

> "Push back against the age as hard as it pushes against you." (Flannery O'Connor)

Chapter 11

Confession and Contrition

Yes, we need to remember that professing Christ is not confessing him, but **to profess Christ is one thing and to confess Christ is another**. Convictions may be worn out over time. Conviction of sin is not equivalent to conversion. **The word *conversion* implies a radically changed life, not simply a changed mind.** A man may mourn for his sin but be unconverted, such as Saul, Esau, and Judas.

King Saul was anointed king of Israel by the prophet Samuel (1 Samuel 10). Saul also had the gift of prophecy. He failed God and was disobedient.

> *"But now your kingdom shall not continue. The LORD has sought for Himself a man after His own heart, and the LORD has commanded him to be commander over His people, because you have not kept what the LORD commanded you."* (1 Samuel 13:14)

Later God totally rejected Saul as king because of his disobedience. So, Samuel said:

> *"Has the LORD as great delight in burnt offerings and sacrifices, As in obeying the voice of the LORD? Behold, to obey is better than sacrifice, And to heed than the fat of rams. For rebellion is as the sin of witchcraft, And stubbornness is as iniquity and idolatry. Because you have rejected the word of the LORD, He also has rejected you from being king."* (1 Samuel 15:22–23)

> *"Then Saul said to Samuel, "I have sinned, for I have transgressed the commandment of the LORD and your words, because I feared the people and obeyed their voice. Now therefore, please pardon my sin, and return with me, that I may worship the LORD. But Samuel said to Saul, "I will not return with you, for you have rejected the word of the LORD, and the LORD has rejected you from being king over Israel." (1 Samuel 15:24–26)*

True mourning for sin is not about fear for the consequences of sin but about sorrow for injury to God and grieving His Spirit. Saul was sorry for invoking the consequences of God's wrath rather than disobeying his Father in heaven. He was not contrite. Judas had 24-hour daily fellowship with Christ and His disciples but was looking for an earthly king. Later after his betrayal of Christ, he was deeply convicted of his sin and saw that he "betrayed innocent blood," yet he will spend eternity in hell. Judas knew Christ personally and had a "personal relationship with Jesus" yet was not submitted to Him. Judas was like many who claim to know God and call Him Lord, **but He will say, "I know you not." (Matt 7:21–23) Judas had conviction without contrition, with faith in a man rather than the true God.** For contrition without faith produces despair and drove Judas to commit suicide. One cannot have true faith without contrition.

Contrition is the mark of a true believer. The definition from the Hebrew [דַּכָּא, *dakka*] is "bruise (Psalm 34:18; Psalm 51:17; Isa 57:15; 66:2); [נָכֵה, *nakheh*], or "smitten" (Isaiah 66:2). Contrite, "crushed," is only the superlative for broken people who have a contrite or broken spirit, weep over wrongdoing, and express genuine sorrow for their sins. *A contrite heart is one in which the natural pride and self-sufficiency have been completely humbled by the consciousness of guilt* and the unmerited forgiveness of God. It is the concept of humility and acceptance of divine providence born out of trials and brokenness.

Historically, there has been considerable debate about *attrition* and *contrition* in repentance and forgiveness. *Attrition* is the sorrow for getting caught doing wrong or "repentance" motivated primarily by fear of punishment. It clings to the mercy of God as a ticket out of hell, an escape from punitive wrath. *Contrition* is very different and is the product of genuine sorrow for having offended God. The New Testament calls us to be contrite in order to receive the forgiveness of God. In the final judgment spoken of in the book of Revelation, the wicked are distinguished from the righteous by the lack of repentance and contrition.

> *"People were severely burned (scorched) by the fiery heat, and they reviled and blasphemed the name of God, who has control of these plagues, and they did not repent of their sins [felt no regret, contrition, and compunction for their waywardness, refusing to amend their ways] to give Him glory."* (Revelation 16:9)

A true believer forsakes his sin and declares that God is right in judging him as a sinner. Those who are in fellowship with the Lord seek to be like Him—His purity and holiness. Some men forsake the obvious and larger sins but retain secret sins. The true believer forsakes all. **For most of us to walk with Christ is to embrace constant revealing of our sin nature that brings continual repentance. This is not a once-time event but a continual process that follows us all our lives.** We tend to let go of the obvious sins and yet are not willing to deal with deeper issues. We need to look into the four mirrors that God has provided daily. The first mirror is the word of God. The second mirror is our wife or husband if we are married. The third mirror is found in the fellowship of the brethren, who in love will show us our faults. Finally, a possible fourth mirror is our enemies who are always there to point out our faults. Sometimes it is the harsh criticism of our enemies that God uses to bring us to repentance and contrition. God looks on those who "have a poor and contrite spirit and tremble at His word."

"The Lord is nigh to them that are of a broken heart, and saveth such as be of a contrite spirit" (Psalm 34:18); and *"The sacrifices of God are a broken spirit a broken and a contrite heart, O God, thou wilt not despise"* (Psalm 51:17); *"To this man will I look, even to him that is poor, and of a contrite spirit, and trembleth at my word"* (Isa 57:15; 61:1; 66:2 KJV).

Contrition leads to humility. The great men of the Bible who have had an experience with God, such as Isaiah the prophet and John the author of the book of Revelation, fell down as dead when they saw Christ. Isaiah said, *"Woe is me for I undone!"* (Isa 6:5). The prophets' prior experience with God, their knowledge of the Holy One, their great learning, and anointed gifting meant nothing. All they could do is but feel unclean and not fit for service to our Lord. To know the Lord is to become aware of our unworthiness and His greatness. Therefore, true knowledge invariably leads to humility and also to holiness. The Lord reminds us in Psalm 101:5, **"The one who has a haughty look and a proud heart, him I will not endure."** Psalm 138:6 says, "For though the Lord is exalted, Yet He regards the lowly, But the haughty He knows from afar."

Confession is a living testimony for Christ, particularly in times like this where the name of Christ and true religion is under constant assault. **To truly confess Christ means persecution and rejection by men.** *To confess Christ is to swim against the stream and recognize that our hope is not in this world but our hope is in the world to come* (John 15:20; 16:33; 2 Tim 3:12). Many use as a rebuttal to Paul's statement, "if we confess our sins to God who is just and faithful to forgive our sins . . ." Indeed, that is true if it's a true confession. There are many who confess sins for fear of consequences but never deal with deeper issues of the heart. God is interested in not just our sins but why we sin, and He wants to show us our sin nature. We must understand we sin because we are sinners, and the heart of man is terribly wicked beyond imagination.

Simon Magnus was a magician, who heard Philip preaching concerning the kingdom of God, and left his sorcery and witchcraft and "believed." Later on, when Peter and John came to Samaria and laid hands on people that they might receive the Holy Spirit, Simon offered to pay money so that he might lay hands on men that they receive the Holy Spirit. Peter rebuked him and said that he had been *"poisoned by bitterness and bound by iniquity"* (Acts 8:13–24). **Simon was a confessed Christian who had a type of belief in God that was superficial and more concerned about receiving and exploiting the gifts of God rather than serving the God of the gifts**, like many of today's TV evangelists! Simon was willing to forsake his sorcery and magic because he lusted after a greater power. Many "faith teachers" are like Simon. Like many TV evangelists, they want the benefits of God, including wealth, the praise of men, and spiritual power without cost and hide their unrepentant spirit of sorcery to appear as angels of light while denying the cross. The Christian life means bearing not only our own cross for our misdeeds but sharing in the infamy of the cross of Christ. His cross includes persecution, intolerance, and rejection by family and friends alike.

> *"Do not think that I came to bring peace on earth. I did not come to bring peace but a sword. For I have come to 'set a man against his father, a daughter against her mother, and a daughter-in-law against her mother-in-law'; and 'a man's enemies will be those of his own household.' He who loves father or mother more than Me is not worthy of Me. And he who loves son or daughter more than Me is not worthy of Me. And he who does not take his cross and follow after Me is not worthy of Me. He who finds his life will lose it, and he who loses his life for My sake will find it."* (Matt 10:34–39)

Our confession should be more than our personal belief, but also what the true church believes. Every confession has crystallized around doctrine (biblical truth). It is critical that we not only know what we believe and why we believe it (theology) but also know the history of our faith. and what the Church Fathers, such as Augustine and Athanasius and the Reformers, believed as well as church confessions such as the Westminster Confession of 1647, the Heidelberg Confession of 1547, or the Baptist Confession of 1689. Theology gives us knowledge about God. Our faith is based on doctrine (biblical teaching), and Christians are urged not to depart from apostolic teaching (1 Tim 1:10; 4:6; Titus 1:9; Gal 1:9; John 2:7, 24, 26; 3:11; Heb 2:1).

The First Great Awakening in America was focused on God's truth and the fear of eternal damnation. The Second Great Awakening in the early nineteenth century was more about a passion for souls rather than gospel truth. The great historian Henry Steele Commager stated, **"During the nineteenth century as well as the twentieth, religion prospered while theology went slowly bankrupt."**

People take salvation today in such a cold, formal, matter-of-fact, business-like sort of way, that it appears as though they are doing God an honor in condescending to receive His offer of Redemption. Their eyes are dry, their sense of sin absent; nor is there any sign of penitence and contrition . . . But oh, if there were conviction! if they came with hearts bowed down, yea! broken and contrite, came with the cry of the guilt-laden soul: "God be merciful to me a sinner!"— came trembling with the burning life and death question of the Philippian jailer: "What must I do to be saved?"—what converts they would be! (Oswald J. Smith)

We must be humble and bow the knee. Many Christians have confused false humility (Col 2:18, 23) with true humility (John 3:30, Rom 12:3, Phil 2:6–8), which in the Greek (ταπεινοφροσύνη) *tapeinophrosune* means "lowliness of mind." True humility is counter-cultural. In the ancient Greek culture, humility was thought to be a vice, to be practiced only by slaves. It is, in reality, the opposite of pride. (Phil 2:6–8)

"God is not looking for brilliant men, is not depending upon eloquent men, is not shut up to the use of talented men in sending His gospel out in the world. God is looking for broken men who have judged themselves in the light of the cross of Christ. When He wants anything done, He takes up men who have come to the end of themselves, whose confidence is not in themselves but in God." (Harry A. Ironside)

Jesus meek and humble heart, hear me. Deliver me, Jesus
from the desire of being loved,
from the desire of being extolled,
from the desire of being honored,
from the desire being praised,
from the desire of being preferred to others,
for the desire of being consulted,
from the desire of being approved,
from the fear of being humiliated,
from the fear of being despised,
from the fear of suffering rebuke,
from the fear of being forgotten
from the fear of being wrong,
from the fear of being suspected,
And Jesus grant me the grace to desire:
that others might be loved more than I,
that others might be esteemed more than I,
that in the opinion of the world others may increase and I may decrease,
that others may be chosen, and I set aside
that others may be praised and I unnoticed,
that others may be preferred to me and everything,
that others may be holier that I, provided I become as fully holy as I should.
(Ancient prayer from unknown author, possibly St. Francis of Assisi)

If you can sincerely pray these words, then you understand humility and what it means to be like Christ Jesus.

Remember, God is not fair, our rewards are not in this world, but there in heaven.

Chapter 12
The Holy Spirit

The "almost a Christian" may know of God the Father and Christ His Son but questions, *"Who is the Holy Spirit?"* He is the third person of the Trinity who eternally proceeds from the Father and the Son and is of the same substance, power, and glory as the Father and the Son. Therefore, He is to be loved, obeyed, honored, and worshiped as equal to the Father and Son. It is the Holy Spirit who enables us to truly know the Father and the Son relationally. The Holy Spirit is not distant or impersonal but relational, warm, trustworthy, and loving. His presence is close enough to be felt like the breeze on our face but remains mysterious, untouchable, and invisible. His purpose is to instruct, equip, guide, love, convict, and heal God's people as well as to teach us the fear of the Lord. He may reveal Himself through dreams and visions, individual illumination, as well as both ordinary and divine providences. Mostly, He reveals Himself through that small, quiet voice that speaks to our hearts. The same spirit that was given to Jesus now has been given to us. Augustine said: **"Without the Spirit we can neither love God or keep His Commandments"** (Ezk 36:26–27; 37:5; John 16:7–11; Acts 2:17–18).

When we say we are a "born-again Christian," we mean we have been transformed into a completely new person in Christ through the work of the Holy Spirit. We were once spiritually dead and now are alive to the things of the Spirit. Many Christians don't fully understand who the person of the Holy Spirit is and what He does through us and for us. I have included necessarily, because of the nature of this book, a very short summary with references to the work of the Holy Spirit.

Our hope is not in ourselves but in the Spirit of God living inside of us. "Blessed be the Lord, who daily bears our burden, The God who is our salvation. Selah. God is to us a God of deliverances" (Psalm 68:19–20).

A Christian is a disciple of Jesus Christ who repents, is baptized, and has saving faith in the Lord, but is also a follower of Christ, evidenced by works produced in him by the Holy Spirit (James 2:14–18). **A true Christian is a fool but wise to salvation. He has responded to the call to give up all, deny himself, including his reputation, wealth, family, and friends to make Christ his first priority. He understands that whoever desires to save his life will lose it, and whoever loses his life for Jesus' sake will find it** (Matt 10:35–40; 16:24–25; Mark 8:34–35; Luke 9:23–24; John 12:25). The Christian has an "exchanged life" (2 Cor 5:21), where he has been transformed from the old man to a new man in Christ. This transformation is radical and no different than the transformation of an ugly worm into a butterfly (2 Cor 5:17). We are born sinners, weak and powerless against a more powerful enemy. We need the Holy Spirit's empowerment to function as God's ambassadors to a lost, dark world. Jesus said it was better if He went away because the Holy Spirit would come. "But I tell you the truth, it is to your advantage that I go away; for if I do not go away, the Helper will not come to you; but if I go, I will send Him to you" (John 16:7), and "I will ask the Father, and He will give you another Helper, that He may be with you forever; that is the Spirit of truth, whom the world cannot receive, because it does not see Him or know Him, but you know Him because He abides with you and will be in you" (John 14:16–17). Jesus ascended to heaven from earth to a much greater cosmic role where He now sits at the right hand of God as High Priest. He intercedes for His Saints; day and night and because of His ascension to his priestly role in heaven. He has now prepared a place for the Spirit-led believer in eternity.

Many Christians don't fully understand who the person of the Holy Spirit is and what He does through us and for us. The words Holy Spirit [*Ruach Ha-Elohim* (Hebrew) or *Pneuma Hagion* (Greek)] literally mean "wind" or "breath of God." The Spirit of God is invisible but powerful and life-giving. I have included a very short summary with references to the major works of the Holy Spirit, and in a later chapter I will discuss the gifts of the Spirit.

The Works of the Holy Spirit

There are three wonderful works performed by the Holy Spirit in preparing unsaved people to become Christians out of a total of at least fourteen important works of the spirit. These first three spiritual works are called by theologians, the "effectual call." (Ephesians 1:11–15)

1. The work of the Holy Spirit in **regeneration**. Regeneration can be equated with "being born again." Regeneration prepares the heart of man to receive the Holy Spirit. It also frees the worldly sinful mind of man for spiritual intellectual illumination. The Holy Spirit teaches us truth (1 John 2:20, 27). Regeneration liberates the will from the bondage of darkness produced by sin in order to by faith receive Christ as Lord and Savior. When regenerated, repenting sinners accept Christ as Savior and Lord.

    They are given a new nature by the Holy Spirit (2 Cor. 5:17, 21). Jesus carefully explained this ministry of the Holy Spirit to Nicodemus (John 3:3–7). It is the work of the Holy Spirit that produces saving faith.

    "And since we have the same spirit of faith, according to what is written, "I believed and therefore I spoke," we also believe and therefore speak, knowing that He

120

who raised up the Lord Jesus will also raise us up with Jesus, and will present us with you. For all things are for your sakes, that grace, having spread through the many, may cause thanksgiving to abound to the glory of God." (2 Cor 4:13–15)

The Holy Spirit alone produces faith in the believer. Saving faith is entirely a monergistic work of God through the Holy Spirit and not in any way a work of man.

2. The work of the Holy Spirit in **restraint.** Satan would enjoy nothing more than to destroy people before they make their decision to accept Christ as Savior, but the Holy Spirit prevents this from occurring (Is. 59:19). *"I do not ask You to take them out of the world, but to keep them from the evil one"* (John 17:15). *"Now is the judgment of this world: now shall the prince of this world be cast out"* (John 12:31). Our Lord in His death upon the cross was judging and defeating Satan. Satan has been bound to allow for the church age. Satan is still able to war on the saints but not defeat them. *"He (Christ) must reign, till He hath put all his enemies under His feet"* (1 Cor 15:25).

3. The work of the Holy Spirit in **conviction.** Humankind's sin and righteousness are exposed by the Holy Spirit. The Holy Spirit will:

"Convict the world of guilt in regard to sin and righteousness and judgment: in regard to sin, because men do not believe in me; in regard to righteousness, because I am going to the Father, where you can see me no longer; and in regard to judgment, because the prince of this world now stands condemned." (John 16:8–11)

You notice that our Lord is very careful to say that when the Holy Spirit has come, He will convict not only individual believers, but the whole world so that no man will have an excuse. When the Holy Spirit was convicting the world of unrighteousness, He was pronouncing to them that in Christ, and in Him alone, could man be made righteous.

4. ***Justification and Sanctification*** come by the power of the Holy Spirit who brings to us a Spirit of Holiness (2 Thess. 2:13; 1 Pet 1:2; cf. Rom. 8:4, 15–16), so that it is "by the Spirit" that we are able to "put to death the deeds of the body" and grow in personal holiness (Rom 8:13). "As He who called you is holy, you also be holy in all your conduct, because it is written, 'Be holy, for I am holy'" (1 Pet 1:15–16).

   "Therefore, my beloved, as you have always obeyed, not as in my presence only, but now much more in my absence, work out your own salvation with fear and trembling; for it is God who works in you both to will and to do for His good pleasure." (Philippians 2:12–13)

   God also provides spiritual gifts for our sanctification and the sanctification of the body of Christ (1 Cor 12:10–11; 14:2, 14–17). It is God alone who justifies His elect. "Those whom God effectively calls He also freely justifies" (Rom 8:30; 3:24), not by infusing any external righteousness into them, but by pardoning their sins and by accounting and accepting their persons as righteous. This is not by any works in them or done by them such as religious works, but for Christ's sake alone they are justified (Rom 4:5–8; 2

Cor 5:19,21; Rom 3:22,24–25, 27–28; Titus 3:5, 7; Eph 1:7; Jer 23:6; 1 Cor 1:30–31; Rom 5:17–19). Sanctification occurs to those justified that they might practice holiness. They, who are at once effectively called and regenerated, are given a new heart, and a new spirit is created in them. They are further sanctified, really and personally, through the virtue of Christ's death and resurrection (1 Cor 6:11; Acts 20:32; Phil 3:10; Rom 6:5–6) by His Word and Spirit dwelling in them (John 17:17, Eph 5:26; 2 Thess 2:13), the dominion of the whole body of sin is destroyed (Rom 6:6, 14). The several lusts thereof are more and more weakened and mortified (Gal 5:24; Rom 8:13), and they more and more quickened and strengthened in all saving graces (Col 1:11, Eph 3:16–19) to the practice of true holiness, *without which no man shall see the Lord*" (2 Cor 7:1; Heb 12:14).

5. The Holy Spirit points always to Christ and the ***glorification of Christ***. The Spirit calls God's elect "in order that we, who were the first to hope in Christ, might be for the praise of his glory" (Eph 1:11).

    "He, the Spirit of Truth (the Truth-giving Spirit) comes, He will guide you into all the Truth (the whole, full Truth). For He will not speak His own message [on His own authority]; but He will tell whatever He hears [from the Father; He will give the message that has been given to Him], and He will announce and declare to you the things that are to come [that will happen in the future. He will honor and glorify Me, because He will take of (receive, draw upon) what is Mine and will reveal (declare, disclose, transmit) it to you. "(John 16:13–14)

6. The sixth work of the Holy Spirit is **church unity**, the making of one new people, the church, out of those who were diverse peoples beforehand.

> "*By abolishing in His flesh, the enmity, which is the Law of commandments contained in ordinances, so that in Himself He might make the two into one new man, thus establishing peace, and might reconcile them both in one body to God through the cross, by it having put to death the enmity.*" (Eph 2:15–16)

Jesus prayed:

> "*I do not ask on behalf of these alone, but for those also who believe in Me through their word; that they may all be one; even as You, Father, are in Me and I in You, that they also may be in Us, so that the world may believe that You sent Me. The glory which You have given Me I have given to them, that they may be one, just as We are one; I in them and You in Me, that they may be perfected in unity, so that the world may know that You sent Me, and loved them, even as You have loved Me.*" (John 17:20–23)

The church consists of saints who are united to Jesus as Head of the Church by the work of the Holy Spirit in producing faith and fellowship with Jesus and each other in order to bring all glory to Him alone. The book of Revelation reminds us that we all will say, "You are worthy, O Lord, to receive glory and honor and power; For You created all things, And by Your will they exist and were created" (Rev 4:11).

7. The Holy Spirit **glorifies Christ in *His Word, the Holy Scripture*** and may not be separated from Him, so also does the Holy Spirit always speak to us through and with the Word of God, the Bible, and cannot be separated from it. His work is to present the cumulative character and history of God's people, as well as the revelation of our trinitarian God Himself through Scripture (2 Tim 3:16–17). The canon of Scripture is closed. This means that God's revelation of Himself and the history of His people in Scripture is finished, and nothing can be added to it or subtracted from it. The Westminster confession of faith states: "The whole counsel of God concerning all things necessary for His own glory, man's salvation, faith and life, is either expressly set down in Scripture, or by good and necessary consequence may be deduced from Scripture: unto which nothing at any time is to be added, whether by new revelations of the Spirit or traditions of men." (See also 2 Tim 3:15–17; Gal 1:8–9; 2 Thess 2:2.) "Nevertheless, we acknowledge the inward illumination of the Spirit of God to be necessary for the saving understanding of such things as are revealed in the Word" (John 6:45; 1 Cor 2:9–12). The Apostle John reminds us in the last chapter of the Bible that the canon of Scripture is closed:

"I testify to everyone who hears the words of the prophecy of this book: if anyone adds to them, God will add to him the plagues which are written in this book; and if anyone takes away from the words of the book of this prophecy, God will take away his part from the tree of life and from the holy city, which are written in this book." (Rev 22:18–19)

The Holy Spirit never speaks or works apart from Scripture and shows us our heart.

For to us God revealed them through the Spirit; for the Spirit searches all things, even the depths of God. For who among men knows the thoughts of a man except the spirit of the man which is in him? Even so the thoughts of God no one knows except the Spirit of God. Now we have received, not the spirit of the world, but the Spirit who is from God, so that we may know the things freely given to us by God, which things we also speak, not in words taught by human wisdom, but in those taught by the Spirit, combining spiritual thoughts with spiritual words. But a natural man does not accept the things of the Spirit of God, for they are foolishness to him; and he cannot understand them, because they are spiritually appraised. But he who is spiritual appraises all things, yet he himself is appraised by no one. For WHO HAS KNOWN THE MIND OF THE LORD, THAT HE WILL INSTRUCT HIM? But we have the mind of Christ. (1 Cor 2:10–16)

Many almost Christians have studied Scripture, some have gone further and studied the oldest Greek and Hebrew manuscripts in the original languages and later became Bible scholars and professors of religion. Yet the spiritual truths have not been opened to them. Spiritual things can only be spiritually discerned through the enabling power of the Holy Spirit. The ultimate issue is not about our knowledge of Scripture but that we know the Author of Scripture as revealed by the Holy Spirit! Paul placed his hope in the power of the Holy Spirit and not the cleverness of men.

"And when I came to you, brethren, I did not come with superiority of speech or of wisdom, proclaiming to you the testimony of God. For I determined to know nothing among you except Jesus Christ, and Him crucified. I was with you in weakness and in fear and in much trembling, and my message and my preaching were not in persuasive words of wisdom, but in demonstration of the Spirit and of power, so that your faith would not rest on the wisdom of men, but on the power of God." (1 Cor 2:1–5)

8.   The Holy Spirit is the **teacher of all spiritual truth**, and He confirms that Scripture is the ultimate standard and authority in matters of faith and that it is inspired, clear, sufficient and without error in the original manuscripts. *Sola Scriptura* was the cry of the reformers meaning that Scripture is the only infallible source of saving knowledge and true wisdom as opposed to the church magisterium.

9.   The work of the Spirit is ***sealing God's people or perseverance of the saints.*** The text says, "Having believed, you were marked in him with a seal," the promised work of the Holy Spirit, who is a deposit guaranteeing our inheritance until the redemption of those who are God's possession.

"In Him, you also, after listening to the message of truth, the gospel of your salvation—having also believed, you were sealed in Him with the Holy Spirit of promise, who is given as a pledge of our inheritance, with a view to the redemption of God's own possession, to the praise of His glory" (Eph 1:11)

10. The sealing of the **Holy Spirit gives us** *assurance*. This perseverance of the saints depends not upon their own free will but upon the immutability or unchangeableness of the decree of His election of His children, flowing from the free and unchangeable love of God the Father (2 Tim 2:18–19, Jer 31:3). The Holy Spirit bears witness "with our spirits that we are children of God and if children, heirs also, heirs of God and fellow heirs with Christ, if indeed we suffer with Him, so that we may also be glorified with Him" (Rom 8:16–17). The Holy Spirit gives evidence of the work of God within us: "And by this we know that he abides in us, by the Spirit which he has given us" (1 John 3:24). "By this we know that we abide in him and he in us, because he has given us of his own Spirit" (1 John 4:13). Because we have been sealed by the Holy Spirit, we are not to grieve the Spirit. "Do not grieve the Holy Spirit of God, by whom you were sealed for the day of redemption" (Eph 4:30).

11. *Prayer* without the empowerment of the Holy Spirit accomplishes little. Effectual prayer is not achieved without the help of the Spirit of God. Just as worship requires "spirit and truth" (John 4:24), so prayer requires the guidance of the Spirit. In the prayer lives of individual believers, we find that the Holy Spirit empowers prayer and makes it effective. "We do not know how to pray as we ought, but the Spirit himself intercedes for us with sighs too deep for words" (Rom 8:26). See also Jude 20: "But you, beloved, building yourselves up on your most holy faith, praying in the Holy Spirit." Paul also writes, "with all prayer and petition pray at all times in the Spirit, and with this in view, be on the alert with all perseverance and petition for all the saints" (Eph. 6:18).

12. The Holy Spirit is our ***teacher and counselor and leader***. "He will teach you all things, and bring to your remembrance all that I have said to you" (John 14:26), and Jesus also said, "He will guide you into all the truth" (John 16:13). "For all who are being led by the Spirit of God, these are sons of God" (Rom 8:14). It is the leading of the Spirit that produces our sanctification. The spiritual man is one who is being led by the spirit, and the solemn warning is that if a man is not being led by the Spirit, he is not a spiritual man or a son of God! Moreover, Jesus promised that when his disciples were put on trial because of persecution, the Holy Spirit would teach them at that time what to say (Luke 12:12; cf. Matt. 10:20; Mark 13:11).

13. **The Holy Spirit is the author and hope for *revival of His Church*.** We often have been guilty of passivity, complacency and, most of all, of quenching the Spirit by our contentment with the status quo! Most churches are not interested in and would be threatened by a fresh move of the Holy Spirit. This grieves God terribly. Every time God brought revival in the past, the majority of churches fought it. This was the experience of Jonathan Edwards, who eventually was fired as pastor of his own church. This was the experience of Israel, whose spiritual life was up and then down like a roller coaster, as exemplified in the book of Judges, and needed periodic revival and deliverance (Judges 2:11–19). We need revival because we are as cracked pots (2 Cor 4:7) that leak the Spirit of God and continually need refreshing. The Holy Spirit is the agent of change and the disrupter of complacency and contentment. If men would humble themselves, confess their sins, and pray for revival, the Holy Spirit would bring revival and refreshing to His church!

14. The Holy Spirit is the ***Protector of the Saints and Deliverer from Evil***. Jesus sent the disciples out with: "power and authority over all demons and to cure diseases" (Luke 9:1). The charge of Scripture is to be strong in the Lord and the power of His might (Eph 6:10–18). We must be humble and not presumptuous but sober and vigilant, and by the power of the Holy Spirit resist the devil and his devious plans (1 Pet 5:6–9). Jesus lives every day to intercede in our behalf (Heb 7:25).

The Holy Spirit is the exact image, love, character, and friend to us as Jesus would have been if He were still on earth. It was better for Jesus to ascend to heaven and leave the Holy Spirit for us because, through His ascension to heaven, He now sits on His throne at the right hand of the Father. Our Lord now intercedes for His Church, and Christ rules and reigns over all things. The crucifixion of Christ defeated Satan, and with His resurrection and ascension, He sealed our atonement as a price paid in full for our sins and the ascension of Christ purchased His enthronement and glorification. Our consummation will occur when Christ returns and judges all things. Thank you, Lord, for giving us the Holy Spirit, who is our friend, guide, helper, protector, illuminator, healer, and discerner of all things and who uses us frail sinners to be Your witness to a fallen world.

Chapter 13

The Holy Spirit as Revealer of Mystery

(Trinitarian Theology of the Holy Spirit)

The concept of the Trinity or tri-unity has been confusing and open to debate for centuries. It took more than 400 years for the church fathers to come to agreement on the nature of the Trinity at the Councils of Nicaea (325), Constantinople (381), Ephesus (431), Chalcedon (451). The Father alone is unbegotten. He alone proceeds from no one and is the source of the Godhead. The fact that the Son is eternally begotten means that there never was a time when the Son was not, the Son existed before the world began. Jesus is said to be consubstantial with the Father or off the same substance as the Father. Jesus, the Father, the Holy Spirit—all three persons are fully God. It does not mean that Jesus's Deity is less than the Father as believed by Arius and called the Doctrine of Subordination. God is not three different modes of the same person (modalism) such as the example of water, steam, and ice being different forms of the same substance as suggested by Sabellius. Each person of the Trinity is a distinct person. This does not mean that there are three distinct Gods or Tritheism. We now agree the Trinity represents God as three distinct Persons who are coequal and coeternal and of the same divine essence. This means that each person of the Trinity is fully and equally God with the same divine attributes such as power, holiness, justice, wisdom, goodness, compassion, justice, truth, and authority etc.

How is this rationally possible? Are you confused? Join the crowd. For many of the world's great thinkers the Trinity seems illogical and mystical. What distinguishes Christian theologians from secular scholars? The answer is FAITH in the revealed word of God through Scripture. To believe in the Trinity one must accept the Bible as the revealed word of God and inerrant and our only source of spiritual truth. Hence the doctrine of the Trinity has been and always will be the great cause of division amongst those that call themselves Christian.

"We as creatures and sinful creatures at that, will never understand this one and three business perfectly. But it is because we cannot fully understand God, that his revelation to us becomes so important. We cannot reason our way to him on our own, so he must reveal himself to us. This kind of thinking should be the building blocks of Christian epistemology." (Van Til)

The Trinity is a mystery that defies a logical explanation and therefore is the great theological divider. Here are some common non-orthodox views on the divinity of Christ and the Trinity of those who would call themselves almost Christian. Many claim Jesus did not exist at all, or if he did, he was nothing more than a good man.

Trinitarian Heresies:

Mormonism ...teaches that Jesus was physically conceived and is the half-brother of Satan.

Jehovah's Witnesses ...teach that Jesus was the first created being and deny the Trinity.

Islam ...teaches that Jesus was a prophet and not divine. (Ref. Surah 4:171, 5:76)

United Pentecostal ...allege that Jesus and the Father are the **same** Person (modalism).

Docetists (literally, "I appear" in Greek) ...charged that Jesus was a mere spirit-being, without a fleshly body; he only "appeared" to be human. This is also taught in Islam.

Ebionitism ...teaches that while Jesus was endowed with particular charismatic gifts which distinguished him from other humans but nonetheless regarded Him as a purely human figure.

Nestorianism or Monophysitism... taught that Jesus had only one nature and denied that Christ had two natures, one divine and the other human.

Macedonianism ...teaches that the Holy Spirit is a created being.

Adoptionism ...taught that Jesus was born totally human and only later was "adopted" – either at his baptism or at his resurrection – by God in a special (i.e. divine) way.

Partialism ...teaches that Father, Son and Holy Spirit together are components of the one God. This led to the belief that each person of the Trinity is only part God, only becoming fully God when they come together.

Tritheism ...confesses the Father, Son and Holy Spirit as three independent divine beings, three separate gods who share the 'same substance'. This is a common mistake because of misunderstanding of the use of the term 'persons' in defining the Trinity.

Arianism ...taught that the preexistent Christ was the first and greatest of God's creatures but denied his fully divine status. Christ is a highly exalted creature, but a created creature nonetheless a lessor divine being. The son is a created being in the first and highest of all created beings. He is neither God nor man nor a mediator between the two. Arias denied Christ's divinity and denied his saving power.

Semi-Arianism ...says the Son is more than a mere creature but less than God or not fully divine. Instead of being of the *same essence* with God (homoousios) basically the Son while still divine has lesser power; the Son is of *similar essence* with the Father. (homoiousios) Semi-Arians believe that the Son while still divine has lesser authority, power, wisdom, than the Father. Since the Son eternally submits to the Father, Christ must be subordinate to the Father. Orthodox theologians have taught that the Father and the Son are coequal and of the same substance or essence.

Pelagianism ...denies original sin; therefore, man can make proper moral choices uncontaminated by an inherited fallen corrupt nature. Salvation becomes dependent simply upon a man's will to choose what is right. It denies God's salvation by election and God's sovereignty. It focuses on man's ability to choose what is right, rather than man's inability to know God except by the grace of God. It gives a boost to man's pride by making him believe that he's able to save himself and distracts man's sense of God's grace and sinful man's inability to help himself. Pelagians don't understand God's grace and think of grace as giving the right instructions for salvation rather than a required empowerment for salvation. Many think they're Christians because they have chosen God or raise their hand at a revival service. When God sovereignly chooses you, you become born again and repent and works follow. When natural man chooses God from his own free will, there's no need for repentance, a changed life, or godly works.

Modalism (i.e., sabellianism, novatianism and patripassianism, monarchianism) ...taught that the three persons of the Trinity are different "modes" of the Godhead. Adherents believed that Father, Son, and Holy Spirit are not distinct personalities but different modes of God's self-revelation. A typical modalist approach is to regard God as the Father in creation, the Son in redemption, and the Spirit in sanctification. In other words, God exists as Father, Son, and Spirit in different eras but never as triune. Stemming from modalism, patripassianism believed that the Father suffered as the Son.

Unitarian Universalism ...is a religious movement that denies the Trinity and believes that God is one. This was popularized by Faustus Socinus (1539-1604). Some Catholic theologians believe the Jews, Muslims, Eastern Orthodox, Protestants etc. all worship the same God in an effort to produce religious unity or oneness. This philosophy morphs nicely into new age spiritualism.

Gnosticism ...is a heretical pagan movement of Greco-Roman roots of the first and second century church that denied the Trinity and taught that matter was evil, and that emancipation comes through special knowledge. Christ was thought to be an emissary of the remote supreme divine being understood only by an esoteric knowledge or gnosis, which enabled the redemption of the human spirit.

Marcionism ...somewhat replaced gnosticism in the second century AD with its dualistic philosophy that the God of the OT was evil a demiurge and a God of wrath, whereas the God of the NT was good and loving and came to save humanity from the OT God. Hebrew Scriptures had no authority and only certain positive NT Scriptures were authoritative. Jesus did not have a physical body (Docetism) was not Jewish and was previously unknown to creation.

Since the NT clearly demonstrates that Jesus is divine, the early Church had to reconcile Jesus's divinity to the Jews with the monotheistic teaching of the OT. Actually, in Hebrew "**God**" (*Elohim*) is a plural word, and the word *one* (the Hebrew, *echad*) refers to one in *a collective sense* (e.g. like one cluster of grapes rather than in an absolute sense or mathematical singularity). In Genesis 2:24 for example, Adam and Eve as two persons are considered to be one.

"Hear, O Israel: The Lord (YHWH) our God (Elohim), the Lord is one (echad)" (Deut 6:4). This can be paraphrased as: "Hear O Israel: The Lord (Singular) our God (plural or the Trinity) is One (in essence in a collective sense)."

One in Essence: The attributes of God are the same and consistent (e.g. eternal, immutable, etc.). The distinction of the three persons does not affect God's essence. **In Salvation:**

> "God—the Triune Jehovah, Father, Son, and Spirit; three Persons work together in sovereign wisdom, power and love to achieve the salvation of a chosen people, the **Father electing**, the **Son** fulfilling the Father's will by **redeeming**, the **Spirit** executing by **renewing**." (J I Packer)

The Father **chooses** us to salvation, the Son **secures** our salvation, and the Spirit **seals** our salvation. The Father originates, chooses, and calls us (John 6:44, Rom 8:28--29, Eph 1:4). The Son reveals the Father, perfects us, and redeems us (Heb 10:10, 14, I Peter 3:18, II Cor 5:21). The Spirit witnesses to Christ, awakens our dead souls, regenerates our hearts, and seals us (Eph 4:30).

In AD 215, Tertullian described God as "three Persons, one Substance" (or "tres Personae, una Substantia" in Latin which was translated from the Greek "treis Hypostases, Homoousios"). Other early third century sources describe the Trinity as "one God existing in three Persons and one substance, Father, Son, and Holy Spirit."

In AD 325, The Nicene Creed described Jesus as "God of God, Light of Light, very God of very God, begotten, not made, being of one substance with the Father." Three Persons: not three individuals, but three personal self-distinctions within the one divine essence. Note that the Trinity is not described as three parts or three beings but three Persons. Each Person is self-conscious and self-directing. Yet the principal elements of the doctrine of the Trinity were not settled until the fourth and in the fifth century. Trinitarian controversies were largely settled under the leadership of Athanasius, Augustine, and the Cappadocian Fathers. Then the grammar of the doctrine was fixed, though the terminology took different forms in the Greek East and the Latin West. Eastern theologians referred to God as one essence in three hypostases, or persons, while Western writers said that God is one substance in three Persons. For some time, this terminology caused considerable confusion because the Greek *hypostasis* was often translated by the Latin *substantia*. Augustine taught that the Holy Spirit proceeded from both the Father and the Son.

As time went on, East and West divided over the way the relations among the Persons were described. The East preferred to speak of the Trinity as having one Source (or Font) and two issues: that is, the Father is the One who begets the Son and from whom the Spirit proceeds. The West attempted to reinforce its reading of the biblical references to the Spirit as the Spirit *of Christ.* Thus, the custom developed in the Latin-speaking church of adding the word "*filioque*" to the Niceno-Constantinopolitan Creed (the Spirit proceeds from the Father *and the Son versus the Eastern creed that the Spirit proceeds from the Father then the Son*). This problem of the filioque and many other theological issues, such as should priests marry, the issue of leaven in communion bread, and finally the seat of Church authority (Rome vs. Constantinople), lead to the AD 1054 church schism and has been a principal cause of East-West division ever since.

There are incomprehensible elements to the Trinity but that does not mean that the doctrine of the Trinity is contradictory. God can be incomprehensible but that does not mean he is utterly unknowable. God's tri-unity is part of His revelation of One who is infinite to us who are finite.

"Bring me a worm that can comprehend a man, and then I will show you a man that can comprehend the triune God." (John Wesley)

"That which is infinite is known only to itself. This is that which gives some notion of God, while yet beyond all our conceptions—our very incapacity of fully grasping Him affords us the idea of what He really is. He is presented to our minds in His transcendent greatness, as at once known and unknown." (Tertullian)

"'For My thoughts are not your thoughts, neither are your ways My ways,' declares the LORD. 'For as the heavens are higher than the earth, So are My ways higher than your ways, And My thoughts than your thoughts'" (Isaiah 55:8--9).

"For now, we see in a mirror dimly, but then face to face; now I know in part, but then I shall know fully just as I also have been fully known" (1 Cor. 13:12)

Here's an excerpt from Robert Letham's contribution to the December issue of *Tabletalk Magazine* on the Trinity entitled "God the Holy Spirit" (December 2019, Vol 43, No 12, pp 19-21; Ligonier Ministries). This is one of the best concise foundational trinitarian theological teachings I have read. For a deeper study of the Trinity, I would suggest reading Robert Letham's excellent book: The Holy Trinity, (551 pages), P&R Publishing, Phillipsburg, N.J. 2004

The Holy Spirit subsists in the indivisible Trinity as one of the three hypostases (persons). As such, He is fully and exhaustively God, one in being eternally with the Father and the Son, one in power and glory. Whatever God does, the Spirit does, since in all God's works all three Persons work together inseparably, whether in creation, providence, or salvation. Therefore, when we speak of the Spirit at work, we must always remember that the Father and the Son are also involved.

Nevertheless, the Holy Spirit is not the Father, and He is not the Son either, for the three are eternally distinct. There is but one God, so the Spirit is identical in being or essence with the Father and the Son, but in terms of personhood, He is irreducibly distinct. Thus, there are actions attributed (or appropriated) peculiarly to the Spirit—only He was sent at Pentecost—but even here He was sent by the Father through and in the Son.

In terms of the eternal relations of the three, the Spirit proceeds from the Father (John 15:26). In this sense, the Spirit is from the Father, a relation that entails no element of subordination, inferiority, or temporal precedence but rather points to a relational and hypostatic (personal) order. This is something beyond our capacity to understand, as it occurs in the mystery of the internal life of God. However, by faith we seek to understand.

In line with this eternal procession, the Father sends the Spirit, through and in the Son, in relation to all His works in creation, including our redemption (Acts 1:8; Gal. 4:4–6). This is known as a *mission* (sending).

As noted, the Son is also actively engaged with the Father in the sending of the Spirit. Jesus refers to the Father sending the Spirit at Pentecost in response to His request or in His name (John 14:16, 26). He also says that He Himself will send the Spirit (16:7), and later He breathes on the disciples and says, "*Receive the Holy Spirit*" (20:22).

Understanding biblical revelation is the work of the Holy Spirit. He is the revelator and teacher of all truth! (John 16:13, I John 2:27) **Remember the Father chooses us to salvation, the Son secures our salvation, and the Holy Spirit seals our salvation**. The Father originates, chooses, and calls us (John 6:44, Rom 8:28--29, Eph 1:4). The Son reveals the Father, perfects us and redeems us (Heb 10:10, 14, I Peter 3:18, II Cor 5:21). The Holy Spirit witnesses to Christ, awakens our dead souls, regenerates our hearts, seals us, and then **glorifies Christ**. (John 16:12-15, Eph 4:30) **Praise the Lord!**

The misunderstanding of the Trinity has resulted in much confusion in Christianity.

> *"In the 1920s, American Protestantism divided into 'modernists' and 'fundamentalists.'* ***The former gave up Christianity for a Pelagian anthropology and Arian Christology, paving the way for today's gnostic secularists.*** *While posing as liberal and open minded, the secular Left exhibits what remains of the revivalist fervor, moral superiority, and censorious finger-wagging—employing a legalistic rhetoric for essentially antinomian principles. There are no moral absolutes, except the ones the priests on the Left agree upon and which they are willing thereafter to persecute others for questioning."* (Michael Horton, Modern Reformation 29;3;33 June 2020.

Chapter 14

The Holy Spirit as Healer

I have practiced medicine for more than a half of a century as a past Director of Intensive Care in a local hospital, a medical school teacher, and a practicing pulmonologist. I also, along with my wife, ran a Christian counseling group where we prayed with many wounded and ill Christians. During my many years of practicing medicine, I have prayed for hundreds of people and comforted many who were dying and hopeless. Prayer can be dangerous since many are captives of Satan, and he doesn't release people easily. This is not to mean that all illnesses are related to a demonic attack, but certainly demonic activity afflicts more people than we realize, particularly those with drug and alcohol addiction. (Luke 9:1-2; 10:17-20) Healing prayer is complicated and requires spiritual discernment and faith in the Lord not in ourselves or our spiritual gifting. It can be costly to set the captives free from bondage.

The practice of healing is very controversial because of the abuse of faith healers who, like Mary Baker Eddy, believe in "mind over matter" or that illness is due to lack of faith. This is unbiblical and has caused much confusion in Christian circles. This short book chapter gathers from several sources and hopefully will provide the reader a better biblical background on healing.

The Greek word for healing is *hugiainō* (hoog-ee-*eye*-no). This noun literally means, "to be in good or sound health." Luke uses the term three times with reference to physical health (5:31; 7:10; 15:27). In the pastoral epistles, however, *hugiainō* is used figuratively to refer to "sound" faith (Titus 1:13; 2:2), "sound" teaching (1 Tim. 1:10; 2 Tim. 4:3; Titus 1:9; 2:1), or "sound" words (1 Tim. 6:3; 2 Tim. 1:13). The Greek word for healing also refers to correct Christian teaching, which engenders a robust faith and gives rise to wholesome values.

"The Hebrew the word *Shalom* speaks not only of peace and well-being but wholeness, health, prosperity and the integration of body, soul, and spirit. The Greek word commonly used or healing is *marpe*, which means restoration of health, remedy, cure, medicine; tranquility, deliverance, refreshing. Occurring thirteen times, *marpe* comes from the verb *rapha*, 'to heal, cure, repair.' Salvation is God's rescue of the entire person, and healing is His complete repair of that person, as *marpe illustrates*."[7]

Healing is described in Scripture following many different actions. Healing is the *restoration of health to spirit, soul, and body resulting from:*

- Salvation and healing from looking at the crucified Christ (Numbers 21: 6-9)
- Intercession (Num. 12:10-15)
- Repentance (1 King. 13:1-6)
- Prayer (James 5:14, 15)
- Supernatural Faith (Matt. 9:20-22, John 4:46-53)
- God's Word (Ps. 107:20)
- Laying on of hands (Acts 28:8)
- Anointing with oil (James 5:14-15)

The apostles themselves seldom used oil in the healing of the sick. Oil was used medicinally in biblical times such as by the Good Samaritan in Luke 10:29-37. A more liberal symbolic interpretation of anointing with oil today could include proper medical treatment and medications such as antibiotics. It also symbolizes the Holy Spirit.

---

7   Hayford, J. W., Thomas Nelson Publishers. (1995). *Hayford's Bible handbook*. Nashville, TN; Atlanta, GA; London; Vancouver: Thomas Nelson Publishers.

In Scripture healing also wrought cures by a touch (Acts 3:7), by the apostle's shadow (Acts 5:15), by handkerchiefs (Acts 19:12), by laying on of hands (Acts 28:8), or by word of mouth (Acts 9:34). It does not appear that the apostles were permitted to employ this gift indiscriminately, no not even among brethren in Christ dear to them, or why should Paul leave Trophimus at Miletus sick (2 Tim. 4:20) or sorrow so much over the illness of Epaphroditus (Phil. 2:27)? As 1 Corinthians 13 plainly intimates, "whether there be prophecies (inspired messages from God) they shall fail (to be given any more); whether there be tongues, they shall cease; whether there be (supernatural) knowledge, it shall vanish away" (v. 8). It was the view of Matthew Henry, Thomas Manton, John Owen, and in fact nearly all of the Puritan divines, that James 5:14, 15 refers to the exercise of one of those supernatural gifts, which the church enjoyed only in the first century. These men were **cessationists** in that they did not believe that the spiritual gifts listed in I Corinthians 12:1-10 continued after the first century. This is an area of continued controversy.

Continuists believe that the spiritual gifts have never ceased and believe that *"Jesus is the same yesterday, today and forever."* (Hebrews 13:8) I am a continuist and have witnessed many transformative answers to healing prayer but no great visible miracles. Unfortunately, many of my Christian brothers demand visible medically documented miracles for themselves or family before believing that the Holy Spirit heals today.

Ancient records reveal that spiritual healing continued under the persecution of the Romans. Saint Gregory of Neocaesarea who died in AD 268 worked many miracles and healings and was later called a wonderworker. Saint Anthony of The Desert (251-356) had only to touch people to heal them. (Francis Macnutt PhD, The Practice of Healing Prayer; The Word Among Us Press, 2010)

When Constantine took over Rome in AD 312. He turned all the pagan temples into churches, this was the beginning of the dark ages and the confusion between true and false pagan religion corrupted Christianity. By AD 350 the practice of healing largely died out in Rome and continued sporadically in the Desert Fathers.

I find there is no scriptural foundation for cessationism. If you believe that spiritual healing occurred only in the first century, then why pray for healing? Or aren't you also saying that the Holy Spirit doesn't heal today? Supernatural healing and gifts have continually but sporadically manifested themselves throughout the centuries, often as exhibition of the flesh more than the spirit. Many of the early anti-baptized leaders were deceived by false prophecy. The First Great Awakening was accompanied by many outbursts of joy and emotion. People fainted and cried out, but Jonathan Edwards was not distracted from preaching about hell and sin. The Second Great Awakening was associated with much spiritual confusion and false spiritual manifestations. The focus was more about what God can do for you, rather than dying to self and man's hopelessness before a Holy God.

Men look for power, wealth, and fame and make many spiritual gifting claims that bring focus on themselves rather than the Holy Spirit. Bad examples from fleshly leaders, such as "Word of Faith" teachers, shouldn't discourage the Christian from recognizing that the Holy Spirit has never left the church but is used by broken people with pure motives around the world to bring healing according to God's will. (John Kennedy; <u>The Torch of the Testimony</u>; Christian Books 1965)

Anointing Oil

First, the "anointing with oil" clearly appears to look back to Mark 6:13 where we are told of the twelve. They "anointed with oil many that were sick and healed them." Second, the positive promise of healing, verse 15, seems to be an unconditional and general one, as though no exceptions, no cases of failure, were to be looked for. Third, "healing" was certainly one of the miraculous gifts specified in 1 Corinthians 12. Moreover, it hardly seems likely that the "faith" here mentioned is an ordinary one: though whether it differed in kind or only in degree is not easy to determine. There was the "faith of miracles"—either to work them or the expectation of them on the part of those who were the beneficiaries, as is clear from Matthew 21:24; Mark 11:24; 1 Corinthians 13:2. The "anointing with oil" after praying over the sick is regarded as a seal or pledge of the *certainty* of healing or recovery.

To illustrate: if I am starting out on a journey, I ask God to preserve me from all harm and danger if that be His holy will (Rom. 1:10), but I make no such proviso when I request Him to deliver me from those who assault my soul (2 Tim. 4:18).

Thus "the prayer of faith" in James 5:15 is not a definite expectation that God *will heal and protect*, but a peaceful assurance that He will do that which is the most for His glory and purpose. That the promise of James 5:15 *is* an indefinite and not an absolute one is clear from this consideration: if it were not so, he could continually claim the promise and so never die—the "and IF they have committed sins" further confirms the indefiniteness of what is here in view.[8]

"Confess your faults one to another, and pray one for another, that ye may be healed" (James 5:16). Here the scope of our passage is widened: in verse 13 the afflicted is to pray for himself, in verse 14 the ministers are to pray for the one seriously sick, now fellow-Christians are to pray for each other. But first they are bidden to confess their faults one to another, which does not mean revealing the secrets of their hearts or acquainting their brethren with that

8   Pink, A. W. (2005). *Divine heali*g: is it scriptural?* Bellingham, WA: Logos Bible Software.

which is suited only for the ear of God, but cases where they have tempted or injured one another or consented to the same evil act—tattling, for example. A mutual acknowledgement of those faults that cause coldness and estrangement, exciting one another to repentance for the same, promotes the spirit of prayer and fellowship. The "healing" here is also wider, referring primarily to that of the soul (Ps. 41:4) and spiritual and physical lameness (Heb. 12:13), being the same term used in 1 Peter 2:24, yet also includes removal of physical chastisements.

A few brief observations on our passage in James 5;13-16 conclusion:

1. Personal prayer (v. 13) is enjoined before ministerial elders (v. 14) and church (v. 16): individual responsibility cannot be shelved.

2. God is not indifferent to the sickness of His people (v. 14) but cares for their bodies as well as their souls.

3. Are not ministers to visit the sick and pray over them instead of waiting until they are sent for (v. 14)?

4. If none but "elders" (ministers) were to anoint with oil, surely, they alone are eligible to administer baptism and the Lord's supper??

5. All sickness is not occasioned by sin, or the "if" of verse 15 would be meaningless.

6. Yet God does sometimes visit with physical chastisements as the "if" denotes.

7. The mutual confession of verse 16 refutes the Catholic error of "auricular confession," for the priest does not confess his sins to those revealing to him the secrets of their souls!

Faith healing

Various terms are currently used to describe healing that occurs without the use of means and in response to faith. Because all true healing comes from God, the term 'divine healing' is not helpful to distinguish this special form. **'Spiritual' healing suggests more the restoration of health to the spirit than the body** and moreover may be confused with the work of spiritists who, in the name of the devil, can produce spurious healing. Faith healing (it is by no means always in Christ since many Eastern Religions believe in faith healing also) is a helpful term so long as the object of faith is Christ alone. **Our faith must be in God not in ourselves or soulish faith. Our faith must be in Christ and Christ alone. Faith comes from a trusting relationship with God and His word. Our faith must not be in our own faith or someone else's faith, such as faith healers, but in the object of our faith, the resurrected miracle-working Christ. Our faith is a gift from God (Eph 2:1-9) and includes trust and submission to His will.** We may not be given faith to perform bold works for God that others have, but we all have a measure of faith, and God will increase our faith for His purpose based on His sovereign will when necessary. Our faith must be in God's promise *"that all things work together for good to those who love God, to those who are called according to His purpose."* (Romans 8:28) **All things include our suffering; and faith trusts that God is in our troubles as well as our blessings.** (I Peter 3:14-17)

Miraculous healing

A miracle essentially consists of "a striking interposition of divine power by which the operations of the ordinary course of nature are overruled, suspended or modified." So far as miraculous healing in Scripture is concerned, the essential features are that the cure is instantaneous (the incident of Mk. 8:22–26 being a notable exception), complete and permanent, and usually without the use of means (the saliva of Mk. 7:33; 8:23; Jn. 9:6 is an exception; also

Mk. 5:27–29; Acts 5:15; 19:12). Divine miracles of healing show no relapses, which typify spurious miracles, except, of course, when dead persons were raised to life who, sooner or later, subsequently died again (*e.g.,* Jairus' daughter, Mk. 5:21–24, 35–43; the widow of Nain's son, Lk. 7:11–15; Lazarus in Jn. 11:1–44, *etc.*).

The purpose of miraculous healing.

Like the other miracles in Scripture, they were dramatized signs and enacted parables intended to teach a double lesson. They were to *authenticate* the word of the person who performed them (*e.g.,* Ex. 7:9; Lk. 5:20–24; Jn. 7:19–22; 10:37–38; Acts 2:22) and to *illustrate* the word. Thus, what happened to the body of the paralytic in Lk. 5:18–26 was a proof and picture of what happened in his soul because he was forgiven his sins. It is important to see, therefore, that the purpose of this healing miracle was theological, not medical. The many who were healed at the beginning of the ministry of Jesus, of the early church and of individual Christians (*e.g.,* Philip, Acts 8:5–8) gradually became fewer as the essential lesson was learned. Many lay ill at the pool of Bethesda, (Jn. 5:3), but Jesus healed only one because one was enough to teach the spiritual truth. If Christ's purpose had been healing all the sick, he would have healed them all.

Thus, a miracle of healing today should not be expected simply when it is medically desirable but rather where the Word of God and his servant needs to be authenticated and illustrated, and such evidence is not already available in the Bible, as in Africa and other third world nations. The fringe of an area of new evangelization on the mission field would therefore seem to be the most likely place for miraculous healing to occur today, the very place where miracles can least be scientifically proven! (But the church in general is now recovering her healing ministry as an integral part of the total gospel of wholeness, and such healings sometimes include the instantaneous as well as the more usually gradual recoveries.

Miraculous healing in the Old Testament.

Even if medical means were also used, recovery in the OT is generally attributed to the intervention of God, *e.g.,* the recovery of Moses (Ex. 4:24–26) from the illness associated with his disobedience over his son's circumcision and is given an entirely spiritual significance. The healing of Miriam's leprosy (Nu. 12:1–15) and of Naaman, through Elisha (2 Ki. 5:8–14), appear to be miraculous. The healing of Jeroboam's suddenly paralyzed hand (1 Ki. 13:4–6) and the raising from the dead of the son of the widow of Zarephath by Elijah (1 Ki. 17:17–24), and of the son of the Shunammite woman by Elisha (2 Ki. 4:1–37) are clearly miraculous. This boy's illness has been attributed to sunstroke; but it could equally well have been fulminating encephalitis or a subarachnoid hemorrhage. (The Jews were conscious of the effects of the sun [see Ps. 121:6], and a case of sunstroke is reported in the Apocrypha [Judith 8:2–3].) The recovery of the Israelites bitten by the serpents when they looked on the bronze serpent is miraculous also, though individuals are not specified (Nu. 21:6–9). The salvation of the Israelites from the later plagues in Egypt (Exodus 12:1-13) is a curious example of what might be termed a "prophylactic miracle," *i.e.,* for them disease was miraculously prevented rather than miraculously healed. The recovery of Hezekiah (2 Ki. 20:1–11) was possibly natural, though it is attributed directly to God (v. 8) and is accompanied by a nature miracle (vv. 9–11)—the illness was probably a severe carbuncle?

Miraculous healing, even counting rising from the dead, is unusual in the OT, and the few cases seem to cluster about the two critical times of the Exodus and the ministry of Elijah and Elisha. See Ex. 7:10–12 for nature miracles performed by Moses and Aaron. The miracles performed by the Egyptian sorcerers (Ex. 7:11, 22; 8:7) mimicked the first three miraculous signs wrought by Moses and Aaron (even though their second and third attempts only added to the sufferings of their people), but they were unable to counterfeit the power of God in the subsequent signs (8:18). Thus, the miracles wrought by Moses achieved their purpose (7:9) of authenticating his word of authority and finally led to the escape of the children of Israel.

Miraculous healing in the Gospels.

Our Lord's miracles of healing are reported by the Synoptists as groups (*e.g.* Lk. 4:40–41) and, in greater detail and more specifically, as individual cases. Demon possession is clearly distinguished from other forms of disease (*e.g.,* Mk. 1:32–34), where *kakōs echōn* (to be in a bad state or sick) is separate from *daimonizomai* which means demon oppression. People came to him in large numbers (Mt. 4:23–24), and all those that came to him were healed (Lk. 4:40). Doubtless cases of mental as well as of physical illness were included, and on one occasion our Lord even restored a severed part of the body (Lk. 22:50–51). At the same time, these recorded instances can represent only a small fraction of those ill in the country at this time.

In the combined narrative of the four Gospels there are over twenty stories of the healing of individuals or of small groups. Some were healed at a distance, some with a word but without physical contact, some with physical contact, and some with both physical contact and a 'means,' *i.e.,* the use of clay made from spittle, which was a popular remedy of the time for blindness (Mk. 8:23; Jn. 9:6) and deafness (Mk. 7:32–35). This may have been to aid the patient's faith or to demonstrate that God does not exclude the use of means, or both. In one unique instance Jesus performed two successive miracles on the same man.

Luke's Gospel is the only one to give the story of the Good Samaritan. It also includes five miracles of healing not recorded by the other Evangelists. These are the raising of the son of the widow of Nain (7:11–16), the healing of the woman 'bowed together' (13:11–16), the man with dropsy (congestive heart failure, possibly liver disease, or kidney failure) (14:1–4), the ten lepers (17:12–19) and the healing of Malchus's ear (22:51). More details of cases are given, and Luke uses the more technical *iaomai* for healing, rather than the non-technical words.

The Fourth Evangelist John, unlike the Synoptists, never refers to healing of people in large numbers, nor to demon possession (though demons are referred to, and the word *daimonizomai* is used only in Jn. 10:21). In addition to the raising of Lazarus from the dead, only three cases are described. These are the healing of the nobleman's son of a serious febrile condition (4:46–54), the man paralysed 38 years (5:1–16), and the man born blind (9:1–14). These miracles of healing in John's Gospel are not only mighty works (*dynameis*) but also signs (*sēmeia*). They demonstrate that Christ's miracles of healing have not only an individual, local, contemporary, and of physical significance; but having a general, eternal, and spiritual meaning as well. For example, in the case of the man born blind, the point is made that individual sickness is not necessarily attributable to individual sin.[9]

The biblical outlook on disease

The topics of suffering and disease in the Bible are closely bound up with the questions of the nature and origin of evil itself. Suffering is a human experience with diverse causes and is one of the results of human sin. In the case of suffering from disease, the link is not usually obvious, though sometimes the illness is directly connected. From the account of the Fall of man in Genesis, it is clear, that soon afterwards man knew insecurity, fear, and pain (Gn. 3:16, 17). Here *'iṣṣābôn* ('sorrow') is better rendered 'pain,' and then mental anguish (Gn. 4:13). The direct connection between sin and suffering becomes rapidly more complex, but nations which obeyed God were, in general, promised freedom from disease (Ex. 15:25–26; Lv. 26:14–16; Dt. 7:12–16 and chap. 28, especially vv. 22, 27, 58–61). On the other hand, pestilence is one of the three sore judgments on the people of God (Je. 24:10; 32:24; Ezk. 14:21) and on other nations, *e.g.,* Philistines (1 Sa. 5:6) and Assyrians (2 Ki. 19:35). There are passages such as Ps. 119:67, where the sinner himself is involved,

---

9   D.T. (1996). Health, Disease and Healing. In D. R. W. Wood, I. H. Marshall, A. R. Millard, J. I. Packer, & D. J. Wiseman (Eds.), *New Bible dictionary* (3rd ed., pp. 453–454). Leicester, England; Downers Grove, IL: InterVarsity Press.

and the case of the impotent man healed (Jn. 5:1–16) where his own fault is perhaps implied (v. 14). David's sin involved the afflictions of others (2 Sa. 24:15–17). **On the whole, human suffering from disease or from any other cause, is the effect on the individual of his spiritual malaise but of the human society as well of which he is an integral part. In Job 1, something is seen of the activity of Satan. This is also apparent in Acts 10:38, where the sick are spoken of as "*all that were oppressed by the devil*" and in the suggestive parable of the wheat and tares ("*An enemy has done this*" Mt. 13:28). Again, Christ himself spoke of "*this woman, whom Satan bound* ..." (Lk. 13:16).**

God does not stand by helplessly, however. Suffering is sometimes used punitively. This may be on a national scale as in Revelation 9:18. Or it may be applied to individuals, as in the cases of Moses (Ex. 4:24), Miriam (Nu. 12:10), Uzziah (2 Ch. 26:16–21), Jeroboam (2 Ch. 13:20), Gehazi (2 Ki. 5:25–27), Ananias and Sapphira (Acts 5:5, 10), Herod (Acts 12:21–23) and Elymas (Acts 13:11).

Much more detail is given when suffering is used constructively (Heb. 12:6–11), as in the case of Jacob, who, after a real physical injury miraculously inflicted, learnt to depend upon God and matured spiritually to fulfill his new name of Israel (Gn. 32:24–32). Hezekiah's illness demonstrated his faith in God and is probably in this category (2 Ki. 20:1–7). The book of Job shows that the real issue is a man's relationship to God rather than his attitude to his own suffering. It is the principal OT refutation of the view, put forward with great skill by Job's 'comforters,' that there is an inevitable link between individual sin and individual suffering. After disposing of the view, which is only partially true, that the reason for the existence of suffering is disciplinary, it leads to the sublime picture of Job: comforted, vindicated and blessed. It is important to realize that the biblical picture is not a mere dualism. Rather, suffering is presented in the light of eternity and in relation to a God who is sovereign, but who is nevertheless forbearing in his dealings with the world because of his love for men (2 Pet. 3:9). Conscious of the sorrow and pain round about them, the NT writers look forward to the final consummation when suffering shall be no more (Rom. 8:18; Rev. 21:4).

This conception is different from the Greek gnostic notion of the body as something inherently evil and the spirit as something inherently good. The biblical conception of the transience yet nobility of the body is best seen in 2 Cor., especially in 5:1–10 and 1 Cor. 6:15. It is an integral part of the complexity of the individual through which the personality is expressed.[10]

In this study of healing, we come to the last set of miracles in Matthew 8 and 9. The first set of three is in Matthew 8:1–17: (1) the healing of a leper, (2) the healing of the sick servant of a Roman centurion, and (3) the healing of Peter's mother-in-law. The second set includes: (4) the quieting of the wind and waves on Galilee, (5) the deliverance of two demon-possessed men from Gadara, and (6) the healing of a paralyzed man. This second set of miracles is in Matthew 8:18–9:8. In Matthew 9:18–34, the miracles include: (7) a double miracle involving the raising of a dead girl to life coupled with the healing of a woman who suffered from a flow of blood, (8) the healing of two blind men, and (9) the healing of a demon-possessed man who had been unable to speak.[11]

Now that we have the overall framework for these chapters, we are ready to look at the three final healings. The first involves the raising of the dead daughter of a synagogue ruler and the healing of the bleeding woman that is joined to it (Matt. 9:18–26). These stories are also told in Mark and Luke, but Matthew's account is the most condensed version. Matthew tells the incidents in nine verses, whereas Mark uses twenty-three verses (Mark 5:21–43) and Luke uses seventeen (Luke 8:40–56).

---

10   D.T. (1996). Health, Disease and Healing. In D. R. W. Wood, I. H. Marshall, A. R. Millard, J. I. Packer, & D. J. Wiseman (Eds.), *New Bible dictionary* (3rd ed., p. 455). Leicester, England; Downers Grove, IL: InterVarsity Press.
11   Boice, J. M. (2001). *The Gospel of Matthew* (pp. 152–154). Grand Rapids, MI: Baker Books.

The case of Jairus.

Matthew says that while Jesus was teaching about fasting (vv. 14–17), a ruler asked him to come and raise his daughter from the dead. In the Gospels, "ruler" almost always means a ruler of the synagogue, which Mark makes this clear in his account, and we also learn that this man's name is Jairus (Mark 5:22). Mark says that at the time the ruler first approached Jesus, his daughter had not yet died but that she died before Jesus reached her: "While Jesus was still speaking, some men came from the house of Jairus, the synagogue ruler. 'Your daughter is dead,' they said. 'Why bother the teacher anymore?'" (v. 35).

Earlier in this series of miracles, when we were studying the healing of the Roman centurion's servant, we remarked on the extraordinary faith of the centurion. He believed that Jesus could heal his servant even without coming to his house. The faith of the synagogue ruler is also striking. True, he asked Jesus to "come and put your hand on her" (Matt. 9:18), which falls short of the centurion's perception, but at some point, in the story, knowing that his daughter had died he still trusted Jesus. Besides, he was from among those religious leaders who were jealous of Jesus and very quickly became hostile to him and tried to destroy him.

What made Jairus appeal to a man most of his peers rejected? No doubt it was utter desperation! His daughter was dying or was already dead, and he had nowhere else to turn. Desperation may not have been the best of motives, but it drove him to Jesus, and that was all that really mattered. It has been the case for many people. They may not have come to Jesus for any other reason but that something in their lives made them desperate. So, they came to Jesus and discovered that he did not scorn them for their inadequate or poor motives but met their needs instead.

The case of the bleeding woman.

Wasn't it desperation that drove this woman to Jesus too? The woman is nameless, but she is introduced as a desperate case since she "had been subject to bleeding for twelve years" (v. 20), to which Luke also adds, "No one could heal her" (Luke 8:43). It is important to think about her condition since it so obviously illustrates our own desperate condition due to sin.

Sickness is sometimes related to sin. In John 5:14, Jesus said to the man healed at the Sheep-Gate pool, "See, *you are well! **Sin no more,** that nothing worse may happen to you."* Jesus told the paralytic: *"And behold, some people brought to him a paralytic, lying on a bed. And when Jesus saw their faith, he said to the paralytic, 'Take heart, my son; **your sins are forgiven.'"*** Sin may be a warning from a loving and discipling father to confess our sin and repent. *"My son do not regard lightly the discipline of the Lord, nor be weary when reproved by him. For the Lord disciplines the one he loves and chastises every son whom he receives."* (Hebrews 12:5-6)

First, she was *unclean*. The words the Gospel writers use are carefully chosen, as we might expect from men who are describing the health problems of a woman. But what we surmise from their accounts is that the woman was suffering from excessive menstrual bleeding which under Jewish law made her unclean (Lev 15:25). Whatever the source, the bleeding would have weakened her—she would have been anemic as well as subject to further diseases—and she would have been considered ceremonially unclean by the Jews, as was the leper whom Jesus healed in chapter 8. The condition of a woman subject to such bleeding and how she was to be treated is described in Leviticus 15:25–33.

Second, she was *isolated*. People could not come into contact with a menstruating woman without being made unclean by that contact. (Lev 15:27) In fact, they could not even lie on a bed where she had lain or sit on a chair where she had sat. No one could touch her, and she was not allowed to touch other people. Sadly, her bleeding would have destroyed her chances for marriage, or if she were married, it would have precluded all sexual relations with her husband. She must have been very, very lonely.

Third, she was *incurable.* Luke makes this clearer than the other two writers when he explains that "no one could heal her" (Luke 8:43), but it is obvious from the other Gospels as well. All three synoptic Gospels say that she had been ill for *"twelve years"* (v. 20), and Mark adds that, in spite of her having seen many doctors, *"instead of getting better she grew worse"* (Mark 5:26).

When we put the story of the synagogue ruler's daughter and the woman who suffered from bleeding together, we have an apt picture of everyone apart from the healing grace of Jesus Christ. I am sure these stories are linked in the Gospels because the circumstances of the cures are intertwined; that is, they actually happened at the same time and were remembered together by the writers. But the stories also reinforce one another (and belong together for that reason) since what was true of the woman was true of the girl too, and vice versa. The dead were as unclean as menstruating women and lepers. They could not be touched. That is why Matthew points out that Jesus overthrew the taboo by taking the dead girl by the hand (v. 25). Again, there is no isolation so utterly complete as death, either for the dead person or for those who have lost the one loved. As far as the woman was concerned, she was bleeding to death even if she was not dead yet. As for being incurable, the condition of the dead girl and the condition of the woman were both clearly beyond hope. But not for Jesus. What we are told is that the woman's contact with Jesus healed her "from that moment" (v. 22) and that as soon as Jesus had taken the dead girl by the hand she got up, being raised from the death that held her. None are too unclean, too isolated, or too hopeless for Jesus to save. He can even raise the dead.[12]

---

12   Boice, J. M. (2001). *The Gospel of Matthew* (pp. 156–157). Grand Rapids, MI: Baker Books.

Hope for the Hopeless

The point of these stories is this is exactly what Jesus does in the case of everyone who is saved from sin. It is what he has done for you if you are a Christian. What does sin do to us after all? Obviously, it makes us *unclean*. It contaminates us, and none of us can come before the purity of God's presence until our sin is dealt with. When Isaiah saw the Lord seated upon his throne in heaven he cried out, "I am ruined! For I am a man of unclean lips, and I live among a people of unclean lips" (Isa. 6:5). He trembled before God until an angel touched his lips with a coal from the altar, saying, "Your guilt is taken away and your sin atoned for" (v. 7).

Sin also *isolates*. It keeps us from God, which is the worst thing about sin, but it also isolates us from other people, creating hurts, hard feelings, and misunderstandings between races, individuals, and even members of one's own family. Isaiah also wrote of our isolation from God: "Your iniquities have separated you from your God; your sins have hidden his face from you, so that he will not hear" (Isa. 59:2).

Then, too, our condition is *hopeless* apart from grace. Nothing could be more hopeless than death, and we are described as being "dead" in our sins (Eph. 2:1). But the same chapter of the Bible that says we were dead in our sins also says, "But because of his great love for us, God, who is rich in mercy, made us alive with Christ even when we were dead in transgressions—it is by grace you have been saved. And God raised us up with Christ and seated us with him in the heavenly realms in Christ Jesus, in order that in the coming ages he might show the incomparable riches of his grace, expressed in his kindness to us in Christ Jesus" (Eph. 2:4–7). There is no finer picture of that love, grace, resurrection power, and salvation than Matthew's account of the healings of the ruler's dead daughter and the bleeding woman.

A Healing of Two Blind Men

We come next to the last part of Mathew chapter 9, which contains two more healing stories. The first, which is the eighth in the overall series, is about the healing of two blind men (vv. 27–31). If we look at them in the same context in which we have been looking at the other miracles, we see that they are concerned with what Jesus does when he saves sinners.

These two men came after him, crying out, *"Have mercy on us, Son of David"* (v. 27). This is the first use of the title "Son of David" in Matthew, and there can be little doubt that it is used here as in other places with strong messianic expectations. Can it be the case that these blind men were confessing Jesus as the Messiah? That is exactly what they were doing! In fact, it was their faith in Jesus as the Messiah that led them to cry out as they did. The messianic age was understood to be a time when "the eyes of the blind [would be] opened and the ears of the deaf unstopped," when "the lame [would] leap like a deer, and the mute tongue shout for joy" (Isa. 35:5–6). "If Jesus was really the Messiah, the blind reasoned, then he would have mercy on them; and they would have their sight," writes D.A. Carson. They may not have been certain that their faith was rightly placed before they cried out, but it was their only chance. Their condition was as hopeless as that of the people in the preceding story. Yet once Jesus turned to them, called them inside, questioned them, and healed them, they knew he was indeed the Savior and the King of Israel.

"'Do you believe that I am able to do this?' he asked.

'Yes, Lord,' they replied. Then he touched their eyes, and their sight was restored completely."

This story and the following one about the man who could not talk are unique to Matthew, though Mark and Luke include stories of the healing of blind men later on in their Gospels (see

Mark 8:22–26; 10:46–52; parallels in Matt. 20:29–34; Luke 18:35–43). Why does Matthew include such a story here? The reason is his understanding of what these healing stories teach. If we have been right in our study thus far, they teach what is involved when Jesus saves men and women from their sin. They portray our spiritual condition—**we are all unclean, isolated, hopeless, even dead in our sins**—and they show that to be saved from sin we need the powerful, forgiving, saving grace of God, which is to be found in Jesus Christ alone. Remember that that **"saving grace represents God's kindness to those who do not deserve it, cannot earn it, and could never repay it."**

What follows then? Clearly, what follows is the opening of our eyes to see Jesus even better than we did before. Before their healing, the blind men saw Jesus in their mind's eye, enough to identify him as the Messiah. But when their eyes were opened, they saw him as He is, and they began to "spread the news about him all over that region" (v. 31).

What happened here reminds us of what happened when Jesus appeared to the two Emmaus disciples when they were making their way back home after the resurrection. They had heard about Christ's resurrection, but they did not believe it. Dead men do not rise. When Jesus appeared to them, they failed to recognize Him. This was a spiritual blindness, illustrated by their inability to see who He was. But He began to teach them from the Old Testament, and when He did, *"their eyes were opened, and they recognized him"* (Luke 24:31). There are three great "openings" in Luke 24: first, the Scriptures (vv. 27, 32); then, their eyes (v. 31); finally, their minds, as they came to understand even the Scriptures in new ways (v. 45).

Does the New Testament Show Common Methods Used in Healing? The methods used by Jesus and the disciples to bring healing varied from case to case, but most frequently they included laying on of hands. In the verse just quoted, Jesus no doubt could have spoken a powerful word of command and healed everyone in the large crowd instantly, but instead, "*he laid his hands on every one of them* and healed them" (Luke 4:40). Laying on of hands seems to have been the primary means Jesus used to heal, because when people came and asked him for healing, they did not simply ask for prayer but said, for example, "come and lay your hand on her, and she will live" (Matt. 9:18).

Laying on of hands: The practice of laying hands on someone or something occurs frequently in the Old Testament—particularly the laying of hands on the head of an animal intended for sacrifice. In the account of the ritual of the Day of Atonement, the priest laid his hands on the scapegoat (Lev. 16:21). This symbolized the transference of the sins and guilt of the people to the goat, which was taken away into the wilderness. Jesus became the scapegoat for us since He took our sins upon Himself! The act of laying on of hands in the Old Testament was also associated with blessing (Gen. 48:18), installation to office (Deut. 34:9), and the setting apart of Levitical priesthood (Num. 8:10). These passages seem to express the idea of transference of authority and quality.

In the New Testament, Jesus laid his hands on children (Matt. 19:13, 15) and on the sick when he healed them (Matt. 9:18). In the early church the laying on of hands was also associated with healing, the reception of the Holy Spirit (Acts 9:17), the setting apart of persons to particular offices and work in the church (Acts 6:6), the commissioning of Barnabas and Paul as missionaries (Acts 13:3), and the setting apart of Timothy (1 Tim. 4:14; 2 Tim. 1:6). The ritual was accompanied by prayer (Acts 6:6).

The laying on of hands was not a magical or superstitious rite that gave a person special power. It expressed the idea of being set apart by God's people for a special task. In the NT, baptism and the reception of the Spirit were, on occasion, accompanied by the laying on of hands. In Acts 8:14–19, the gift of the Spirit was conferred only when baptism had been followed by apostolic laying on of hands. It is unlikely that the laying on of hands by Ananias in Acts 9:12, 17 (where it precedes baptism) is to be understood similarly. Acts 19:6 links laying on of hands with baptism and the gift of the Spirit expressed in tongues and prophecy, and Heb. 6:2 refers to teaching about baptisms and laying on of hands, probably as instruction given to new converts. Elsewhere, however, the gift of the Spirit was given without mention of laying on of hands and once even before baptism (Acts 10:44–48), and it is unlikely that in the NT period baptism was always accompanied by laying on of hands.

When hands were laid on new believers in Samaria and they received the Holy Spirit, Simon assumed that a neutral power was involved that was effective through the hands of the apostles (8:17–19; cf. 9:17; 19:6), but the apostles' response shows that it was the attitude of the recipient's heart rather than the laying on of hands (8:20–21) that was instrumental for receiving the Holy Spirit (10:44–47). At Heb. 6:2 "the laying on of hands" denotes the receiving of the Holy Spirit, here listed among "the elementary doctrines of Christ" and taken by some as a reference to the rite of confirmation.

The practice of laying on of hands in connection with ordination was probably closely related to its use in connection with the giving of the Holy Spirit and its gifts to new believers (1 Tim. 4:14; 2 Tim. 1:6; cf. Acts 6:6; 13:3; 1 Tim. 5:22).

Anointing with oil: Another physical symbol of the Holy Spirit's power coming for healing was anointing with oil. Jesus's disciples "*anointed with oil* many that were sick and healed them." (Mark 6:13; 16:17-18) The Greek word used is *chrio* (χριο). It is never used here in connection with oil but uniformly of the anointing with the Holy Spirit. Although in the secular documents it had the same meaning as *aleipho*, which is the other Greek word used for anointing. *Chrio* (ἀλειφο. Χριο) is used in "The Spirit of the Lord is upon me, for he hath anointed me" (Luke 4:18), a quotation from Isaiah 61:1, where the same Greek word appears in the Septuagint translation. It is used in Acts 4:27, 10:38, of the anointing of our Lord through the Holy Spirit. In 2 Corinthians 1:21 the word is used in connection with the anointing of the believer with the Spirit. Hebrews 1:9 presents a seeming deviation of the rule that *chrio* (χριο) is used in the New Testament in connection with the anointing with oil. We have "God hath anointed thee (the Lord Jesus) with the oil of gladness," and *chrio* (χριο) is used. How true the inspired writer was to the genius of the two words as they are used in the New Testament, for the word "oil" here does not refer to literal oil but is symbolic of the Holy Spirit. In I John 2:20, 27, "unction" and "anointing" are from the noun form that comes from *chrio* (χριο) and refer to the anointing of the believer with the Holy Spirit.

The anointing oil also represents the seal or promise of the Holy Spirit: *"And these signs will accompany those who believe: in my name they will cast out demons; they will speak in new tongues; they will pick up serpents with their hands; and if they drink any deadly poison, it will not hurt them;* **they will lay their hands on the sick, and they will recover**.*"*[13]

Anointing with oil signifies the presence of the Holy Spirit. This practice does have medicinal value, but the religious import of such anointing would have been more significant for the Jews. It was a symbol of God's grace being poured on them. It also signified that the one who applied the oil was a conduit of God's grace and healing power[14] (Mark 6:13). James attributes healing power not to the oil but to the "prayer of faith" and the action of God. This removes the activity from the arena of magic and places it squarely in that of prayer and miracle.

---

13   The Holy Bible: English Standard Version. (2016). (Mk 16:17–18). Wheaton, IL: Crossway Bibles.
14   Cooper, R. L. (2000). *Mark* (Vol. 2, p. 110). Nashville, TN: Broadman & Holman Publishers.

Anointing with oil also was performed in preparation for death. "You did not anoint My head with [cheap, ordinary] oil, but she has anointed My feet with [costly, rare] perfume."[15] (Luke 7:46)

The New Testament often emphasizes the role of faith in the healing process—sometimes the faith of the sick person (Luke 8:48; 17:19), but at other times the faith of others who bring the sick person for healing. In James 5:15 it is the elders who pray, and James says it is "the prayer of faith" that saves the sick person—this then must be the faith of the elders praying, not the faith of the one who is sick. When the four men let down a paralytic through a hole in the roof where Jesus was preaching, we read, "And when Jesus saw *their* faith …" (Mark 2:5). At other times Jesus mentions the faith of the Canaanite woman regarding the healing of her daughter (Matt. 15:28) or of the centurion for the healing of his servant (Matt. 8:10, 13).[16]

How Then Should We Pray for Healing? How then should we pray regarding physical illness? Certainly, it is right to ask God for healing, for Jesus tells us to pray, "Deliver us from the evil one" (Matt. 6:13). And the apostle John writes to Gaius, "I pray that all may go well with you and *that you may be in health*" (3 John 2). Moreover, Jesus frequently healed *all* who were brought to him, and he never sent people away, telling them it would be good for them to remain ill for a longer time! In addition to this, whenever we take any kind of medicine or seek any medical help for an illness, *by those actions we admit that we think it to be God's will that we seek to be well.* If we thought that God wanted us to continue in our illness, we would never seek medical means for healing! So, when we pray it seems right that our first assumption, unless we have a specific reason to think otherwise, should be that God would be pleased to heal the person we are praying for—as far as we can tell from Scripture, this is God's revealed will.

15   *The Amplified New Testament.* (1987). (Lk 7:46). La Habra, CA: Zondervan; The Lockman Foundation.
16   Grudem, W. A. (2004). *Systematic theology: an introduction to biblical doctrine* (pp. 1065–1066). Leicester, England; Grand Rapids, MI: Inter-Varsity Press; Zondervan Pub. House.

Ken Blue has a helpful observation here. He argues that if we want to understand God's attitude toward physical healing, we should look at Jesus's life and ministry. Blue says, **"If Jesus truly reveals the character of God to us, then we may cease speculating about and arguing over God's will in sickness and healing. Jesus healed people because he loved them.** Very simply, he had compassion for them; he was on their side; he wanted to solve their problems." This is a strong argument, especially when coupled with the realization that Jesus came to inaugurate the presence of the kingdom of God among us and to show us what the kingdom of God would be like.

How then should we pray? Certainly, it is right to ask God for healing, and we should go to him with the simple request that he give physical and emotional healing in time of need. James warns us that simple unbelief can lead to prayerlessness and failure to receive answers from God: *"You do not have, because you do not ask"* (James 4:2). But when we pray for healing, we should remember that we must pray for God to be glorified in the situation, whether he chooses to heal or not. And we also ought to pray out of the same compassion of heart that Jesus felt for those whom he healed. When we pray this way, God will sometimes—and perhaps often—grant answers to our prayers.

Someone may object at this point that, from a pastoral standpoint, much harm is done when people are encouraged to believe that a miracle of healing will occur and then nothing happens—disappointment with the church and anger at God may result. Those who pray for people to be healed today need to hear this objection and use wisdom in what they tell people who are ill.

But we also need to realize that there is more than one kind of mistake to make: (1) *Not praying for healing at all* is not a correct solution, for it involves disobedience to James 5:14. (2) Telling people that *God seldom heals today* and that they should expect nothing to happen is not a correct solution either, for it does not provide an atmosphere conducive to faith and is inconsistent with the pattern we see in the ministry of Jesus and the early church in the New Testament. (3) Telling people that *God always heals today* if we have enough faith is a cruel teaching not supported by Scripture. Peter reminded the church after healing the lame man who had been laid at the temple gate probably for many years in Acts Chapter 3:12. It is very likely that Christ passed him by many times, but God used Peter to heal him, and Peter said "Men of Israel, why are you amazed at this, or why do you gaze at us, as if by **our own power or piety** we had made him walk?" Jesus is the source of healing, not man, or his special apostles, or his faith! The prayer of faith is more about giving Jesus permission to heal according to his divine plan and purpose and sometimes according to His sovereign will not to heal at all.

The pastorally wise solution, it seems, lies between (2) and (3) above. We can tell people that God frequently heals today (if we believe that is true), and that it is very possible that they will be healed, but that we are still living in an age when the kingdom of God is "already" here but "not yet" fully here. Therefore, Christians in this life will experience healing (and many other answers to prayer), but they will also experience continuing illness and eventual death. In each individual case it is God's sovereign will that decides the outcome, and our role is simply to ask Him and wait for Him to answer (whether "yes" or "no" or "keep praying and wait").

The key to proper healing practice is listening to God. When I lay hands on people, I ask God: "What are you doing?" Before we pray for anybody, we need to remind ourselves that we don't know what or how to pray! Anything we pray using man's wisdom is worthless! The Holy Spirit is the source of all healing in Spirit-led prayer (2 Cor 3:5). Scripture reminds us not to lay hands on somebody suddenly. We must not be led

by compassion but be led by the Holy Spirit. **Unless we ask the Holy Spirit for leadership and discernment to minister His will through us, as the healer of all diseases, (Psalm 103:3) our prayers are useless, counterproductive, and powerless.** Many are deceived and believe that they own or possess the gift of healing. All gifts of the spirit are borrowed from the Holy Spirit who alone is the true gift of healing. Above all show love, compassion, and affirmation. Many of those ill with a terminal condition need permission to die. Often the healing prayer is helping loved ones to release their beloved with a terminal illness.

Some suggestions for those who pray for the sick.

1. Never be in a hurry to pray.

2. Decide whether to pray FOR or to pray WITH a sick person.

3. If serious issues are present, then don't pray alone. Men should pray for women always with others and have an open door in their office and women should not pray alone with men

4. Choose a safe, neutral, quiet, place to pray where confidentiality is protected.

5. Turn off phones, remove distractions, etc.

6. Put on the whole armor of God. (Eph 6:10-20)

7. Be quiet and listen to the Holy Spirit and not men.

8. Pray and minister with faith, if you don't have faith, don't pray. (Matt 8:17)

How to pray with discernment for the sick or those suffering.
(James 5:13)

1. First ask the recipient of prayer; "What do you want us to pray for?"
2. Then ask God, "Show me how to pray for this person and their problem."
3. Is this sickness a sickness unto death? Then I pray for comfort and peace.
4. Often it is the one asking for prayer for another who is the one who needs prayer.
5. Is there unconfessed and unrepented sin? (Matt 9:5-6, John 5:14)
6. Ask, do you think God is punishing you for a past sin?
7. Is this a demonic attack or mental illness?
8. Is there a root of bitterness and anger? (Matt 11:25)
9. Is this for the glory of God? (John 9:1-5)
10. Is there a family curse such as alcoholism or drug addiction? (Exodus 20:5-6)
11. Is there a problem from dabbling in the occult?
12. Is there a curse from a witch doctor, family member, etc.? (Luke 6:28)
13. Is this related to sexual or physical abuse?
14. Is this an illness from which they will recover and just need encouragement?
15. Is this a person who wants sympathy and attention, not healing?
16. Is this a person being used by Satan to be disruptive and distractive?
17. Some want direction from the Lord in the midst of a difficult situation.
18. Some come because of feeling trapped in guilt and depression. (James 5:15-16)
19. Some may struggle with suicidal thoughts.

20. Some have anxiety attacks. (Prov 12:2; Mark 4:19; 2 Cor 11:28-9:

21. Ps 37:8: Phil4:6; 1 Peter 5:7; Matt 6:25-31)

22. Some struggle with their salvation and need assurance. (Isa 42:1-4)

23. Look for spiritual archetypes.

24. Some struggle with guilt and need confession, repentance, and then absolution.

25. Some struggle with fear of problems related to a chronic illness such as finances.

26. Some struggle with fear of epidemics, earthquakes, famines, judgments of God.
    Some struggle with spiritual abuse, bullying.

27. Some struggle with a "bitter root expectation." (Heb 12:15; Jer 4:18; Deut 29:18)

28. Some live with the sin of their fathers (Ex 20:5, 34:7; Deut 5:9, Ezk 18; Gal 1:26).

29. Some illnesses have been allowed for God's Kingdom purpose, and prayer and encouragement are needed; not healing prayer! (John 9:1-39; II Cor 12:7-10; James 1:2-4)

30. Some illnesses are due to failure to discern the body. (I Cor 11:27-28) "*Whoever, therefore, eats the bread or drinks the cup of the Lord in an unworthy manner will be guilty concerning the body and blood of the Lord.* [28] *Let a person examine himself, then, and so eat of the bread and drink of the cup.* [29] *For anyone who eats and drinks without discerning the body eats and drinks judgment on himself.* [30] *That is why many of you are weak and ill, and some have died.*"

What often is missing in modern biblical Christian prayer for healing? It is **the prayer of absolution.** (ab-so-lū'shun (tr of vbs. λύω, *lúō*, "loose," and ἀφίημι, *aphíēmi*, "release," "give up," etc.) meaning to designate the official act described in Mt 16:19: *"Whatsoever thou shalt loose on earth, shall be loosed in heaven."* James reminds us: *"And the prayer of faith will save the one who is sick, and the Lord will raise him up. **And if he has committed sins, he will be forgiven.**"* (James 5:15). The Catholic church got it right here in spite of its many other doctrinal errors. Absolution proclaims the atoning work of Christ as the only way a sinner may receive "absolution" or forgiveness (Luke 7:36–50; Col. 1:13–14). Elders need to proclaim **Forgiveness** by the saving work of Christ on the cross **to the truly repentant sinner** by virtue of Christ's gift of the Holy Spirit to the Apostles empowering them to forgive or to retain sins (John. 20:23)

How do we approach someone who **has an illness related to the discipline of God**? The church since the time of Job and his friends has recognized that sometimes an illness is related to disobedience resulting in godly discipline. For example, a man may develop a venereal disease as a consequence of extra-marital sex. The Book of Proverbs affirms that God's love requires God's discipline. "*My son, do not despise the* LORD's *discipline or be weary of his reproof, for the* LORD *reproves him whom he loves, as a father the son in whom he delights*" (Prov 3:11-12) Hebrews 12:6-8 also reminders us that "For *the Lord disciplines the one he loves and chastises every son whom he receives. It is for discipline that you must endure. God is treating you as sons. For what son is there whom his father does not discipline? If you are left without discipline, in which all have participated, then you are illegitimate children and not sons.*" Paul warned the Corinthians about their lust and behavior at the communion table: "*Let a person examine himself, then, and so eat of the bread and drink of the cup. For anyone who eats and drinks without discerning the body eats and drinks judgment on himself. That is why many of you are weak and ill, and some have died. But if we judged ourselves truly, we would not be judged. But when we are judged by the Lord, **we are disciplined so that we may not be condemned along with the world.**"* (I Cor 11:28-32)

Unfortunately, well-meaning Christians often pray against illnesses and problems that are ordained by God. In contrast, many others are like Job's friends and imply that every illness is a punishment for sin and should suffer the consequences of sin. In order to pray properly, ask if the recipient of prayer believes that their illness is a judgment from God related to an unconfessed sin.

R C Sproul said, "When we suffer the consequences of our sin or when we suffer for reasons that are totally unknown to us, we might think that God is against us, in both cases, however, the Lord is for us, and he is using our suffering to cultivate in us, the holiness we must have in order to see the Lord (Heb 12:14). Let us keep that in mind when we suffer, remembering that God is with us and is using our pain for our final good and his ultimate glory." (R C Sproul, Living Before the Face of God) We need to pray for comfort and courage during this type of trial (Isa 40:1-2) and remind those that suffer that their iniquity has been pardoned. Often, we believe that the discipline of the Lord proves that He does not love us, when the opposite is true. Our Father is a loving God who cares so much for His children that He lovingly protects us and disciplines us yet amazingly simultaneously comforts us by His Holy Spirit. The Book of Lamentations reminds us that, *"though he causes grief, he will have compassion according to the abundance of his steadfast love."* (Lam 3:32; see also Ps 30:2; Ps 4:1; 2 Cor 4:9; Ps 116:1-4)

The Greek word used for comfort or encouragement with alleviation of grief is *paraklesis*, which means "a calling to one's side" (*para*, "besides," *kaleo*, "to call"); hence, either "an exhortation, consolation, and comfort"[17] speaks of the work of the "*paraclete*" or Holy Spirit to comfort and stand with us during the trials of life. He is our attorney that protects us from the accuser of the brethren. We like little

17   Vine, W. E., Unger, M. F., & White, W., Jr. (1996). Vine's Complete Expository Dictionary of Old and New Testament Words (Vol. 2, p. 110). Nashville, TN: T. Nelson.

children of God go crying to our mothers when hurt or wounded; so, we are comforted by the Holy Spirit who in a sense holds us in his arms and comforts us and protects us. John Owen reminds us that "spiritual fruit will come in due season." "*For the moment all discipline seems painful rather than pleasant, but later it yields the peaceful fruit of righteousness to those who have been trained by it.* (Hebrews 12:11)"

Those with "gifts of healings" (a literal translation of the plurals in 1 Cor. 12:9, 28) will be those people who find that their prayers for healing are answered more frequently and more thoroughly than others. When that becomes evident, a church would be wise to encourage them in this ministry and give them more opportunities to pray for others who are ill. We should also realize that gifts of healing could include ministry not only in terms of physical healing, but also in terms of emotional healing. And it may at times include the ability to set people free from demonic attack, for this is also called "healing" sometimes in Scripture (see Luke 6:18; Acts 10:38). Perhaps the gifts of being able to pray effectively in different kinds of situations and for different kinds of needs are what Paul referred to when he used the plural expression, "*gifts of healings.*"

Who is qualified to pray for the sick? Some quote Mark 2:7 "Who can forgive sins but God alone?" Catholics believe that only ordained priests can forgive sin and pronounce absolution. The Westminster Confession (1647) declared: "*To those officers (Elders and Deacons) the keys of the Kingdom of heaven are committed, by virtue whereof they have power respectively to retain and remit sins.*" Jesus said to the disciples, "Receive the Holy Spirit and if you forgive the sins of any, they are forgiven them, if you retain the sins of any they are retained." (John 20:22-23) This statement was probably addressed to all of Jesus's followers. Peter reminds us of our calling to be a Holy Priesthood. (I Peter 2:9-10) "*But you are a chosen generation, a royal priesthood, a holy nation, His own* *special people, that you may proclaim the praises of Him who called you out of darkness into His marvelous light; who once were not a people but are now the people of God, who had not obtained mercy but now have obtained mercy.*"[18] Jesus first sent the twelve apostles out in Luke 9 and then the seventy out in Luke 10. These men were given divine authority by Jesus. (Matt 10:1) "*And when He had called His twelve disciples to Him, He gave them power over unclean spirits, to cast them out, and to heal all kinds of sickness and all kinds of disease.*" Jesus is quoted in Mark 16:17-18 "*These are the signs that will be associated with **believers**: in my name they will cast out devils…they will lay hands on the sick, who will recover.*" Notice this promise of God is not addressed to super-saints but to all believers. Many church leaders fear what might happen if immature believers pray for the sick! Certainly, many involved in church work may not be true Christians at all but have compassion for the sick and the oppressed. Many evangelical churches are afraid of the priestcraft of the Catholic Church and in turn have rejected requiring biblical qualifications of elders on those who pray for the sick as laid out in Scripture. (I Tim 3: 1-13, Titus 1: 5-9)

You may ask what and who is an elder? In most civilizations, authority has been vested in those who by reason of age or experience have been thought best qualified to rule. It is not surprising therefore that the leaders in many ancient communities have borne a title derived from a root meaning 'old age.' In this respect the Heb. 'elder' (*zāqēn*) stands side by side with the Homeric *gerontes*, the Spartan *presbys*, the Roman *senatus* and the Arab *sheikh.*[19]

18   *The New King James Version.* (1982). (1 Pe 2:9–10). Nashville: Thomas Nelson.
19   Taylor, J. B. (1996). In D. R. W. Wood, I. H. Marshall, A. R. Millard, J. I. Packer, & D. J. Wiseman (Eds.), *New Bible dictionary* (3rd ed., p. 305). Leicester, England; Downers Grove, IL: InterVarsity Press.

In the Old Testament, an older person, usually white haired, (Heb. *zāqēn* "beard"), was exceptional because the age of death for men was well under the age of fifty, and ancients gave special honor to the elderly and considered them as leaders in a community. The elders were heads of households, representatives, and leaders of tribes, and at times, the most prominent men of a tribe. On the eve of the Exodus, Moses explained to Israel's elders God's plan of deliverance (Exod. 4:29); later he consulted them during the wilderness wanderings (e.g., Lev. 16:25). At Lev. 4:15; 9:1 the elders are said to have assisted in cultic ceremonies (cf. Exodus. 24:1, 14). On the advice of his father-in-law, Moses appointed "rulers" over the people who would assist him in administering justice (Exod. 18:24–26), and later, at God's prompting, he selected seventy elders to alleviate his own extensive judicial responsibilities (Num. 11:16, 24).

The Christian church followed the Jewish custom of granting authority to older persons *(Greek* πρεσβύτερος, *presbyteros)* who had shown laudable wisdom (e.g., 1 Tim. 5:1, "older men" [KJV "elder"]; Heb. 11:2, "men of old." Almost from the birth of the Church there were elders who offered leadership (e.g., Acts 11:30; 21:18; cf. Jas. 5:14). The book of Acts cites their influence on the Apostolic Council at Jerusalem (15:6, 22) and afterward (16:4). At what stage of church growth, the elders became actual office bearers, alongside deacons and bishops, remains uncertain Paul appointed elders in the Galatian churches (14:23) and conferred with the Ephesian elders (20:17). Certainly, the office of elder was in existence at least as early as the end of the apostolic age (e.g., 1 Tim. 5:17; Tit. 1:5). [20]

Unfortunately, today many "church elders" are appointed because of their financial and/or business positions, community leadership positions, or church positions, not their walk with the Lord or their tested spiritual maturity.

20   Myers, A. C. (1987). In *The Eerdmans Bible dictionary* (p. 319). Grand Rapids, MI: Eerdmans.

Many pastors are afraid of losing control and authority by appointing men with godly authority, wisdom, and anointing. Some denominations do not appoint biblical elders. (I Tim 3:1-13, Titus 1:1-10) So, where does this leave us? A weak church with impoverished leaders and immature lay people. James reminds us, "*Is anyone among you sick? Let him call for the elders of the church and let them pray over him.*" Those praying for the sick must be able to hear the voice of the Holy Spirit for guidance and discernment on how, when, where, and what to pray. What qualification is the most important for those praying for the sick? The answer is **brokenness, teachableness, and humility.** (I Cor 4:10-16) "*We are fools for Christ's sake, but you are wise in Christ. We are weak, but you are strong. You are held in honor, but we are in disrepute. To the present hour we hunger and thirst, we are poorly dressed and buffeted and homeless, and we labor, working with our own hands. When reviled, we bless; when persecuted, we endure; when slandered, we entreat. We have become, and are still, like the scum of the world, the refuse of all things.*" And "*God chose what is foolish in the world to shame the wise; God chose what is weak in the world to shame the strong; God chose what is low and despised in the world, even things that are not, to bring to nothing things that are, so that no human being might boast in the presence of God*" (I Cor 1:27-29)

Remember, "*Let no one deceive himself. If anyone among you thinks that he is wise in this age, let him become a fool that he may become wise. For the wisdom of this world is folly with God. For it is written, 'He catches the wise in their craftiness,' and again, 'The Lord knows the thoughts of the wise, that they are futile.' So, let no one boast in men.*" I Cor 3:18-21)

If you do pray and hear nothing from the Holy Spirit then please don't pray! Please be quiet and just listen to what God might be saying through others!

But What If God Does Not Heal? Nonetheless, we must realize that not all prayers for healing will be answered in this age, but all prayers will be answered in the age to come in heaven. Sometimes God will not grant the special "faith" (James 5:15) that healing will occur, and at times God will choose not to heal because of his own sovereign purposes. Paul prayed for himself for healing but was denied because of God's sovereign purpose. (2 Cor 12: 7-10) In these cases we must remember that Romans 8:28 is still true: though we experience the "sufferings of this present time," and though we "groan inwardly as we wait for … the redemption of our bodies" (Rom. 8:18, 23), nonetheless, *we know that in everything God works for good with those who love him, who are called according to his purpose" (*Rom. 8:28). His sovereign will may include fatal or chronic illness in some individuals. Many sincere but naive believers pray for healing for all individuals believing that it is God's will to heal everybody, not recognizing that they may be praying directly against God who is using an illness or trial for His divine purpose!

Whatever Paul's "thorn in the flesh" was (centuries of work by Bible-believing interpreters have failed to turn up a definitive answer), Paul realized that God allowed it to remain with him "to keep me from being too elated" (2 Cor. 12:7), that is, to keep Paul humble before the Lord. So, the Lord told him, "*My grace is sufficient for you, for my power is made perfect in weakness*" (2 Cor. 12:9). There are indications in the early church that even in the presence of the apostles not all people were healed. Paul recognized that "our outer nature is wasting away" (2 Cor. 4:16), and sometimes disease and illness will not be healed. When Epaphroditus came to visit Paul, he had an illness that brought him "near to death" (Phil. 2:27). Paul indicates in the narrative of Philippians chapter two that it appeared as though Epaphroditus was going to die—that God did not heal him immediately when he became ill. But eventually God did heal (Phil. 2:27) in answer to prayer. Paul told Timothy that he should drink a little wine "for the sake of your stomach and your frequent ailments" (1 Tim. 5:23). He said, "Trophimus I left ill at Miletus" (2 Tim. 4:20). And both Peter (1 Peter 1:6–7; 4:19) and James (James 1:2–4) have words of encouragement and counsel for those who are suffering trials of various kinds:

> *"Count it all joy, my brethren, when you meet various trials, for you know that the testing of your faith produces steadfastness. And let steadfastness have its full effect, that you may be perfect and complete, lacking in nothing."* (James 1:2–4)

When God chooses not to heal, even though we ask him for it, then it is right that we *"give thanks in all circumstances"* (1 Thess. 5:18) and realize that God can use sickness to draw us closer to himself and to increase in us obedience to do his will. Paul's "thorn in the flesh" is a wonderful example of God's refusal to heal Paul for God's glory and His ultimate purpose. (2 Cor 12:7-10) So the psalmist can say, "*It is good for me that I was afflicted* that I might learn your statutes" (Ps. 119:71), and "*Before I was afflicted, I went astray; but now I keep your `will teach you all things and bring to your remembrance all that I have said to you. (Psalm 119:67-68)* **"Peace I leave with you; my peace I give to you. Not as the world gives, do I give to you. Let not your hearts be troubled, neither let them be afraid."** (John 14:26-27 ESV)

Therefore, God can bring increased sanctification to us through illness and suffering—just as he can bring sanctification and growth in faith through miraculous healing. But the emphasis of the New Testament, both in Jesus's ministry and in the ministry of the disciples in Acts, seems to be one that encourages us in most cases eagerly and earnestly to seek God for healing, and then to continue to trust him to bring good out of the situation, whether he grants the physical healing or not. Emotional or spiritual healing is available to all who call on our Lord. The point is that in everything God should receive glory and our joy and trust in him should increase.

> "*Finally, in the book of Revelation no one is described as ill and then healed, since healing occurs during our resurrection accompanied by new perfect bodies. However, the book contains several references to eschatological healing. In Revelation 3:17–18 illness and anointing with eye salve are used as a metaphor for the lukewarm state of the church and its remedy in Christ. In Revelation 22:2 the leaves of the tree of life bring "healing to the nations," although what this healing consists of is never described. It is only in Revelation 7:16–17 (with reference to those coming out of the great tribulation) and Revelation 21:4 (with reference to the inhabitants of the new Jerusalem) that physical healing is clearly included in the description of heavenly existence. Believers may have suffered pain and gone through sickness on earth, but in the resurrection "God will wipe away every tear from them" (Rev 21:4); pain and death will have been banished. There is no need of a human agent of this healing; God (the Lamb in Rev 7) is its only agent, **reminding the readers that ultimate healing awaits the return of Christ and the resurrection of the Saints**.*" [21]

21   Martin, R. P., & Davids, P. H. (Eds.). (1997). In *Dictionary of the later New Testament and its developments* (electronic ed., pp. 437–438). Downers Grove, IL: Inter Varsity Press.

Chapter 15
The Root of Bitterness

The Root of Bitterness: possibly the most common cause of physical, emotional illness. Many people are ill because of a "**Bitter Root Judgment**." Scripture emphasizes that if we pass judgement on another, we in return will receive judgement. (Mathew 7:1-5) Today approximately one out of four to one out of five women will have suffered some type of sexual abuse. Many of whose who have suffered some type of physical, mental, or sexual abuse have not unexpectantly made harsh judgment on the abuser. This intense anger results in what is called a "Bitter Root Judgement." This retained anger may result in a **"Bitter Root Expectancy."** A typical example is when an abused woman marries, she expects her husband to be like her abuser. Her husband turns out just like her alcoholic sexual predator father, for example. She divorces her husband and remarries, but her second, third, fourth, fifth, etc. husbands all turn out like her abusive father. What is happening? A bitter root of judgment results in an expectancy that all men will be like her childhood abuser. The husbands receive a subliminal message from their wife that they will drink too much and be abusive. This cycle of dysfunctional relationships repeats itself over and over until the victim of the original abuse is able to forgive her original abuser and confess and repent of the sin of a bitter root judgment. (Heb 12:15; Jer 4:18; Deut 29:18)

> "*Repay no one evil for evil but give thought to do what is honorable in the sight of all. If possible, so far as it depends on you, live peaceably with all. Beloved, never avenge yourselves, but leave it to the wrath of God, for it is written,*

"Vengeance is mine, I will repay, says the Lord." To the contrary, "if your enemy is hungry, feed him; if he is thirsty, give him something to drink; for by so doing, you will heap burning coals on his head." Do not be overcome by evil but overcome evil with good." (Romans 12:17-21)

"You have heard that it was said, "You shall love your neighbor and hate your enemy." But I say to you, love your enemies and pray for those who persecute you, so that you may be sons of your Father who is in heaven. For he makes his sun rise on the evil and on the good and sends rain on the just and on the unjust. For if you love those who love you, what reward do you have? Do not even the tax collectors do the same? And if you greet only your brothers, what more are you doing than others? Do not even the Gentiles do the same? You therefore must be perfect, as your heavenly Father is perfect." (Matt 5:43-48)

Matthew Henry comments about Matt 5:44: "But I say unto you, I, who come to be the great Peace-Maker, the general Reconciler, who loved you when you were strangers and enemies, I say, Love your enemies,". Though men are ever so bad themselves and carry it ever so basely towards us, yet that does not discharge us from the great debt we owe them, of love to our kind, love to our kin. We cannot but find ourselves very prone to wish the hurt, or at least very coldly to desire the good, of those that hate us and have been abusive to us; but that which is at the bottom hereof is a **root of bitterness**, which must be plucked up, and a remnant of corrupt nature which grace must conquer. Note, it is the great duty of Christians to love their enemies; we cannot have complacency in one that is openly wicked and profane, nor put a confidence in one that we know to be deceitful, nor are we to love alike. But we must pay respect to the human nature and so far, honour all men. We must take notice, with pleasure, of that even in our enemies which is amiable and commendable: ingenuousness, good temper, learning, and moral

179

virtue, kindness to others, profession of religion, etc., and love that, though they are our enemies. We must have a compassion for them and a good will toward them. We are here told:

1. That we must speak well of them. Bless them that curse you. When we speak to them, we must answer their revilings with courteous and friendly words and not render railing for railing; behind their backs we must commend that in them which is commendable. And when we have said all the good, we can of them, not be forward to say anything more. See 1 Pt. 3:9. They, in whose tongues is the law of kindness, can give good words to those who give bad words to them.

2. That we must do well to them. "Do good to them that hate you, and that will be a better proof of love than good words. Be ready to do them all the real kindness that you can, and glad of an opportunity to do it, in their bodies, estates, names, families; and specially to do good to their souls." It was said of Archbishop Cranmer, "that the way to make him a friend was to do him an ill turn; so many did he serve who had disobliged him."

3. We must pray for them. "Pray for them that despitefully use you and persecute you. Note, (1.) It is no new thing for the most excellent saints to be hated, and cursed, and persecuted, and despitefully used, by wicked people; Christ himself was so treated. (2.) That when at any time we meet with such usage, we have an opportunity of showing our conformity both to the precept and to the example of Christ, by praying for them who thus abuse us. If we cannot otherwise testify

our love to them, yet this way we may without
ostentation, and it is such a way as surely, we
durst not dissemble. We must pray that God will
forgive them, that they may never fare the worse
for anything they have done against us, and that he
would make them to be at peace with us; and this
is one way of making them so."[22] (Matthew Henry)

The Holy Spirit is waiting to help us forgive what seems unforgivable. I know of a local woman who was born out of wedlock by a prostitute in another city. The mother of this beautiful child was unable to care for her baby and gave her child to her mother, the grandmother, to raise. The grandmother had many abusive men visiting her home, and the grandmother allowed men to begin abusing this child at the age of six. This continued until this woman was twelve, and she ran away with her brother and lived on the streets. Prostitution and drugs became a way of life, and she eventually went to prison. She was found by the Lord in prison, and after finishing a Christian rehabilitation and discipleship program, she got a good job. When funds were available, she went back to the east coast city where she was originally raised to forgive her grandmother and mother. She understood that after she was released from a physical prison she still remained in a spiritual prison of anger, bitterness, depression, and low self-worth. Freedom, joy, victory, and release from spiritual bondage come from forgiveness of those who have injured us. Many people have been amazed by her story of victory and would think it would be impossible to forgive such terrible abuse. **What is impossible for man is possible through the work of the Holy Spirit to bring forgiveness and reconciliation. Praise the Lord!**

---

22   Henry, M. (1994). Matthew Henry's commentary on the whole Bible: complete and unabridged in one volume (p. 1635). Peabody: Hendrickson.

Finally, I might mention our experience in a deliverance ministry with the demonically oppressed. The root of the problem that was an open door for demonic activity seems nearly always to have been unforgiveness. Not only do we need to forgive others, we often need to forgive ourselves. When we forgive, we close the door to demonic activity.

> *"When the unclean spirit has gone out of a person, it passes through waterless places seeking rest, but finds none. Then it says, 'I will return to my house from which I came.' And when it comes, it finds the house empty, swept, and put in order. Then it goes and brings with it seven other spirits more evil than itself, and they enter (*The open door of judgment and unforgiveness*) and dwell there, and the last state of that person is worse than the first. So also, will it be with this evil generation."* (Matt 12:43-45)

Be reconciled to God through Christ by the Holy Spirit and know the healing power of God and His peace.

> *"All this is from God, who through Christ reconciled us to himself and gave us the ministry of reconciliation; that is, in Christ God was reconciling the world to himself, not counting their trespasses against them, and entrusting to us the message of reconciliation. Therefore, we are ambassadors for Christ, God making his appeal through us. We implore you on behalf of Christ, be reconciled to God. For our sake he made him to be sin who knew no sin, so that in him we might become the righteousness of God."* (2 Cor 5:18-21)

Chapter 16
What is a Spiritual Archetype?

Arche is the Greek word for ruler such as used in Archbishop. A spiritual archetype is a group of demonic spirits grouped together for mutual benefit. For instance, an individual with a spirit of adultery needs the help from a deceiving spirit, spirit of control, and lying spirit to protect the participant's deception so that their duplicity will not be discovered. Also, with the spirit of adultery comes the spirit of lust and the spirit of greed to finance his or her affair. Another example might be homosexuality which is often associated with a spirit of anger, depression, deception, suicide, spirit of control, lying spirit, spirits of frustration, lust, and a spirit of murder often manifested by character assassination, slander, and blackmail. A spirit of homosexuality has many other evil spirits associated with it such as listed in Romans 1:28-32.

> *"And since they did not see fit to acknowledge God, God gave them up to a debased mind to do what ought not to be done. They were filled with all manner of unrighteousness, evil, covetousness, malice. They are full of envy, murder, strife, deceit, maliciousness. They are gossips, slanderers, haters of God, insolent, haughty, boastful, inventors of evil, disobedient to parents, foolish, faithless, heartless, ruthless. Though they know God's righteous decree that those who practice such things deserve to die, they not only do them but give approval to those who practice them."*

God is not mocked. Homosexual behavior has serious health consequences causing adults to struggle with depression, guilt, suicide, substance abuse, AIDs, hepatitis, syphilis, and other venereal diseases, anger, violence and murder, social isolation, and lack of acceptance compared to their heterosexual counterparts.

This understanding that demonic spirits often move together in groups for self-help and protection in order to gain or maintain power is helpful to the prayer counselor as he begins to see some part of the problem of the counselee who presents with spiritual oppression. The counselor may begin to understand that the spirit commonly manifested such as the spirit of control or anger is part of a much larger problem and just the tip of the iceberg of a much larger issue. I have chosen three Biblical illustrations from Revelation chapter two to demonstrate how demonic spirits exercise their power collectively: like Balaam, the Nicolaitans, and Jezebel.

Many pastors and elders are guilty of the doctrine of the Nicolaitans and think of themselves as apostles far above and not co-equal with the average Christians; *"Yet this you have: you hate the works of the Nicolaitans, which I also hate."* (Rev 2:6; 2:15) This means literally to have "victory" (Nikos) over the laity (laos). **Nicolaitan** also could be the Greek equivalent of *niką laon* ("he has conquered the people") who, according to Irenaeus, originated from Nicolaus, the proselyte of Antioch who was given church leadership in Acts 6:5. The Nicolaitans had disseminated doctrine similar in kind to the gnostic heresy of Cerinthus. Their teaching could have been based on a dualism claiming that what was done in the body had no bearing on the soul. The Nicolaitan and Balaam teaching included two moral errors: open practice of sexual immorality (perhaps at a pagan temple) and open participation in eating food that had been sacrificed to idols (probably also at a pagan temple). Both of these actions were routine activities for typical pagans. They could be interpreted as duties of a loyal citizen of Ephesus. The Nicolaitans disobeyed the command issued to the Gentile churches by the apostolic council held at Jerusalem in AD 49–50, that they should refrain from the eating of "things sacrificed to idols" (Acts 15:29). Such a restriction, though seemingly hard, prevented the Christian communities from joining in public festivals, and so brought upon them suspicion and dislike, yet was necessary to prevent a return to a pagan laxity of morals.

The Nicolaitans are not merely a subgroup in the church who were more lenient toward pagan religion and society. In the letters, their thought is called a teaching (Gk *didachē*; 2:14, 15, 20, 24), and they may have claimed inspiration for this teaching (2:20). Their leaders may have called themselves apostles (2:2) and prophets (2:20) and been actively seeking disciples. **The sin that God hates is division of His church into two classes: the laity and leadership, or priestly class.** Because of the lack of education in the early church, it became easy for some church leaders to claim supernatural revelation in the early church that led into what eventually became the schismatic error of Roman Catholic church with its Magisterium, Popes Cardinals, priestly class, etc. and a biblically ignorant laity who were not encouraged to read Scripture until 1960. It was Martin Luther who returned the church back to reading Scripture in the local language and the equal standing of all Christians before God. "*But you are a chosen race, a royal priesthood, a holy nation, a people for his own possession, that you may proclaim the excellencies of him who called you out of darkness into his marvelous light. Once you were not a people, but now you are God's people; once you had not received mercy, but now you have received mercy.*" (I Peter 2:9-10)

It has been proposed that Nicolaitan is an etymological play on the Hebrew name "**Balaam.**" (Num 25:1–2; 31:16, Rev 2:14) Balaam (*bilʿām*) can be the contracted form of *bālaʿʿam* ("he has destroyed the people") or *baʿal ʿam*, ("lord of the people"). Balaam is known to tradition as a *seer of the gods or diviner.*[23] It is

<hr>

23   Achtemeier, P. J., Harper & Row and Society of Biblical Literature. (1985). In <u>Harper's Bible dictionary</u> (1st ed., p. 90). San Francisco: Harper & Row.

evident that, though dwelling among idolaters, Balaam had some knowledge of the true God and was held in such reputation that it was supposed that he whom he blessed was blessed, and he whom he cursed was cursed. Moab King Balak sent for Balaam *"from Aram, out of the mountains of the east,"* to curse Israel. But by the remarkable interposition of God, he was utterly unable to fulfil Balak's wish, however desirous he was to do so. The apostle Peter refers (2 Pet. 2:15, 16) to this as an historical event. In Micah 6:5 reference also is made to the relations between Balaam and Balak that Israel might remember the *"saving acts of the Lord."*

Though Balaam could not curse Israel, yet he suggested a mode by which the divine displeasure might be caused to descend upon them through pagan lust (Num. 25). Balaam was known as a biblical example of a spiritually gifted leader with an inner lust for wealth and position, not unlike many gifted spiritual leaders today. His words to the Balak's messengers, however, were very pious: "*Though Balak were to give me his house full of silver and gold, I could not go beyond the command of the Lord my God, to do less or more*" (Num 22:18). Although Balaam would do only what the Lord allowed, he became a prime example of someone who does the right thing for the wrong reason: a religious spirit. The account of Balaam is incomplete without the sequel to the story. Numbers 25 tells how the Moabite King almost succeeded in turning the Israelites against the Lord. It describes a scene at Peor where Israelite men engaged in debauchery with Moabite women. That may have meant participation in the common heathen practice of temple prostitution, for according to Numbers 31:14–16, that was Balaam's advice to Balak and the Moabites on how to weaken Israel.

All the gifts of the spirits have their counterfeits. Some men are naturally very gifted, and their gifting may be falsely assumed to be from the Holy Spirit. They use their gifts to gain the acclamation of men and to gain wealth like Balaam. Balaam (Arabic *balam,* "glutton") was a *"prophet of God"* or diviner or soothsayer and was asked to curse God's people by Balak, king of Moab. The Israelites were forbidden by the Lord to consult diviners or practice divination (Deut 18:10–11). Balaam was a non-Israelite prophet known from both biblical and extra biblical sources as a person from the region of the Transjordan, skilled not only in divination but also in performative acts. His fame in the culture of the ancient world places him alongside Noah, Daniel, and Job as a folk hero in the repertoire of the storyteller. Balaam was a man who knew God and did only what the Lord allowed him to do. His heart was corrupt because he wanted to curse Israel, but God would not allow it. Though Balaam could not curse Israel, yet he suggested a mode by which God's divine displeasure might be caused to descend upon Israel. (Num 22–25) Balaam's heart was full of deceit and greed and he "*loved the reward of wickedness*" (2 Pet 2:15). Balaam apparently told the Moabite leader that Israel could be defeated if its people were seduced to worship Baal-peor, who was the god of prosperity. The sacrifice to Baal-peor included sexual immorality.

Apostle John writes to the church of Pergamum and tells us that:

> Nevertheless, I have a few things against you: you have some people there who are clinging to the teaching of Balaam, who taught Balak to set a trap and a stumbling block before the sons of Israel, [to entice them] to eat food that had been sacrificed to idols and to practice lewdness [giving themselves up to sexual vice] (Rev 2:14, AMP)

Balaam taught antinomianism or lawlessness. He exhibited great prophetic gifting, but his heart was not converted. He was a hireling.

Balaam is characterized as a man "*who loved gain from wrongdoing but was rebuked for his own transgression; a dumb ass spoke with human voice and restrained the prophet's madness*" (2 Pt 2:15, 16). Jude said of certain religious leaders that they **"abandon themselves for the sake of gain to Balaam's error and perished in Korah's rebellion."** (Jude 11).

Who was **Korah but a rebellious leader**, a son of Levi and one of the principal families involved in leadership in the Jerusalem tabernacle. Korah felt that he should have had equal leadership responsibilities to Moses. In Hebrew tradition, Korah was a bold, haughty, and ambitious man, considered to have possessed great wealth, adding to his own sense of self-importance. *"Now Korah the son of Izhar, son of Kohath, son of Levi, and Dathan and Abiram the sons of Eliab, and On the son of Peleth, sons of Reuben, took men. And they rose up before Moses, with a number of the people of Israel, 250 chiefs of the congregation, chosen from the assembly, well-known men. They assembled themselves together against Moses and against Aaron and said to them, 'You have gone too far!* <u>For all in the congregation are holy, every one of them, and the LORD is among them. Why then do you exalt yourselves above the assembly of the LORD?</u> *"* (Numbers 16:1-3) After their attempted revolt, Korah and his supporters are swallowed by the earth and delivered alive to Sheol (Num 16:32–33). This fate demonstrates the severe consequences of challenging leaders appointed by our Lord and disobeying His rules for worship. God appoints His leaders like Moses. Many ambitious men strive for power and preeminence, and there will be severe consequences for blindness ambition like Balaam and Korah.

Incidentally, Korah's descendants are credited with writing eleven psalms (Pss 42; 44–49; 84–85; 87–88). The manner of Korah's demise likely influenced their approach to composing psalms, which include many references to Sheol. David uses Korah's fate to describe what he wishes for his enemies (Psa 55:15).[24]

The spirit of Jezebel (Rev 2:20). Jezebel is the Anglicized transliteration of the Hebrew לְ *'Izebel,* best understood as meaning "where is the prince?" (אְי זִוּעָב לְ *'ēyzō ba'al*), a ritual cry from worship ceremonies in honor of Baal. The Spirit of Jezebel is an archetype,

24   Fleenor, R. (2016). <u>Korah, Son of Izhar.</u> In J. D. Barry, D. Bomar, D. R. Brown, R. Klippenstein, D. Mangum, C. Sinclair Wolcott, … W. Widder (Eds.), *The Lexham Bible Dictionary.* Bellingham, WA: Lexham Press.

or a collection of demonic spirits, similar to the Balham and the Nicolaitans heresy. She was a woman who called herself a prophetess, and she used this title to convince those in the "church" to commit immorality and pagan worship. Jezebel has stamped her name on history as the representative of all that is designing, lustful, crafty, malicious, revengeful, and cruel. She is the first great instigator of persecution against the saints of God. Guided by no moral principle, restrained by no fear of either God or man, she was passionate in her attachment to her heathen worship.

Her background in ancient history was she was the daughter of Ethbaal, king of the Sidonians, and wife of Ahab the son of Omri and king of Israel (1 Kgs 16:29–31). Jezebel had two sources of power. The first was her status in her Phoenician homeland. As the daughter of Ethbaal, king of the Sidonians, she was a princess by birth. According to Josephus (*Ant* 8.13.2), Ethbaal was also a priest in the Phoenician cult of the goddess Astarte (Ashtoreth). Historians suggest that Phoenicia followed the Mesopotamian practice of appointing the king's daughter as the high priestess of the chief local god, in this case, Baal Melqart. With the king as high priest and his daughter serving as high priestess, links between the monarchy and the state religion were considerably strengthened. Together, the two were able to wield substantial political, economic, and religious power over the land. Hence, when Jezebel came to Israel, she was accustomed to being an active participant in government. She promoted the cult of Baal who was a god of prosperity and fertility, which had long enjoyed extensive support in Israel. She fostered the worship of other Canaanite fertility deities, supporting 450 prophets of Baal and 400 prophets of the goddess Asherah at her royal table (1 Kgs 18:19). In the meantime, she ruthlessly persecuted the rival prophets of Yahweh, causing them to go into hiding (1 Kgs 18:4).

By Jezebel's influence, most Israelites in the northern kingdom left the worship of the true God for Baal and Ashtoroth. The prophet Elijah laments that only 7000 men in the entire nation were not swayed by her control.

Jezebel's unscrupulous nature is revealed in the account of Ahab's desire for Naboth's vineyard (1 Kgs 21:1–16). Although Ahab desired the vineyard, he recognized Naboth's right to retain the family property. Jezebel recognized no such right in view of a monarch's wishes. She arranged to have Naboth falsely accused of blaspheming God and consequently executed, leaving the vineyard for Ahab to seize. Jezebel demonstrates her archetype of demonic helping demons, which includes a lying spirit, spirit of character assignation and blackmail, spirit of murder, spirit of manipulation, spirit of hate of the righteous and God, spirit of covetous, spirit of jealousy of the righteous etc. For this heinous crime Elijah pronounced a violent death for Ahab and Jezebel (1 Kgs 21:20–24), which was ultimately fulfilled (1 Kgs 22:29–40; 2 Kgs 9:1–37).

The corrupt influence of Jezebel spread to the southern kingdom of Judah through her daughter Athaliah, who married Jehoram, king of Judah. Thus, the idolatry of Phoenicia infected both kingdoms of the Hebrews through this evil Sidonian princess.

Ashtaroth, or Astaroth for the Philistine and Phoenician like Jezebel, was the same female pagan god as the Semite Astarte, both modelled from the Babylonian Ishtar. Her other counterparts are Isis and Hathor of Egypt, Kali of India, and Aphrodite and Demeter of Greece. The Roman counterpart was Diana (the same as in Act 19:35). Indeed, the same goddess in these days goes by the name of Mary, mother of Jesus.

The Council of Ephesus in AD 431 had to deal with the cult of Diana the virgin goddess (in Greek, Artemis, in Phoenician, Astarte. Her cult continued in Ephesus until 431, being supplanted by the cult of Mary by the Roman Catholic Church, to legitimize that Mary was the "mother of god" and the "mother of all" and note that Diana also had these attributes. They also gave to Mary all the other attributes of Diana such as: "queen of heaven" and "divine virgin" etc. Before AD 431, Mary was recognized only as the very human mother of Jesus but not divine. The church fathers effectively paganised Christianity at Ephesus. Diana, still spiritually alive, had her name changed to that of the Virgin Mary, mother of Jesus. From this heretical error comes the doctrine of the Immaculate Conception or the doctrine that God preserved the Virgin Mary from the taint of original sin from the moment she was conceived. To many Catholics Mary had to be pure and without sin to be the mother of Jesus. The doctrine of Immaculate Conception was defined as official dogma of the Roman Catholic Church in 1854.

The Spirit of Jezebel is basically a ruthless controlling spirit working through the lust of the flesh, and the lust of the eyes, and the pride of life. It has, in general, two aims: one, to gain identity, glory, recognition, power, and satisfy the need for the "praises of men." This is a narcissistic consequence of the desire for love and self-worth focused on SELF. It seeks public and private office and will use any devious means to gain office and power to control men.

Secondly, the Jezebel spirit is a man-hater and seeks to emasculate all men and divest them of their authority and power over others. It fosters a distrust and hatred of men in general. The "Jezebel spirit" is in a constant agitation, terribly aggressive, ambitious, domineering, power hungry, critical, bitter, demanding, possessive, very determined, callous, very controlling, seducer, lustful and commonly homosexual or bisexual, selfish, greedy, prideful, manipulative, unrepentant, deceitful spirit, an overwhelmingly evil spirit, with a predilection of character assignation and murder as well as witchcraft. These are some of the collections of demonic spirits or archetypes that comprise the Jezebel archetype. Indeed, these collective spirits can be definitely named "Satan's woman" as in Revelation 17:4-6. "*The woman was arrayed in purple and scarlet, and adorned with gold and jewels and pearls, holding in her hand a golden cup full of abominations and the impurities of her sexual immorality. And on her forehead was written a name of mystery: 'Babylon the great, mother of prostitutes and of earth's abominations.' And I saw the woman, drunk with the blood of the saints, the blood of the martyrs of Jesus.*"

What are we to do with these collections of serious spiritual principalities and powers coming against Christ's church? Christ exposes them and rebukes them in His letter to the seven churches of Asia and others in Romans chapter one. He rebukes the church for allowing these poisonous groups of spirits to flourish in His church. We must beware of the devices of the enemy and stand firm against them!

> "*I wrote to you in my letter not to associate with sexually immoral people—not at all meaning the sexually immoral of this world, or the greedy and swindlers, or idolaters, since then you would need to go out of the world. But now I am writing to you not to associate with anyone who bears the name of brother if he is guilty of sexual immorality or greed, or is an idolater, reviler, drunkard, or swindler—not even to eat with such a one. For what have I to do with judging outsiders? Is it not those inside the church whom you are to judge? God judges those outside. 'Purge the evil person from among you.'*" (I Cor 5:9-13)

Chapter 17
Gifts of the Spirit

Spiritual gifting is usually seen as evidence of a spiritual transformation and conversion. God has given gifts to his church, some of which are listed in Romans 12:6–12: prophecy, service, teaching, giving, exhortation, leadership, and mercy. Ephesians 4:11–12 lists the gifts of the Spirit God uses to build His Church: apostles, prophets, evangelists, pastors, and teachers. First Corinthians 12:4–10 lists 9 other equipping gifts of the Spirit: [*Thoughts*] word of wisdom, word of knowledge, discernment of different spirits, [*Words*] prophesy, interpretation of tongues, various types of tongues, and [*Deeds*] miracles, healing, and faith. Later in 12:28, Paul lists gifts of the Spirit to the Church again: *"And God has appointed in the church, first apostles, second prophets, third teachers, then miracles, then gifts of healings, helps, administrations, various kinds of tongues."* Peter lists *"speaking and serving"* as gifts of the Spirit (1 Pet 4:11). There are many other gifts to the church implied but not specifically mentioned such as the gifts of hospitality, encouragement, intercession, kindness, mercy, friendship, teaching, generosity, leadership, and others as in Romans 12. We are to *"desire earnestly spiritual gifts but especially that we may prophesy"* and "So also you, since you are zealous of spiritual gifts, seek to abound for the edification of the church" (1 Cor 14:1, 12). Edification means to build up the Church, not individual members of the church who have inflated egos because they possess certain spiritual gifts. *"Therefore, my brethren, desire earnestly to prophesy, and do not forbid to speak in tongues. But all things must be done properly and in an orderly manner"* (1 Cor 14:39–40). Many ask what prophecy is today. Some teachers claim that the gifts of the Spirit ceased with the age of the apostles (secessionism). Others loudly claim that the gifts of the Spirit have never ceased and continue today. (continueism)

Paul warned the Thessalonian church:

> "*That is, the one whose coming is in accord with the activity of Satan, with all power and* <u>signs and false wonders</u>, *and with all the deception of wickedness for those who perish, because they did not receive the love of the truth so as to be saved.* For this reason, God will send upon them a deluding influence so that they will believe what is false, in order that they all may be judged who did not believe the truth but took pleasure in wickedness." (2 Thess 2:9–12)

Today we have many false prophets for hire, performing healings, miracles, and false wonders designed to deceive the almost Christians. We are not to reject the spiritual gifts outright but await the witness of the Holy Spirit to authenticate what is true versus what is false, knowing that Satan can counterfeit all the gifts of the Spirit. The true man of God seeks to bring glory to God and not himself. He does not seek fame or fortune like Balaam.

Elisha healed Naaman, the commander of the Syrian army, of leprosy but refused the offer of great wealth in order not to steal any glory from God who is: "the healer of all our diseases" (2 Kings 5:16, Psalm 103:3)**. I am not aware of any man of God accepting money for a reward for using the spiritual gift of healing or prophesy in the entirety of Scripture.** In 2 Kings 5:26-27 Elisha rebuked and cursed his servant Gehazi for his greed and implying that God's prophet was a hireling. The biblical prophet was not popular and faced estrangement and misunderstanding from the religious community. Ahab called Elijah: "You troubler of Israel." Most biblical prophets received imprisonment or death for using their spiritual gifts as exemplified by the story of Micaiah (2 Chron 18:13–27).

Jonathan Edwards wrote in his *Treatise Concerning Religious Affections* about the revival in the early- to mid-1700s in New England that was called the First Great Awakening:

> **"There is indeed something very mysterious in it, that so much good, and so much bad, should be mixed together in the church of God; as it is a mysterious thing,** and what has puzzled and amazed many a good Christian, that there should be that which is so divine and precious, as the saving grace of God, and the new and divine nature dwelling in the same heart, with so much corruption, hypocrisy, and iniquity, in a particular saint. Yet neither of these is more mysterious than real. **And neither of them is a new or rare thing. It is no new thing, that much false religion should prevail, at a time of great reviving of true religion; and that at such a time multitude of hypocrites should spring up among true saints."**

Later he commented about the transient effect of revival: "It appears plainly to have been in the visible church of God, in times of great reviving of religion, from time to time, as it is with the fruit trees in the spring; there are a multitude of blossoms, all of which appear fair and beautiful, and there is a promising appearance of young fruits; but many of them are but of short continuance; they soon fall off, and never come to maturity" . . .

> Matt. 24:12, 13: *"And because iniquity shall abound the love of many shall wax cold. But he that shall endure unto the end, the same shall be saved."* "And so, it is ever likely to be in the church, whenever religion revives remarkably, till we have learned well to distinguish between true and false religion, between saving affections and experiences, and those manifold fair shows, and glistering appearances, by which they are counterfeited; the consequences of which, when they are

not distinguished, are often inexpressibly dreadful. By this means, the devil gratifies himself, by bringing it to pass, that that should be offered to God, by multitudes, under a notion of a pleasing acceptable service to him, that is indeed above all things abominable to him. By this means he deceives great multitudes about the state of their souls; making them think they are something, when they are nothing; and so eternally undoes them; and not only so but establishes many in a strong confidence of their eminent holiness, who are in God's sight some of the vilest of hypocrites."

Revival and the true outward expression of the gifts of the Spirit often brings mixture, confusion, and counterfeit expression of the same gifts. In time the true nature of many of the so-called gifted church leaders will be discovered. True expression of the Holy Spirit is simplicity with joy, peace, humility, and agape love. It is not concerned about worldly affairs, money, fame, or sensual delights. Psalm. 146:5, *"Happy is he that hath the God of Jacob for his help, whose hope is in the Lord his God."* Matt. 5:6: *"Blessed are they that do hunger and thirst after righteousness; for they shall be filled."* Psalm. 89:15, 16, *"They shall walk, O Lord, in the light of thy countenance. In thy name shall they rejoice all the day: and in thy righteousness shall they be exalted."*

Today many men today call themselves prophets of God and teach and preach false visions and do not prophesy what is the right or the hard sayings of the already-revealed Word of the Lord. **Today's prophetic voice should always be directly from Scripture spoken with the conviction of and anointing of the Spirit without guile. It is not a new revelation but a fresh expression of old revelation.** The true prophet gift does not add to the Bible but unfolds God's truth with power and anointing through ordinary men such as Martin Luther, John Calvin, John Knox, Jonathan Edwards, George Whitfield, Charles Wesley,

Charles Spurgeon, Martyn Lloyd-Jones, and many others. These men spoke with such anointing that men fell on their faces and repented of their sins. Satan deceives many through false prophets who subtly add to or subtract from God's word and seek disciples, fame, and fortune for themselves. (Isa 30:10: Matt 24:11, 24; Mark 13:22; 1 Tim 4:1–2, 2 Tim 3:1–7, 13; 1 John 4:1)

A prophet cannot be judged by miraculous signs, revivals, and wonders alone, but by the fruits of the spirit. "We must remember that Satan has his miracles, too" (John Calvin).

The Lord spoke to the false prophets through Isaiah:

"Who say to the seers, "You must not see visions" and to the prophets, "You must not prophesy to us what is right, speak to us pleasant words, prophesy illusions "Get out of the way, turn aside from the path, let us hear no more about the Holy One of Israel." Therefore, thus say Holy One of Israel, "Since you have rejected this word and have put your trust in oppression and guile and have relied on them." Therefore this iniquity will be to you like a breach about to fall, a bulge in a high wall, whose collapse comes suddenly in an instant. . . . For thus the Lord GOD, the Holy One of Israel, has said, **"In repentance and rest you will be saved, In quietness and trust is your strength. But you were not willing.** *"(Isaiah 30:10–13, 15)* Jeremiah warned about the false prophets in his day.

"As for the prophets: My heart is broken within me, all my bones tremble; I have become like a drunken man, even like a man overcome with wine, Because of the LORD And because of His holy words. For the land is full of adulterers; For the land mourns because of the curse. The pastures of the wilderness have dried up. Their course also is evil and their might is not right. "For both prophet and priest are polluted;

Even in My house I have found their wickedness," declares the LORD. "Therefore, their way will be like slippery paths to them, they will be driven away into the gloom and fall down in it; For I will bring calamity upon them, the year of their punishment," declares the LORD. "Moreover, among the prophets of Samaria I saw an offensive thing: They prophesied by Baal and led My people Israel astray. "Also, among the prophets of Jerusalem I have seen a horrible thing. The committing of adultery and walking in falsehood; And they strengthen the hands of evildoers, So that no one has turned back from his wickedness. All of them have become to Me like Sodom, And her inhabitants like Gomorrah. "Therefore, thus says the LORD of hosts concerning the prophets, 'Behold, I am going to feed them wormwood and make them drink poisonous water. (Jer 23:9–15, NASB)

Ezekiel prophesied to the false shepherds of Israel in Ezekiel 13 and 34:

"Son of man, prophesy against the shepherds of Israel. Prophesy and say to those shepherds, 'Thus says the Lord GOD, "Woe, shepherds of Israel who have been feeding themselves! Should not the shepherds feed the flock? "You eat the fat and clothe yourselves with the wool, you slaughter the fat sheep without feeding the flock. "Those who are sickly you have not strengthened, the diseased you have not healed, the broken you have not bound up, the scattered you have not brought back, nor have you sought for the lost; but with force and with severity you have dominated them. "They were scattered for lack of a shepherd, and they became food for every beast of the field and were scattered. "My flock wandered through all the mountains and on every high hill; My flock was scattered over all the surface of the earth, and there was no one to search or seek for them." Therefore, you shepherds, hear the word of the LORD: "As I live," declares the Lord GOD, "surely because My flock has become a prey,

198

My flock has even become food for all the beasts of the field for lack of a shepherd, and My shepherds did not search for My flock, but rather the shepherds fed themselves and did not feed My flock; therefore, you shepherds, hear the word of the LORD: 'Thus says the Lord GOD, "Behold, I am against the shepherds, and I will demand My sheep from them and make them cease from feeding sheep. So, the shepherds will not feed themselves anymore, but I will deliver My flock from their mouth, so that they will not be food for them." (Ezk 34:2–10)

Later the Lord speaks again:

"I will feed My flock and I will lead them to rest," declares the Lord GOD. I will seek the lost, bring back the scattered, bind up the broken and strengthen the sick; but the fat and the strong I will destroy. I will feed them with judgment. "As for you, My flock, thus says the Lord GOD, 'Behold, I will judge between one sheep and another, between the rams and the male goats. 'Is it too slight a thing for you that you should feed in the good pasture that you must tread down with your feet the rest of your pastures? Or that you should drink of the clear waters, that you must foul the rest with your feet? 'As for My flock, they must eat what you tread down with your feet and drink what you foul with your feet!" Therefore, thus says the Lord GOD to them, "Behold, I, even I, will judge between the fat sheep and the lean sheep. "Because you push with side and with shoulder and thrust at all the weak with your horns until you have scattered them abroad, therefore, I will deliver My flock, and they will no longer be a prey; and I will judge between one sheep and another. "Then I will set over them a shepherd, My servant David, and he will feed them; he will feed them himself and be their shepherd. "And I, the LORD, will be their God, and My servant David will be prince among them; I the LORD have spoken." (Ezekiel 34:15–24)

The prophetic voice is the voice of God speaking through men that convicts the church of sin and often shakes nations. The prophetic voice has never died and was heard through Polycarp, Tertullian, Athanasius, Augustine, and other church fathers. The prophetic voice has been heard more recently through the writings of Martyn Luther, John Calvin, John Knox, Bishops Ridley and Latimer, Jonathan Edwards, George Whitfield, John Wesley, Robert Murray M'Cheyne, Søren Kierkegaard, Catherine and William Booth, Watchman Knee, A. W. Tozer, C.S. Lewis, Paul Washer, Dave Wilkerson, J. C. Ryle, T. Austin Sparks, Arthur Wallis, Dietrich Bonhoeffer, C. H. Spurgeon, J. Gresham Machen, Martyn Lloyd Jones, Leonard Ravenhill, Oswald Chambers, Andrew Strom, David Wells, and many others.

The prophetic voice confronts Christians with their sin and then calls them to repent. It makes us uncomfortable by upsetting the status quo. We think of ourselves as good Christians, not in the need of repentance. **We are comfortable and usually content in our churches and not interested in change and threatened by confrontation**. Jeremiah was called by God to *"To root out and pull down, to destroy and to throw down, to build and plant"* (Jer 1:10). No wonder prophets were persecuted and killed.

Os Guinness wrote:

> "All too often we have trumpeted the gospel of Jesus, but we have replaced biblical truths with therapeutic techniques, worship with entertainment, discipleship with growth in human potential, church growth with business entrepreneurialism, concern for the church and for local congregation with expressions of the faith that **our churchless and little better then vapid spirituality, meeting real needs with pandering to felt needs, and mission principles with marketing precepts. In the process we have become known for commercial,**

diluted, and feel-good Gospels of health, wealth, human potential, and religious happy talk, each of which is indistinguishable from the passing fashions of the surrounding world. All too often we have set out high, clear statements of the authority of the Bible, but flouted them with the lives and lifestyles that are shaped more by our own sinful preferences and by modern fashions and convenience."

Ouch, the truth hurts, but that is the prophetic voice of truth that calls men to bow the knee and cry out to God and call for mercy, mercy, then repent. We live in an age of many false prophets, and we need to pray for discernment. Some claim that we are:

"More corrupt than the dark days before Luther; more importantly intellectual than during the heyday of Calvinism; more financially perverted than the days that caused John the Baptist to explode; more intoxicated with the drive for spiritual power than any age, yet exercising that outward power with less internal transformation than anyone since King Saul; enamored with the gifts, yet hardly knowing the Giver, our age has produced the most commercial, materialistic, fad-oriented people ever to claim His name." (Gene Edwards)

Chapter 18
Listen and Obey

The infilling of the Holy Spirit is necessary to hear God's voice and then be empowered to obey it. What then is *obedience*? The dictionary definition of obedience is compliance with an order, request, or law, or submission to another's authority. God's definition of obedience is very different. It is obedience to His Holy Spirit's voice as well as the written commandments: "And if you *faithfully obey the voice of the Lord your God, being careful to do all his commandments that I command you*" (Deut 28:1 ESV). I can remember that as a child my common excuse for my rebellion was, "You never told me that I couldn't do that." Often obedience to the letter of the law is an excuse for sin!

The non-Christian considers Christian obedience, as some form of bondage or about a list of can't do's. He thinks of himself as having freedom or liberty to do whatever he pleases. In actuality, the biblical view is that non-Christians are in bondage since they are in bondage to sin. "Jesus answered them, '*Most assuredly, I say to you, whoever commits sin is a slave of sin*'" (John 8:34). In contrast Paul spoke of the liberty to the legalistic Galatian church:

> "*Stand fast therefore in the liberty by which Christ has made us free, and do not be entangled again with a yoke of bondage. . . . For you, brethren, have been called to liberty; only do not use liberty as an opportunity for the flesh, but through love serve one another . . . But if you are led by the Spirit, you are not under the law.*" Gal 5:13, 18)

Pagans have no spiritual freedom because of the bondage of sin and cannot see that true liberty is found only in Christ.

There always is tension in the call to obey God's voice versus our own sinfulness. I can still remember my mother's voice saying, "You just don't listen!" Yes, how many times I have said as an excuse to my wife, "I am too busy to listen right now, but please remember what I do is important!" Listening to the Holy Spirit requires brokenness. The Greek word used for obedience is ὑπακούω or *hupo akouo*, literally meaning to "hear under." In other words, we must humble ourselves like slaves, putting all other things aside, and then *listen* to the quiet, still voice of our Lord. **Biblical obedience is *about listening first and then doing or we can say that biblical obedience is about* hearing rightly then doing rightly.** "When He had called all the multitude to Himself, He said to them, "*Hear Me,* everyone, and understand" and "If anyone has ears to hear, let him hear" (Mark 7:14–16; Luke 8:18, 21; 16:31). Jesus spoke to the multitude in John chapter 8:47 **"Whoever is of God *listens* to God. [Those who belong to God hear the words of God.] This is the reason that you do not *listen* [to those words, to Me]: because you do not belong to God and are not of God or in harmony with Him."** (John 8: 47 10:3, 8, 16) but to those "who are able to hear, let him *listen* to and heed what the Holy Spirit says to the assemblies (churches). (Rev 2:7, 29; 3:6, 13, 22; 13:9)

> "*Hear, O My people, and I will admonish you!*
> *O Israel, if you will* **listen** *to Me!*
> *There shall be no foreign god among you.*
> *Nor shall you worship any foreign god.*
> *I am the* LORD *your God,*
> *Who brought you out of the land of Egypt.*
> *Open your mouth wide, and I will fill it.*
> "*But My people would not* **heed** *My voice,*
> *And Israel would have none of Me.*
> *So I gave them over to their own stubborn heart,*
> *To walk in their own counsels.*

*"Oh, that My people would **listen** to Me,*
   That Israel would walk in My ways!
I would soon subdue their enemies,
And turn My hand against their adversaries.[25]
   (Psalm 81:8–14)

Like so many men, I often have started doing what I thought was good work for the Lord before listening, and then I have had to ask the Lord for help to get me out of the mess I made by getting ahead of Him. This is what the Psalmist called "*presumptuous sin*" (Psalm 19:13). I have often thought I knew God's will or plan without seeking Him or waiting for His timing and anointing. I went ahead of Him, not only being unfruitful, but embarrassing our Lord by my presumption.

As a physician, many times the choices I make may potentially jeopardize someone else's life. I have used my profession "of being busy doing God's work" as an excuse to avoid hearing from God. It is an exaggerated self-importance that dulls the mind to the prompting of the Holy Spirit. I must die to self and my self-imposed agendas to hear the voice of God. I must examine myself, repent of my stubbornness, and listen. *"We know that God does not listen to sinners; but if anyone is God-fearing and a worshiper of Him and does His will, He listens to him."* (John 9:31)

The commandments are objective, verifiable, unchangeable statements passed on by apostolic tradition. Since they are verifiable, we know we have missed the mark. "If we say that we have no sin (Missed the mark), we deceive ourselves, and the truth is not in us" (1 John 1:8). However, the Bible teaches us that if we know Him, we obey Him.

"Now by this we know that we know him, if we keep his commandments. He, who says, I know Him and does not keep His commandments, is a liar and the truth is not in him. But whosoever

25   *The New King James Version.* (1982). (Ps 81:8–14).
      Nashville: Thomas Nelson.

keeps His word; truly the love of God is perfected in him. By this we know we are in Him. He who says he abides in Him ought himself also to walk just as He walked." (1 John 2:3–5)

It seems that our obedience is always incomplete and in tension with the Word. Self-examination brings contrition. However, we believers must remember that we have complete sufficiency in Christ; in other words, what we can't do, Christ can do through us by the working of the Holy Spirit. What freedom to have our hope in God for our perfection and not in ourselves! The verifiable proof of our salvation is a changed life and obedience to His spoken and written Word produced by the Holy Spirit.

Many postmodern churches, new emergent leaders, encourage contemplative prayer. Contemplative prayer is a New Age, Eastern Religious deception that allows the incursion of demonic spirits into our souls by mimicking the voice of God. Visualization is also an ancient occult practice to get spiritual guidance that allows demonic incursion into our minds. Christian prayer is focused on knowing God through Scripture. Any voice that is in conflict with God's Word is not the voice of God. Beware of prophetic dreams, visions, and words of knowledge and wisdom that are inconsistent with Scripture. We are to meditate on Scripture and not our navel! We are not to empty our mind but to fill it with God's Word. God speaks through His Word. The enemy is awaiting to speak lies to Christians.

"Be sober, be vigilant; because your adversary the devil walks about like a roaring lion, seeking whom he may devour. Resist him, steadfast in the faith." (I Peter 5:8)

"Finally, brethren, whatever things are true, whatever things are noble, whatever things are just, whatever things are pure, whatever things are lovely, whatever things are of good report, if there is any virtue and if there is anything praiseworthy—meditate on these things. The things which you learned and received and heard and saw in me, these do, and the God of peace will be with you." (Phil 4:8)

"The coming of the lawless one is according to the working of Satan, with all power, signs, and lying wonders, and with all unrighteous deception among those who perish, because they did not receive the love of the truth, that they might be saved. And for this reason God will send them strong delusion, that they should believe the lie, that they all may be condemned who did not believe the truth but had pleasure in unrighteousness." (2 Thess 2:9–11)

We live in an age of increasing deception. Those who do not love and study Scripture will be deceived and perish. Christians need to be aware of the danger of demonic deception. There are many voices speaking but only one is the Holy Spirit. "He who has an ear, let him hear what the Spirit says to the churches. To him who overcomes I will give to eat from the tree of life, which is in the midst of the Paradise of God."(Rev 2:7).

The work of the "almost a Christian" man has attempted obedience to the written law only, since he does not hear God's voice and does not depend on the Holy Spirit. We can have assurance that we know Him if we obey (keep) his commandments by *listening to His voice alone* as He speaks to us through Scripture. Our obedience is always imperfect yet growing, which deepens our love for such a merciful God who never gives up on us. Our God is light and there is no darkness in Him His Light exposes the darkness in us.

"If we say that we have fellowship with Him and yet walk in the darkness, we lie and do not practice the truth; but if we walk in the Light as He Himself is in the Light, we have fellowship with one another, and the blood of Jesus His Son cleanses us from all sin. If we say that we have no sin, we are deceiving ourselves and the truth is not in us. If we confess our sins, He is faithful and righteous to forgive us our sins and to cleanse us from all unrighteousness. If we say that we have not sinned, we make Him a liar and His word is not in us." (1 John 1:6–10)

Yes, we are saved by grace alone, and our salvation was purchased entirely by the merit and righteousness of Jesus without any works on our part. However, God loves those He purchased through the blood of His Son Jesus Christ and promises to bring us through *progressive sanctification* and obedience to bring Him glory as we are submitted to Him. Too many Christians think they have arrived and do not need further sanctification. It is His Spirit that *continually* works through us to produce works pleasing to God (James 2:24). Our walk with Christ always has some tension. Paul reminds the Galatians:

> *"Do not be deceived, God is not mocked; for whatever a man sows, that he will also reap. For he who sows to his flesh will of the flesh reap corruption, but he who sows to the Spirit will of the Spirit reap everlasting life. And let us not grow weary while doing good, for in due season we shall reap if we do not lose heart. Therefore, as we have opportunity, let us do good to all, especially to those who are of the household of faith."* (Gal 6:7–10)

"The spiritual man habitually makes eternity-judgments instead of time-judgments. By faith he rises above the tug of earth and the flow of time and learns to think and feel as one who has already left the world and gone to join the innumerable company of angels and the general assembly and Church of the First-born which are written in heaven. Such a man would rather be useful than famous and would rather serve than be served. And all this must be by the operation of the Holy Spirit within him. No man can become spiritual by himself. Only the free Spirit can make a man spiritual." (A. W. Tozer)

Chapter19

True and False Compassion

Jesus speaks about **true compassion** in Luke chapter 10 with the parable of the Good Samaritan. A lawyer asked Jesus what do I have to do to inherit eternal life? Jesus answered what is written in the law? And he answered, *you shall love the Lord your God with all your heart and with all your soul and with all your strength and with all your mind and your neighbor as yourself.* And Jesus said to him you've answered correctly do this and you will live. But the lawyer tried to justify himself and asked Jesus who is my neighbor? Jesus goes on to tell the story of the good Samaritan and concludes with the answer *"the one who showed him mercy is the good neighbor. You go and do likewise"*

What is the difference between empathy and compassion? One of the great questions of today is what is the Christian response to homelessness, drug addiction, poverty, crime, and many other problems. The City Council in cities such as Seattle, San Francisco, Los Angeles has struggled with homelessness and drug abuse. Drug users are very vulnerable to hepatis, AIDS, tuberculosis, and many other infectious diseases. From a public health perspective many would choose to minimize disease spread by providing free clean needle exchange, drug therapy, meals, tents, housing, no bail for minor crimes, and other community services. Others look at this dilemma and feel that offering many of these services suggest that the user is a victim that has community approval and needs community support. In today's post modern culture any type of physical or emotional suffering is considered intolerable. **A Christian worldview understands that suffering and pain are normal consequences of not only bad behavior but of life itself. The Christian understands that God uses suffering always in a positive way that is redemptive.** When we inject our own feelings of compassion into a situation that God is using for his own redemptive purposes, we are trying to be like God and violating the first commandment by telling God "we know better" and He can't chasen someone through trials and troubles for His own redemptive purpose. The Christian most ask himself what is it really mean to love my brother? This is a question that we all struggle with and there are no simple answers since every situation is a little different. My wife and I have worked with many who have been in prison and subsequently have come to know the Lord. Their testimony has often been that the best thing that ever happened to them was that they were arrested and placed in prison. This chapter does not provide a clear answers to societal problems but is designed to provoke thought and a biblical world view.

Compassion motivates people to go out of their way to help the physical, mental, or emotional pains of another and themselves. Compassion is often regarded as having sensitivity, an emotional aspect to suffering, though when based on cerebral notions such as fairness, justice, and interdependence, it may be considered rational in nature and its application understood as an activity also based on sound judgment. There is also an aspect of equal dimension, such that an individual's compassion is often given a property of "depth", "vigor", or "passion". The etymology of "compassion" is Latin, meaning "co-suffering." Compassion involves "feeling for another" and is a precursor to empathy, the "feeling as another" capacity for better person-centered acts of active compassion; in common parlance active compassion is the desire to alleviate another's suffering.

Compassion involves allowing ourselves to be moved by suffering and experiencing the motivation to help alleviate and prevent it. An act of compassion is defined by its helpfulness. Qualities of compassion are patience and wisdom; kindness and perseverance; warmth and resolve. It is often, though not inevitably, the key component in what manifests in the social context as altruism. Expression of compassion is prone to be hierarchical, paternalistic, and controlling in responses. Difference between sympathy and compassion is that the former responds to suffering from sorrow and concern while the latter responds with warmth and care and action when possible.

The English noun *compassion*, meaning *to suffer together with*. Compassion is thus related in origin, form and meaning to the English noun patient (= one who suffers). Ranked a great virtue in numerous philosophies, compassion is considered in almost all the major religions as among the greatest of virtues.

Empathy refers to the ability to relate to another person's pain vicariously, as if one has experienced that pain themselves: For instance, people who are highly egoistic and presumably lacking in empathy keep their own welfare paramount in making moral decisions.

What is the best example of **true compassion** but God Himself? "*For God so loved the world, that he gave his only Son, that whoever believes in him should not perish but have eternal life. For God did not send his Son into the world to condemn the world, but in order that the world might be saved through him.*" (John 3:16-17) What a compassionate example of love to give up your son to humiliation, shame, rejection, pain, and suffering to a world that would largely reject Him, yet he still forgives those who place their faith in Him; how wonderful! Micah 7:18-20 speaks of God's compassion.

> *"Who is a God like you, pardoning iniquity and passing over transgression for the remnant of his inheritance? He does not retain his anger forever, because he delights in steadfast love. He will again have compassion on he will tread our iniquities underfoot. You will cast all our sins into the depths of the sea. You will show faithfulness to Jacob and steadfast love to Abraham, as you have sworn to our father from the days of old."*

God sees our sin but His love draws us to Himself like a mother with a child near a hot stove to protect her children. **True compassion doesn't condone sin but reaches out a hand of help and hope to us to leave our sin and find Christ as the only solution for our fallen nature.** This compassion we are called to is not emotive only but is a call to action. True compassion encompasses both a gut level feeling of sympathy and pity as well as positive action taken on our part to relieve the suffering we observe (1 John 3:18). **True compassion feels empathy for those caught up in sin but does not approve of sin but presents the answer for the sinner, Jesus Christ**. One of the most compassionate acts we can do is to share the good news of the gospel of Jesus Christ with those who do not know Him so that they might be restored to fellowship with Him. However, our compassion is not to be limited to the lost. We are commanded to have compassion on all people, but especially those who belong to the household of faith (Galatians 6:10) and more especially to those who are poor and powerless among us (James 1:27, Col 3:12-15).

> *If anyone says, "I love God," and hates his brother, he is a liar; for he who does not love his brother whom he has seen cannot love God whom he has not seen. And this commandment we have from him: whoever loves God must also love his brother.* (I John 4:20)

Here is the root of the problem. As Christians we are called to be compassionate but not to have false compassion. Christians understand that **God's law is a product of God's love and condemns sin. True compassion does not enable sin but restrains sin.** Good works such as giving free needles and syringes to drug addicts is well meaning but enabling. Scripture is Clear evil will be punished.

> "Stolen water is sweet, and bread eaten in secret is pleasant." (Prov 9:17)

> But he does not know that the dead are there, that her guests are in the depths of Sheol. [26]

> Whoever heeds instruction is on the path to life, but he who rejects reproof leads others astray. (Prov 10:17)

> Those of crooked heart are an abomination to the LORD,but those of blameless ways are his delight. Be assured, an evil person will not go unpunished, but the offspring of the righteous will be delivered. (Prov 11:20)

> Righteousness exalts a nation, but sin is a reproach to any people. (Prov 14.34)

The sluggard says, "There is a lion in the road!

> There is a lion in the streets!" As a door turns on its hinges, so does a sluggard on his bed. The sluggard buries his hand in the dish; it wears him out to bring it back to his mouth. The sluggard is wiser in his own eyes than seven men who can answer sensibly. (Prov 26:13)

Work produces Joy, contentment, self-esteem, purpose, and busyness that keeps people out of trouble. Idleness gives opportunity for many types of sins like drug abuse.

---

26   The Holy Bible: English Standard Version (Pr 9:17–18). (2016). Crossway Bibles.

For you yourselves know how you ought to imitate us, because we were not idle when we were with you, [8] nor did we eat anyone's bread without paying for it, but with toil and labor we worked night and day, that we might not be a burden to any of you. [9] It was not because we do not have that right, but to give you in ourselves an example to imitate. [10] For even when we were with you, we would give you this command: **If anyone is not willing to work, let him not eat.** [11] For we hear that some among you walk in idleness, not busy at work, but busybodies. [12] Now such persons we command and encourage in the Lord Jesus Christ to do their work quietly and to earn their own living. (2 Thes 3:7-13)

True inner peace and prosperity occur when we are obedient to God's law. God's ten commandments are necessary for a functioning society. Where would we be if murder, lying, stealing, adultery, coveting, and disrespect for authority were allowed? God's law restrains the sinfulness that is in all men therefore it is a reflection of His love. We, out of love, must encourage men to obey His law and restrain disobedience.

"False Compassion" enables sin. For example, it holds that it is a benefit to women to promote abortion; an act of dignity to perform euthanasia; a scientific breakthrough to "produce" a child by genetic engineering. **It is considering as a right to abort a child, rather than seeing a child a gift to be welcomed. It avoids biblical language such as murder or that abortion is about killing babies. Instead, it avoids the truth about life beginning at conception. It simply substitutes the words fetus for baby, termination, or abortion for murder!**

Many feel that the "greatest destroyer of peace today is 'Abortion', because it is a war against the child... A direct killing of the innocent child, 'Murder' by the mother herself... And if we can accept that a mother can kill even her own child, how can we tell other people not to kill one another? How do we persuade a woman not to have an abortion? As always, we must persuade her with love... And we remind ourselves that love means to be willing to give until it hurts..."

"The so-called right to abortion has pitted mothers against their children and women against men. It has sown violence and discord at the heart of the most intimate human relationships. It has aggravated the derogation of the father's role in an increasingly fatherless society. It has portrayed the greatest of gifts--a child--as a competitor, an intrusion and an inconvenience. It has nominally accorded mothers unfettered dominion over the dependent lives of their physically dependent sons and daughters. And, in granting this unconscionable power, it has exposed many women to unjust and selfish demands from their husbands or other sexual partners."

—Mother Theresa of Calcutta

"Their false compassion is called true compassion and their false understanding is called true understanding, for this is their most potent spell." (Aleister Crowley)

"Christian compassion" does not oblige one to feel sorry for someone who has what he needs to live in a manner suited to his social level. Some chose to live on the street not in regular housing. Paul reminds us in 2 Thessalonians 3:10 that "If anyone is not willing to work, let him not eat." Christian compassion simply elicits the desire to help those who lack the means to lead a dignified life according to the demands of human nature and their status while respecting their choice. **Unfortunately, many refuse help but instead want approval and support for their self-destructive choices. Accordingly, there is no reason for someone to feel guilty for not supporting a homeless person simply because he is richer or has a higher social standing than others. This is so called "White Guilt."** Nor does having less than others make the upright man suffer; rather, he is satisfied at seeing that others have more than he.

The erroneous interpretation of compassion affects some members of the traditional elites in a curious manner. They deem it their duty to disguise their high station, education and splendor. In doing so they misguidedly believe they are fulfilling their Christian duty to prevent others from suffering the humiliation of seeing people who are higher than themselves. This is false guilt. **White guilt is the goal of critical race theory. It is this false sense of guilt that is the prime motivator of false compassion**. This was well understood by Marxist Saul Alinsky as espoused in his book *Rules for Radicals: A Pragmatic Primer for Realistic Radicals* published in 1971.

False compassion has manipulated the concept of justice to righting society inequities. Critical Race Theory as predicted has become the father for complete societal disruption. It espouses the concept that whites have unearned privileges related to the historic subjugation of blacks by slavery. This means that blacks are victims of white racial prejudice. Since blacks are victims then of course they deserve reparations and various entitlements. Blacks demand equity with whites without the deeper understanding that equity is not the same as equality. **Equity is a Marxist term that requires government intervention to satisfy racial and societal inequities; whereas equality is given by God and our constitution that all men are created equal. The terminology of equity is from the communist manifesto that told the lower classes that need they need to rise up against the suppressing upper classes.** The term analogy of equity is the term analogy of social revolution and class warfare and is cultural Marxism. The only solution for the modern-day Marxist is more and more government eventually leading to a complete dictatorship. Marxism leads to destruction of the nuclear family, radical feminism, down grading of education, lawlessness, and immorality. To discuss Critical Race Theory adequately will take another book so for more information please read (We Will Not be Silenced by Erwin Lutzer, Harvest House, 2020, and Red White and Black: American History from Revisionists and Race Hustlers by Robert L. Woodson, Emancipation Press, 2021, Dinesh D'Souza, <u>The United States of Socialism,</u> St. Martin's Press 2020; <u>American Marxism</u>, Mark R. Levin. Amazon Books 2021, <u>Christianity and Wokeness,</u> Owen Strachan, Salem Books, 2021)

The higher social classes have the duty to shine in the eyes of the lower classes. The latter have the right to contemplate the splendor of the higher classes and to be inspired by it to make appropriate educational, trade school, and other vocational training to gain upward mobility. I was taught in school "*Noblesse Oblige*" or priviledge requires an obligation to help the less fortunate. In effect, the condition of the higher classes should stimulate members of the lower classes to improve their own situations, be ambitious, and help them when possible.

"The contemplation of the higher classes can inspire members of the lower classes who are gifted with exceptional talents to aspire legitimately to a higher condition and higher education. his desire must not be confused with the reprehensible "coveting of thy neighbors' goods" prohibited by the tenth Commandment. Such coveting occurs when someone becomes envious because another person is or has more than he; or when he comes to hate his neighbor and is consumed with a passion to deprive him of what is justly his. Envy is a product of radical race theory that teaches that blacks are victims and deserve reparations Base sentiments like these should not be confused with the noble desire to equal, or even surpass, through diligent effort, the situation one admires in another." (Plinio Corrêa de Oliveira)

Thomas Sowell writes about this modern error: "At least as far back as the 18th century, the left has struggled to avoid facing the plain fact of evil… Every kind of excuse, from poverty to an unhappy childhood, is used by the left to explain and excuse evil." Christianity teaches that Christian people are victors not victims through Christ.

We spend a lot of effort on making our Churches feel more welcoming and "economic mobility" more accessible, but those efforts are mostly superficial and do little for our country's aching soul. As Thomas Sowell puts it: "What if the problem is internal? What if the real problem is the cussedness of human beings?"

False compassion makes excuses for immoral behavior. Immoral sexual behaviors are not only unhealthy but offend a righteous God! We are obligated to call for righteous moral behavior because we love people and hate their self-destructive behavior. Yes, we are called in love to call sin, SIN as does Paul in I Cor 5:9-13.

> *⁹I wrote to you in my letter not to associate with sexually immoral people— not at all meaning the sexually immoral of this world, or the greedy and swindlers, or idolaters, since then you would need to go out of the world. But now I am writing to you not to associate with anyone who bears the name of brother if he is guilty of sexual immorality or greed, or is an idolater, reviler, drunkard, or swindler—not even to eat with such a one. For what have I to do with judging outsiders? Is it not those inside the church whom you are to judge? God judges those outside. "Purge the evil person from among you."*

With regard to *sexual and gender mores*, while we must exercise compassion and concern and genuine love for those involved in sexual sins such as adultery, promiscuity, and homosexuality, we must also clearly articulate the words "go and sin no more" (John 8:11). Grace without truth is false piety of the second worst kind (legalism and self-righteousness being the worst).

However, if you have migrated to the current theological position that *adultery, promiscuity, homosexuality, transgenderism, or bestialism are acceptable norms*, I suppose you could attempt to condemn conservatives for rejecting transgenderism as ethically supportable. **The world is lost in sin and by rejecting God's law we are rejecting God Himself. We live in a world that doesn't believe in Hell or eternal damnation and are creating a Hell on earth.**

The false understanding of compassion is used to create a false understanding of diversity. God loves diversity since he created all diversity. Racial, ethnic, and sexual diversity has become an effort to blame God as malevolent. Some claim that God has made a mistake and caused confusion and anxiety since some transgender people claim a desire to change their sexual identity to correct God's mistake! Others would like to change their skin color, birth parents, birthplace, etc. Satan uses every opportunity to create jealousy, envy, confusion, and misplaced anger at our creator. The falsely enlightened post-modern thinks that equity means fairness and protection of the oppressed. Equity means everyone gets the same reward, income, housing, education, etc., to make the perfect communist state where the government owns everything and controls all housing, education, and income so that no one gets ahead but are all equal.

Jesus prayed to his Father for unity of His people in John 17:20-23

We are all united by Sin. We are all lost and without hope except for Jesus and His death on the cross. (Romans 3:10-20, 23) There is no distinction between rich or poor, black, or white, gay, or straight, educated, or ignorant, men versus women, we are all sinners and there is no distinction when we stand guilty before a Holy God at the foot of the cross. Human distinctions based on race, gender, wealth, education, religion, and other cultural distinctions are simply foolishness and meaningless at the foot of the cross. Efforts to divide by trying to redress past societal injuries only creates victimhood, confusion and anger and misses the big picture that we all live in a fallen world, without hope, except for Christ. (White Guilt)

Many progressive Christians draw their line regarding sexual morality based on whether both parties can legitimately enter into sexual affairs without coercion, and without harming another. They would argue that this rule effectively condemns adultery, rape, pedophilia, incest, and bestiality. But gays and transgenders, it is argued, are not harming anyone from entering into unforced mutually agreeable sexual encounters. **Progressives have no absolutes** and therefore these sexual sins are evaluated by contemporary moral standards focused on the self-life and excuses for immorality. **Christian absolutes frighten the lost as does the potential of God's wrath and eternal destruction.**

More importantly, what's missing in this contemporary definition of morality is *harm to oneself* and rejecting the design of their creator. Being true to oneself is a great truism, but as psychology and faith both teach, there is a false self, an "ego," a fallen self, that should not be affirmed. And rejecting one's gender (he made them male and female) is rejecting the image of God in us:

> "*So, God created mankind in his own image, in the image of God he created them; male and female he created them.*" (Gen 1:27)

> "*For this reason, God gave them up to dishonorable passions. For their women exchanged natural relations for those that are contrary to nature;* and *the men likewise gave up natural relations with women and were consumed with passion for one another, men committing shameless acts with men and receiving in themselves the due penalty for their error. And since they did not see fit to acknowledge God, God gave them up to a debased mind to do what ought not to be done. They were filled with all manner of unrighteousness, evil, covetousness, malice. They are full of envy, murder, strife, deceit, maliciousness. They are gossips, slanderers, haters of God, insolent, haughty, boastful, inventors of evil, disobedient to parents, foolish, faithless, heartless, ruthless. Though they know God's righteous decree that those who practice such things deserve to die, they not only do them but give approval to those who practice them.*" (Romans 1:26-32)

Progressives criticize hateful attitudes towards others deemed sinners, or of patriarchal abuses, or of Phariseeism. But in the case of the current sexual revolution, they do not have the moral high ground upon which to condemn those who have good reasons of their own to limit the influence of trangenderism on our public schools and bathrooms. And in accepting such sexual and gender practices as norms, thy almost certainly are abandoning Biblical truth for the false piety. If they really loved others, they would protect children from victimization.

Blind compassion: ignores the consequences of enabling sin by helping avoid the consequences of sin. It is a specious rendering of the progressive/humanitarian ideal. It purports to improve the human condition but ignores the risks and costs of its actions. It seeks to relieve distress but excuses the opposite results as well-intentioned. It promises betterment but frequently produces disappointment.

> **"Let grace be shown to the wicked, yet he will not learn righteousness. In the land of uprightness, he will deal unjustly."** (Isaiah 26:10)

> "There is severe discipline for him who forsakes the way, **whoever hates reproof will die.**" (Proverbs 15:10)

Blind compassion has turned the attention of the public schools away from readiness for college or the job market and toward student enjoyment and self-fulfillment. In an effort for students to feel good about themselves, everyone is a winner, there are no losers. Graduating High School and college students are not prepared for a demanding, competitive job where they will not be coddled. **Unfortunately, many expect rewards without responsibility**.

Since the early 20th century, American educators have idealized a style of schooling that tries to optimize learning by means that are, first and foremost, well received by the student. Its aim has been to shield students from the stresses and pressures associated with rigorous curricula in favor of "student-friendly" experiences that seek to capture attention and boost self-esteem. **Christ came to slay the self and humble us, not buildup false self-esteem!** The message of the cross is death to self in exchange of a new life in Christ.

Blind compassion promises betterment but frequently produces disappointment. Blind compassion has turned the attention of the public schools away from readiness for college or the job market and toward student enjoyment. When everyone is a winner than no one wins. It has turned public conversations about human problems away from solutions to wokness, frustration, and rebellion. Civil discourse is not allowed because it presents alternate opinions and solutions.

> *"In the absence of faith, we govern by tenderness. And tenderness leads to the gas chamber."* — Flannery O'Connor

Beware of the compassionate governments. (Euthanasia) The economics of many governments, particularly where socialized medicine means health care services are rationed; the question inevitably surfaces: Is this life worth saving? This has been a prominent feature of Western Europe, particularly France, Holland, and Belgium. One European doctor noted, "Keep in mind that the cost to treat chronic conditions, such as COPD, heart disease, cancer, or chronic renal failure where treatment can be cost prohibitive, but with good medical care, patients can lead decent lives, and have a social-economic impact despite a chronic illness. It has been reported that in various European nations during the Covid Health Crisis; elderly patients over the age of 80 were not hospitalized because healthcare was rationed. They simply were left to die at home. Because of the societal cost of healthcare, when it is run by the state, there will always be economic incentives to minimize the number of intensive care beds and healthcare supplies in socialized nations. When there is a great increase in demand like a pandemic, there is no elasticity in a socialized system. The elderly, mentally ill or chronically ill receive no treatment. Europe had much higher death rates from Covid particularly in the elderly as compared to the free-market healthcare system in the United States. However, we have become progressively utilitarian, where the actual measure of human worth is, 'how much do you add to, or subtract from our common projects and costs.' **In Holland after many years after the passage of "Right to Die" legislation, the current understanding of compassion is the "Duty to Die." The elderly and infirmed must make way for reducing medical costs for the younger generation!**

> The truth that lies underneath the "rights" rhetoric is who will decide what constitutes a quality of life and at what cost. Theodore Dalrymple is an English doctor, psychiatrist, and author of *Our Culture—What's Left of It.* Dalrymple wrote, **"Euthanasia has a tendency to slide from the voluntary to the compulsory, as people increasingly make judgments on behalf of others as to what is a human life worth living."**

Finally, we see the work of false compassion worked out in the criminal justice system. Men without fathers, born in poverty with low educational achievement floundering in a society with no answers. The solution is not early release, no bail, or minimum sentencing. The solution is the discipline and love of Christ. Reducing or removing consequences of sin simply produces lawlessness and ultimately complete societal disruption and disintegration! Consequences produce self-reflection and societal protection that hopefully will produce repentance.

Man, inherently understands recompense or retaliation "The Lex Talionis" or an eye for an eye or a tooth for a tooth or a just retaliation for Law breakers. (Exodus 21:23-25). "The crime and retribution must be commensurate with the nature of the offense. This is the central meaning of justice. Dr Joseph Boot (Jubilee Magazine, Ezra Institute Fall 2022) reminds us that "retribution is the foundation of love, and its moral sense. **We cannot love her neighbor, while denying them all that is due them, including justice. (Romans 13:8-10) Justice is the central foundation of love in all that it protects the week and the wronged. It restores order when distracted by wickedness.** To set love and justice and opposition to each other would be a false dichotomy, and an artificial contradiction that leads the world into tyranny". Crime is not a disease. Disobeying God's law – order demands retribution and restitution…. **Mercy detached from justice grows unmerciful.** The humanitarian theory is if we are to kind to lawbreakers and have considered their rights that this will be a recipe for solution to their rebellious behavior is in fact is a great delusion."

> *Whoever says to the wicked, "You are in the right,"*
> *will be cursed by peoples, abhorred by nations,*
> *but those who rebuke the wicked will have delight,*
> *and a good blessing will come upon them.* (Prov 24:24-25)

Chapter 20
Judgement versus Discernment

Recent surveys of young people concluded that the number one negative impression of Christianity is that we are *"judgmental."* Many pastors who are trying to reach young people emphasize the compassion of Christ and paint a picture of a "Big Tent" where Christ accepts everyone, regardless of ongoing unrepentant sin. Some pastors teach that God accepts unrepentant sinners without requiring repentance as a condition of salvation. However, the biblical message is "***Repent or you shall perish***" (Luke 13:5) and "*Repent and believe,*" not get saved now and then repent later. Repentance is inextricably connected to salvation by faith because God does not allow a converted man to continue in sin. Remember the eight "Rs" of repentance:

> **R**epentance begins with
> **R**ecognition of an offense against God, then
> **R**emorse or
> **R**egret and proceeds through
> **R**enunciation of the sin and
> **R**eversal by
> **R**eliance on God and then
> **R**estitution wherever possible.

If there is no repentance, then there never was a changed heart or true salvation by saving faith. ***A changed heart always results in changed behavior and a call to personal repentance, confession***

and contrition. The call to repent is universal to all that believe. "Truly, these times of ignorance God overlooked, but now commands *all men everywhere to repent"* (Acts 17:30–31; 26:20; Luke 24:47). Biblical repentance is a work of grace by the Holy Spirit that brings conviction of sin and empowerment to change. It is not a work of man.

The word *sin* is no longer politically correct since it reflects absolute truth and the biblical standard for life. The postmodern church is confused about compassion. **Secular compassion responds to human needs such as hunger, homelessness, and so on. Christian compassion is based on the biblical understanding that man faces the wrath of God for his sin unless he repents. The focus of Christian compassion is helping the lost find God through acts of mercy as exemplified by the parable of the Good Samaritan (Luke 10:29–37).**

How then do we live in a world that has become increasingly secular? We are called to judge those inside the church but not those outside of the church. Paul rebuked the Corinthian church for failing to purge out the gross immorality of a man having an adulterous affair with his father's wife. Here again the problem was the common fear of judging a brother. In 2 Corinthians, Paul mentions the restoration of this sinning brother who repented of his sin and was restored (2 Cor 2:6–8). If Paul had not rebuked the church and demanded punishment, this brother would likely have gone to hell.

> "*Do you not know that a little leaven leavens the whole lump? Therefore, purge out the old leaven, that you may be a new lump, since you truly are unleavened. For indeed Christ, our Passover, was sacrificed for us. Therefore, let us keep the feast, not with old leaven, nor with the leaven of malice and wickedness, but with the unleavened bread of sincerity and truth. I wrote to you in my epistle not to keep company with sexually immoral people. Yet I certainly did*

not mean with the sexually immoral people of this world, or with the covetous, or extortioners, or idolaters, since then you would need to go out of the world.[1] *But now I have written to you not to keep company with anyone named a brother, who is sexually immoral, or covetous, or an idolater, or a reviler, or a drunkard, or an extortioner—not even to eat with such a person. For what have I to do with judging those also who are outside? Do you not judge those who are inside? But those who are outside God judges. Therefore "put away from yourselves the evil person."*[27] (1 Cor 5:6–13)

Later in chapter 6 Paul tells us:

"Do you not know that the unrighteous will not inherit the kingdom of God? Do not be deceived. Neither fornicators, nor idolaters, nor adulterers, nor homosexuals, nor sodomites, nor thieves, nor covetous, nor drunkards, nor revilers, nor extortioners will inherit the kingdom of God. And such were some of you. But you were washed, but you were sanctified, but you were justified in the name of the Lord Jesus and by the Spirit of our God." (1 Cor 6:9–11)

When we look at others, we must be careful about *improperly judging, but we must be discerning.* Pagan critics want to impose on Christians their own version of "judge not" in an effort to be able to continue to sin and avoid public rebuke and moral guilt. In a post Christian culture no one is allowed to judge since there are no moral absolutes. They ask, "who are you to judge?" We must explain that we aren't judging but discerning and we all are accountable to Scripture and a righteous God. It is God's business to judge but we have a responsibility to discern and warn of God's coming judgement, and He says in Romans 14:4–10:

27   *The New King James Version.* (1982). (1 Co 5:6–13). Nashville: Thomas Nelson.

"Who are you to judge another's servant? To his own master he stands or falls. Indeed, he will be made to stand, for God is able to make him stand. One person esteems one day above another; another esteems every day alike. Let each be fully convinced in his own mind. He who observes the day, observes it to the Lord; and he who does not observe the day, to the Lord, he does not observe it. He who eats, eats to the Lord, for he gives God thanks; and he who does not eat, to the Lord he does not eat, and gives God thanks. For none of us lives to himself, and no one dies to himself. For if we live, we live to the Lord; and if we die, we die to the Lord. Therefore, whether we live or die, we are the Lord's. For to this end Christ died and rose and lived again, that He might be Lord of both the dead and the living. But why do you judge your brother? Or why do you show contempt for your brother? For we shall all stand before the judgment seat of Christ."

James again warns about judging:

"Do not speak evil of one another, brethren. He who speaks evil of a brother and judges his brother, speaks evil of the law and judges the law. But if you judge the law, you are not a doer of the law but a judge. There is one Lawgiver, who is able to save and to destroy. Who are you to judge another?" (James 4:11–12)

Many Christians *confuse discernment with judging*. We are called to discern sin and not to judge or pass judgment on an individual. "For what have I to do with judging those also who are outside? Do you not judge (discern evil and sin) those who are inside (1 Cor 5:12)? Paul admonishes the Corinthian elders for not discerning and allowing sin in the church as well as not disciplining the individuals involved in sin. Church discipline requires discernment of sin and then taking corrective action. For example, in a jury trial, the individual juror *discerns the guilt* of the

227

perpetrator of a crime. This is not judging, in the sense of passing sentence on an individual, but only discerning guilt or innocence. The judge (an image of God) then *pronounces the sentence* for the crime. The Greek word for judgment *krino* means to *pass judgment* for a sin or *pass a sentence* or wish harm on a person for their behavior. We must discern sin and theological error in the church. **"He who says to the wicked 'you are righteous,' him the people will curse, nations will abhor him, but those who rebuke the wicked will have delight and good blessing will come upon them"** (Prov 24:24–25). God will *pass sentence* or punishment on an individual and his or her sin when He returns for His church at the final judgment (Prov 24:19–20). Christians can have confidence that all sin will be exposed and finally judged by God. We are to be gentle to our brothers and not ignore sin, but "in humility correcting those who are in opposition, if God perhaps will grant them repentance, so that they may know the truth, and that they may come to their senses and escape the snare of the devil, having been taken captive by him to do his will" (2 Tim 24–26). **Ultimately, the discerning of error in a brother makes us feel very vulnerable, but the attempt to bring correction is the ultimate measurement of our love for our brother.** Pray that every Christian would discern sin rather than give tacit approval to sinful behavior by keeping silent. We are the hope of the lost, and in gentleness and humility, we bring the only solution for sin, which is a saving faith in Jesus Christ followed by confession, repentance, and submission to the healing and delivering power of the Holy Spirit.

> *"When I say to the wicked, "You shall surely die," and you give him no warning, nor speak to warn the wicked from his wicked way to save his life, that same wicked man shall die in his iniquity: but his blood I shall require at your hand."* (Ezek 3:18)

Proverbs instructs us *"Not to rejoice when our enemy falls and do not let your heart be glad when he stumbles, lest the Lord see it, and it displeases Him, and then He turns away His wrath from him"* **(Prov 24:17–18). Christians have been given the power**

from God to bind or loose. *"Assuredly, I say to you, whatever you bind on earth is bound in heaven, and whatever you loose on earth will be loosed in heaven"* **(Matt 18:18).** Ultimately, all sin will be punished. It is so easy to wish evil on evildoers rather than blessing so that they might come to repentance. Most Christians are totally unaware that we are to release and give others to God for punishment, rather than binding them by our unforgiveness, less God withholds his wrath on those who have injured us. *"Do not rejoice when your enemy falls, and do not let your heart be glad when he stumbles; Lest the Lord see it, and it displease Him, And He turn away His wrath from him."* (Proverbs 24:17-18)

The practical question is how do we deal with a "Christian" brother in sin in our Christian fellowship? Paul tells us that: *"For what have I to do with judging those who are outside? Do you not judge those who are inside? But those who are outside God judges"* (1 Cor 5:12–13). First, we must earn the right to in love to confront a brother by developing a relationship with him. Next, at the appropriate time and after much prayer, we need to discuss the problem with our brother. If he does not confess his sin and ask for repentance, we need to return with another brother and offer support where indicated, such as enrolling in a support group such as Alcoholics Anonymous as well as the threat of church discipline. If the brother remains unrepentant, then we must bring him before the church and then administer appropriate discipline. (Matt 18:15-20)

> *"Moreover, if your brother sins against you, go and tell him his fault between you and him alone. If he hears you, you have gained your brother. But if he will not hear, take with you one or two more, that 'by the mouth of two or three witnesses every word may be established. And if he refuses to hear them, tell it to the church. But if he refuses even to hear the church, let him be to you like a heathen and a tax collector."*[28] (Matt 18:15–17)

---

28   *The New King James Version.* (1982). (Mt 18:15–17). Nashville: Thomas Nelson.

Chapter 21
Love of God

Love for God is the great and basic demand made by Jesus. (Mt 22:39) Love is neither an extravagant, universal, overly idealistic love of humanity that ignores man's sinful nature nor a high-flown superficial love. But it is a love that requires loving one's neighbor as oneself. Christ frees the shallow understanding of neighbourly love once and for all from its restriction to His followers. He concentrates it again on the helpless man whom we meet on our way. He makes the legal and contentious question of what it means to love like God; a question of the heart attitude with an urgency and compassion, which there can be no escaping.

By itself, the title *"Golden Rule"* is not found in Scripture but is a popular way of referring to (Mt 7:12; Lk 6:31): *"And as you would like and desire that men would do to you, do exactly so to them."* This might be misunderstood in terms of general philanthropy and good character, and it has in fact been wrongly evaluated along such lines throughout the whole course of humanistic ethics from Aristotle to Kant.

Many other world religions have similar admonitions in their holy writ, but each articulation has important nuances. The golden rule is to be understood qualitatively rather than quantitatively. Rules of reciprocity can be motivated by self-interest rather than Christian love. But the story of the Good Samaritan makes such an understanding impossible (Lk 10:29). The scribe asks: *"Who is my neighbour?"* Jesus does not answer by giving a systematic list of the various classes of men from my fellow-national who is nearest to me to the foreigner who is farthest away. Nor does He reply by extolling the eccentric love of those who are most distant, to which all men are brothers. He answers the question by reversing the question: "Who is nearest to the one in need of help?" This means that He shatters the older concentric grouping in which the **"I"** is at the center, but maintains the organizing concept of the neighbour, and by means of this concept sets up a new grouping in which the **"Thou"** is at the center. This order, however, is not a system, which applies schematically to all men and places. It consists only in absolute concreteness. It is built up from case to case around a man in need. Whoever stands closest to the man in need, the same has a neighbourly duty towards him. Three men are equally near to the man who has fallen among thieves in his distress. Which of them fulfils his neighbourly duty? The Christian understanding of love involves self-sacrifice as exemplified by Jesus. It was very costly and probably inconvenient to the Good Samaritan to interrupt his travel plans to care for the wounded man, who was likely a Jew who hated Samaritans, and would likely be ungrateful. We Christians may think of ourselves as being loving but ignore the cost of God's sacrificial *agape* love. **Agape love is not cheap. It cost Christ His life and by the grace of God will cost ours also. A postmodern popular pseudo-Christianity preaches costless love or "Sloppy Agape".**

The proof of salvation is that we love our brother with the unique type of love, (*agape*), that comes only from God. The world doesn't need man's love *phileo* or brotherly love, or *storge* (A Greek word not used in the New Testament for the love of things like I love my dog, home, or car etc.), or *eros* or sexual sensual love but the type of love (*agape*) that only can come from God. *"He who says he's in the light, and hates his brother, is in darkness until now. He who loves (agape) his brother abides in the light and there is no cause for stumbling in him. But he* *who hates his brother is in darkness and walks in darkness and does not know where he is going, because darkness has blinded his eyes."* (I John 2:9–11), Leviticus 19:8, Matt 5:43, 19:19, 22:39; Mark 12:33; Luke 10:27; John 13:34; Romans 12:19) We are called to reflect God's love *"Agape"* as in Luke 10:25, Mark 12:28, Matt 22:37–40 *And a lawyer stood up and put Him to the test, saying, "Teacher, what shall I do to inherit eternal life?" And He said to him, "What is written in the Law? How does it read to you?" And he answered, "YOU SHALL LOVE (**AGAPE**) THE LORD YOUR GOD WITH ALL YOUR HEART, AND WITH ALL YOUR SOUL, AND WITH ALL YOUR STRENGTH, AND WITH ALL YOUR MIND; AND YOUR NEIGHBOR AS YOURSELF." and he said to him, "you have answered correctly; DO THIS AND YOU WILL LIVE."*[29]

At first reading we miss that Jesus was mocking the lawyer because He understood that no man can *agape* his brother since *agape* love is that perfect unconditional sacrificial love that is only from God alone and is meant to flow through a Christian man from God by the work of the Holy Spirit to a lost world. This type of love cannot happen by carnal man's strength but by only the work of the Holy Spirit. The work of *agape* love through the Holy Spirit is the mark of a true Christian. **If a man thinks he can give that unconditional selfless godly agape love by his own effort; he is indeed deceived**. *Agape* love is supernatural and is meant to flow through the believer in such a way that the watching world would see Jesus and give glory to God and not man. The object of Christian love is to give glory to God alone. *Agape* love is not a subjective emotional feeling or experience detached from reality, commitment, or covenant, but the outflow of an abiding and the deep work of the Holy Spirit. See also (Leviticus 19:8, Matt 5:43, 19:19, 22:39; Mark 12:33; Luke 10:27; John 13:34; Romans 12:19). **To focus only on God's agape love is unbalanced**

---

29   *New American Standard Bible: 1995 update.* (1995). (Lk 10:25–28). LaHabra, CA: The Lockman Foundation.

without integrating His love with His justice, wrath, and holiness. Biblical love is sacrificial and costly to those who reach out to those who are lost. Jesus is our example of sacrificial agape love. *"For God so loved the world that He* <u>gave</u> *His only begotten son…"* He gave His life for us on the cross bearing not only pain but disappointment and humiliation. **Agape love may require sacrifice, humiliation and tremendous personal cost** as exemplified by not only our Lord but the apostles in the book of Acts and particularly Paul in II Cor 11:23-27.

But whatever anyone else dares to boast of—I am speaking as a fool—I also dare to boast of that. [22] Are they Hebrews? So am I. Are they Israelites? So am I. Are they offspring of Abraham? So, am I. [23] Are they servants of Christ? I am a better one—I am talking like a madman—with far greater labors, far more imprisonments, with countless beatings, and often near death. [24] Five times I received at the hands of the Jews the forty lashes less one. [25] Three times I was beaten with rods. Once I was stoned. Three times I was shipwrecked; a night and a day I was adrift at sea; [26] on frequent journeys, in danger from rivers, danger from robbers, danger from my own people, danger from Gentiles, danger in the city, danger in the wilderness, danger at sea, danger from false brothers; [27] in toil and hardship, through many a sleepless night, in hunger and thirst, often without food, in cold and exposure. [28] And, apart from other things, there is the daily pressure on me of my anxiety for all the churches. [29] Who is weak, and I am not weak? Who is made to fall, and I am not indignant? (ESV)

First Corinthians 13 is one of the favorite Bible chapters for many Christians and is called the "Love Chapter." Many Christians think Paul is calling men to love that unconditional *agape* love of God by human effort, when in actuality, **Paul demonstrates that *agape* love comes only from God and not man. We think we can love like God, but we can't. We are simply a conduit of agape love to others, who hopefully will see Jesus, and God get the glory, not us.** In the New Testament, the word *agape* acquires a special connotation because of the kind of special sacrificial love revealed in

Christ, which should be taken as an indication of an essential quality of God and as a model for human imitation. God often calls us to do something, which is impossible to do in our own strength without the help of the Holy Spirit. The Christian is to be a recipient of the gift of God's supernatural *agape* love and then spread His *agape* love to a lost world as well as our brothers and sisters. In actuality, Paul is showing Christians what *agape* love is in chapter thirteen.

The Greek word for love used in chapter 13 of 1 Corinthians is "*agape*." Paul reminds us that:

> *"If I speak with the tongues of men and of angels, but do not have (agape) love, I have become a noisy gong or a clanging cymbal. If I have the gift of prophecy and know all mysteries and all knowledge; and if I have all faith, so as to remove mountains, but do not have (agape) love, I am nothing. And if I give all my possessions to feed the poor, and if I surrender my body to be burned, but do not have (agape) love, it profits me nothing."* (1 Cor 13:2–3)

In 1 Corinthians 16:22 God reminds us that *"If anyone does not love (phileo) the Lord, he is to be accursed. Maranatha. The grace of the Lord Jesus be with you. My love (agape) be with you all in Christ Jesus. Amen." And in Ephesians 5:1, **Paul reminds us to "be imitators of God, as beloved children; walk in (agape) love, just as Christ also (agape) loved you and gave Himself up for us, an offering and a sacrifice to God as a fragrant aroma."***

God's love or agape is defined by Paul in I Corinthians 13:4–8:

> *"Love is patient, (agape) love is kind and is not jealous; (agape) love does not brag and is not arrogant, does not act unbecomingly; it does not seek its own, is not provoked, does not take into account a wrong suffered, does not rejoice in unrighteousness, but rejoices with the truth; bears all things, believes all things, hopes all things, endures all things. Love (agape) never fails."*

That definition of God's perfect, unselfish love defines our Lord Jesus and the sacrificial, perfect love of the Father who sent His Son to the cross to die for us that we might have eternal life. Sinful selfish man cannot demonstrate this type of perfect love without the infilling of the Holy Spirit. Jesus asked Peter if Peter loved (*agape*) Him.

> *"So when they had finished breakfast, Jesus said to Simon Peter, "Simon, son of John, do you love (agape) Me more than these?" He said to Him, "Yes, Lord; You know that I (phileo) love You." He said to him, "Tend My lambs." He said to him again a second time, "Simon, son of John, do you love Me?" He said to Him, "Yes, Lord; You know that I (phileo) love You." He said to him, "Shepherd My sheep." He said to him the third time, "Simon, son of John, do you (phileo) love Me?" Peter was grieved because He said to him the third time, "Do you (phileo) love Me?" And he said to Him, "Lord, You know all things; You know that I (phileo) love You." Jesus said to him, "Tend My sheep." (John 21:15–18)*

Peter honestly responded that he loved Jesus with *phileo*, or brotherly love, but understood that he couldn't *agape* his Lord with the same type of sacrificial love (*agape*) that the Lord loved him. After all, Peter had just denied Christ three times before Jesus asked him if he loved Him. Why was this? Our ability to *agape* love Christ comes by the resurrection power of the Holy Spirit, since no unregenerate man can possess the love of God (*agape*) in his own power or ability. Peter was not a Christian, nor were any of the disciples until the infilling of the Holy Spirit, which did not occur until after the resurrection at Pentecost. ***Agape* love is the exclusive privilege of Spirit-filled Christians. Pentecost was the birth of the church and the supernatural filling of man with *agape* love through the gift of the Holy Spirit and the**

resurrection power of Christ. Peter became a man filled with agape love and power of the Holy Spirit at Pentecost. The fruit of the Spirit's work is *(agape)* love is that it marks believers and shines as a light before the world (Matt 5:16; John 13:35; Gal 5:22; Phil 1:9–11).

> *"And this I pray, that your (agape) love may abound still more and more in real knowledge and all discernment, so that you may approve the things that are excellent, in order to be sincere and blameless until the day of Christ; having been filled with the fruit of righteousness which comes through Jesus Christ, to the glory and praise of God."* (Phil 1:9–11)

Chapter 22

Suffering and Persecution

It is often suffering that separates the "Almost Christian" from the "True Christian". Many claim to know and love God but when trouble comes, they fall away. Post Modern Christianity produces admirers not followers. The biblical cry of "give up all and follow me," is not taught but caught by watching the lives of fellow believers take up the cross daily. (Matt 10:38-39, Matt 16:24-28, Luke 9:24-27) They love the fellowship and emotional high of Christian worship but are unwilling to pay the cost. Soren Kierkegaard in his book *Provocations: Spiritual Writings of Kierkegaard* p 88 remarks:

"The admirer (The Almost Christian) never makes true sacrifices. He always plays it safe. Though in words, phrases, songs, he is inexhaustible about how he praises Christ, he renounces nothing, will not reconstruct his life, and will not let his life express what he supposedly admires. Not so for the follower. (The True Christian) No, no. The follower aspires with all his strength to be what he admires. (He is willing to pay any price, including death, isolation, prison, scandal etc. He knows the cross) And then, remarkably enough, even though he is living amongst a "Christian people," he incurs the same peril as he did when it was dangerous to openly confess Christ."

So often Almost Christian church goers demean those who suffer for Christ and believe that if you live the Christian life, you will receive blessings, not troubles! If you suffer for Christ, you brought it on yourself because you offended some one. Jesus promised *suffering and persecution* to his followers. Suffering takes many forms: physical pain, frustrated hopes, depression, isolation, loneliness, grief, anxiety, rejection, poverty, spiritual crisis, and persecution of self as well as friends and family by torture and death. Jesus reminds us in the beatitudes:

> *Blessed are those who have been persecuted for the sake of righteousness, for theirs is the kingdom of heaven. Blessed are you when people insult you and persecute you, and falsely say all kinds of evil against you because of Me. Rejoice and be glad, for your reward in heaven is great; for in the same way, they persecuted the prophets who were before you.* (Matt 5:10–12)

Paul told Timothy: *"Indeed, all who desire to live godly in Christ Jesus will be persecuted"* (2 Tim 3:12). Paul spoke of his afflictions, weaknesses, and suffering over sixty times. Suffering and persecution produce proven character and hope. *"And not only this, but we also exult in our tribulations, knowing that tribulation brings about perseverance; and perseverance, proven character; and proven character, hope"* (Rom 5:3–4). The purpose of the Gospel is to defeat the Devil and his evil works, *The Son of God was revealed for this purpose to destroy the Devil's works* (I John 3:8) We can expect spiritual warfare and many battles with "principalities and powers" (Eph 6:12-14) as we share the good news of a defeated enemy.

"The biblical gospel will often be divisive and cause great offense, even we take care to be gracious in our manner, because it confronts spiritual darkness (John 3:19–21) speaks to the heart space (Matthew 5:19) and comes to the root of our religious rebellion against God (Ist Corinthians 2:14). Every way it makes men self-conscious of the great antithesis, often provoking a strong or hostile reaction." (Joseph Boot, Gospel Witness 2017, p33)

The persecuted suffering church in China is praying for the American church that it might experience suffering and persecution in order that it might also experience the faithfulness of God through many trials. **Most Western Christians are wimps and fear trials, troubles, and persecution. The mature church must be tested with fire if it is to become the light to the world.** The epistle of 1 Peter teaches us that all suffering is redemptive and will be used for God's purpose and demonstrates the genuineness of our faith. The true Christian receives troubles and trials gladly as he identifies with the cross of Christ and has fellowship with His suffering (Phil 3:10).

Perhaps one of my greatest concerns for the church is the misunderstanding of the character of a loving God. **God allows persecution, troubles, and trials in our lives because He loves us. Suffering produces wisdom and maturity on our journey through this life.** That is a theme of Hebrews. Hebrews 10:33 particularly speaks of the "public insult and persecution" these Jewish believers experienced in the early days of their faith. Hebrews 12 considers God's superintendence of our suffering.

It is for discipline that you endure; God deals with you as with sons; for what son is there whom his father does not discipline? But if you are without discipline, of which all have become partakers, then you are illegitimate children and not sons. **(Hebrews 12:7–8)**

If you are not disciplined by God, then you are not a true son of God.

C. S. Lewis's autobiography is aptly titled "*Surprised by Joy.*" Sometimes God does surprise us with joy. But sometimes *He surprises us with suffering*. If we knew that suffering was coming, we might be able to grit our teeth and bear it. If in the midst of the suffering, we were able to remain above our circumstances, suffering would be less intense. Our culture commends such a stoic attitude. But we experience our most real and deep grief and trauma in suffering when it surprises us. When we are surprised by suffering, we often lack the inner resources to cope with it. We may fall apart. A so-called philosophical attitude is not possible. The only possible attitude is the attitude of faith. Real suffering drives us to place all our cares upon God and so gives us a valuable lesson in living. I feel sorry for those who have not suffered for their faith, for they know not the comfort and joyful fellowship with God!

First Peter chapter four tells us not to be surprised at suffering. Peter does not mean the initial surprise and horror at bad news. He means that suffering is not something strange, and we ought not think we are immune from it or reject its purpose. Suffering is part of the life of God's people. We must come to grips with it and see God's hand in it. The psalmists cry out to God in the midst of suffering. Their words do not try to ignore it; they wrestle with God for relief. Such wrestling builds our faith; it keeps us close to the only One who can give us deliverance. Psalm 119:71 says, **"It is good for me that I have been afflicted that I may learn your statutes."** Such words as these are helpful, but what is also helpful to people who are suffering is the knowledge that other people care for them. Often the touch of a caring hand is worth more than a sermon. In this way, we make God's presence tangible to others who are surprised by suffering. We often flee from those in distress because their suffering makes us uncomfortable. It reminds us that we, too, may be called to suffer. If you know people who are suffering, remember that God does not call on you to speak some magic words that make all the pain go away. He calls on you to be present, to listen, and to share their burden as your own. Who can you visit this week to show the love of Christ?

***Believers ought to expect to suffer as an inevitable part of their calling.* To believe is not to evade suffering; it is to face it with new confidence and hope**. Rightly approached, suffering develops the character of believers, equips them for more effective service, draws believers closer to Jesus Christ, and prepares them for eternal life. Those in Christ are inevitably at odds with their culture and society. All Satan-energized systems are actively at odds with the things of Christ. Our dark world resents and is often hostile toward those who represent the Lord Jesus Christ. That resentment and hostility may be felt at certain times and places more than others, but it is always there to some extent as a part of the privilege of being His own. The apostle John said a person can't love both God and the world (1 John 2:15), and James said, ***"Whoever therefore wants to be a friend of the world makes himself an enemy of God"* (James 4:4). *"When you do good and suffer, if you take it patiently, this is commendable before God"* (1 Pet 2:20). When Christians endure suffering with patience, it pleases God.**

In Greek culture, suffering was viewed as an evil afflicting humanity that was beyond mankind's ability to control. The Greek and Roman gods were capricious and often unpredictable. Thus, suffering was considered a matter of fate, and Greek tragedies typically portrayed individuals who were victims of life's blind injustice. The New Testament, however, takes a radically different approach. Key words for suffering in the New Testament are frequently used in descriptions of the death of Christ. There the strongest possible language is used to remind us that Jesus suffered by God's express will (Matt 16:21; Mark 8:31; Luke 17:25; 24:26; Acts 3:18; 17:3; 1 Pet 1:11).

In Jesus, we learn that suffering, though painful, is not an unmixed evil. Peter writing in First Peter, particularly picks up and emphasizes this thought. A person who suffers for doing wrong has no comfort: He has brought his suffering on himself.

But whenever a Christian suffers *despite doing what is good*, he or she becomes a companion of Jesus, who also suffered despite doing nothing but good. In this case, the believer can be sure that God is actively involved in his situation, permitting injustice and suffering for a good purpose of His own. We may not understand that purpose. But looking at the wondrous good God accomplished through the suffering of our Lord and His glorification, we can be sure that when we suffer as Christians, both good and glory will result.

Another consequence of a firm belief in the return of Jesus Christ should be a transformed understanding of suffering. ***For suffering strengthens our hope and makes our present fellowship with Jesus more wonderful***. This is why Paul writes of the believer's hope in Romans saying, "Not only so, but we also rejoice in our sufferings, because we know that suffering produces perseverance; perseverance, character; and character, hope" (Rom 5:3–4). In Paul's experience hope had transformed suffering, and suffering had intensified his hope.

The Hebrew language contains many different words for pain and suffering. Some express intensity, others are synonyms with slightly different shades of meaning. These may focus on physical pain, on sadness or sorrow, on mental anguish, grief, troubles, or general stress. The New Testament vocabulary is more limited. In general, words for suffering in the New as in the Old Testament tend to focus more on mental distress than the physical pain The word *suffering*, which occurs in Romans 5:3, means any tribulation, persecution, or hardship—like that which Paul lists of himself in 2 Corinthians 11: beatings, imprisonments, stoning, shipwrecks, perils, weariness, thirst, and hunger. It includes the cruelest oppressions. The Greek word Paul used, and its Latin translation carried the most vivid of images in Paul's day, was *thlipsis,* (to press, squash, rub, hem in, afflict, oppress, harass, or that which causes pain, physical or mental),[30] which means the kind of oppression that a conquered people would receive from a cruel conqueror. The Latin translation was based on the noun *tribulum,* which meant a threshing sled and implied severe torture. A *tribulum* was generally several feet wide and five or six feet long and was studded with sharp spikes on the bottom; it was pulled over the grain on a threshing floor by an animal. The Latin word *tribulare* compared oppression to experiencing such a thrashing.

It is easy to see how the early Christians conceived of their suffering. They knew themselves to be often pressed as wheat while the *tribulums* of the world passed over them. They knew the feel of the spikes and the lash of the flail. But they endured such suffering. They had learned that it was the way God separated the wheat in their lives from the chaff and made them more useful and more obedient servants. All of God's children learn this sooner or later.

> *"Most assuredly, I say to you, unless a grain of wheat falls into the ground and dies, it remains alone; but if it dies, it produces much grain. He who loves his life will lose it, and he who hates his life in this world will keep it for eternal life."* (John 12:24–25)

Certainly, the persecuted prophet Jeremiah knew tribulation. What had persecutions done for Jeremiah? In Jeremiah 17, he intimates that they had actually drawn him closer to the Lord and strengthened him for his work. He is contrasting two types of people. The first is the person who trusts in human beings and thereby departs from the Lord. Jeremiah says this person *"will be like a bush in the wastelands; he will not see prosperity when it comes.*

---

30   Kittel, G., Bromiley, G. W., & Friedrich, G. (Eds.). (1964–). *Theological dictionary of the New Testament* (electronic ed., Vol. 3, p. 139). Grand Rapids, MI: Eerdmans.

He will dwell in the parched places of the desert, in a salt land where no one lives" (v. 6). The other type of person is the one who trusts God and whose hope is in him. What is he like? Jeremiah says, *"He will be like a tree planted by the water that sends out its roots by the stream. It does not fear when heat comes; its **leaves are always green. It has no worries in a year of drought and never fails to bear fruit"** (v. 8). **In other words, Jeremiah had found that suffering had strengthened his roots and had actually drawn him closer to the Lord.*** Jeremiah knew what it meant to be in the pit of despair and cried out to God.

> *"This I recall to my mind; Therefore, I have hope. The LORD'S loving kindnesses indeed never cease, For His compassions never fail. They are new every morning; Great is Your faithfulness. "The LORD is my portion," says my soul "Therefore I have hope in Him. The LORD is good to those who wait for Him."* (Lam 3:21–25)

Affliction is only temporary. We live in this world for only a mini-second compared to the timelessness of eternity, which we will spend with our Lord if He is our Savior.

All Christians should experience some suffering. Tribulations will come. Job spoke truthfully when he said, *"Yet man is born to trouble as surely as the sparks fly upward"* (Job 5:7). But the Christian can have a hope in the midst of tribulation that transforms suffering and is strengthened by it.

> *"But they will do all this to you [inflict all this suffering on you] because of [your bearing] My name and on My account, for they do not know or understand the One Who sent Me* (John 15:21)

> Rejoice and exult in hope; be steadfast and patient in suffering and tribulation; be constant in prayer." (Romans 12:12)

"Indeed all who delight in piety and are determined to live a devoted and godly life in Christ Jesus will meet with persecution [will be made to suffer because of their religious stand." (2 Tim 3:12)

*"Blessed (happy, blithesome, joyous, spiritually prosperous)— with life-joy and satisfaction in God's favor and salvation, regardless of their outward conditions) are the **meek (the mild, patient, long-suffering), for they shall inherit the earth!"*** [Ps. 37:11] (Matt 5:5)

"When they persecute you in one town [that is, pursue you in a manner that would injure you and cause you to suffer because of your belief], flee to another town; for truly I tell you, you will not have gone through all the towns of Israel before the Son of Man comes." (Matt 10:23)

"For it was an act worthy [of God] and fitting [to the divine nature] that He, for Whose sake and by Whom all things have their existence, in bringing many sons into glory, should make the Pioneer of their salvation perfect [should bring to maturity the human experience necessary to be perfectly equipped for His office as High Priest] through suffering." (Heb 2:10)

"This is positive proof of the just and right judgment of God to the end that you may be deemed deserving of His kingdom [a plain token of His fair verdict which designs that you should be made and counted worthy of the kingdom of God], for the sake of which you are also suffering." (2 Thess 1:5)

"Consider it wholly joyful, my brethren, whenever you are enveloped in or encounter trials of any sort or fall into various temptations. Be assured and understand that the trial and proving of your faith bring out endurance and steadfastness and patience. But let endurance and

steadfastness and patience have full play and do a thorough work, so that you may be people perfectly and fully developed with no defects, lacking in nothing." (James 1:2–4)

"You should be exceedingly glad on this account, though now for a little while you may be distressed by trials and suffer temptations, So that [the genuineness] of your faith may be tested, [your faith] which is infinitely more precious than the perishable gold which is tested and purified by fire. [This proving of your faith is intended] to redound to [your] praise and glory and honor when Jesus Christ (the Messiah, the Anointed One) is revealed." (1 Pet 1:6–7)

"So since Christ suffered in the flesh for us, for you, arm yourselves with the same thought and purpose [patiently to suffer rather than fail to please God]. For whoever has suffered in the flesh [having the mind of Christ] is done with [intentional] sin [has stopped pleasing himself and the world, and pleases God. So that he can no longer spend the rest of his natural life living by [his] human appetites and desires, but [he lives] for what God wills." (1 Pet 4:1–2)

Perhaps one of the best dialogues on Christian persecution and the normal Christian life was written during the second century AD by an unknown author.

"For Christians cannot be distinguished from the rest of the human race by country, color, or language, or custom. They do not live in cities of their own; they do not use a peculiar form of speech; they do not follow an eccentric manner of life. This doctrine of theirs has not been discovered by the ingenuity and deep thought of inquisitive men, nor do they put forward a merely human teaching, as some people do. . ... They busy themselves on earth, but their citizenship is in

heaven. They obey established laws, but in their own lives they go far beyond what the laws require. They love all men, and by all men are persecuted. They are unknown, and still they are condemned; they are put to death, and yet they are brought to life. They are poor, and yet they make many rich; they are completely destitute, and yet they enjoyed complete abundance. They are dishonored, and in their very dishonor are glorified; they are defamed and are vindicated. They are reviled, and yet they bless; when they are fronted, they still pay due respect. When they do good, they are punished as evildoers; undergoing punishment, they rejoice because they are brought to life. They are treated by the Jews as foreigners and enemies and are hunted down by the Greeks; and all the time those who hate them find it impossible to justify their enmity." ("Epistle of Mathetes to Diognetus," Anonymous, circa AD 130–190, Beloved Publishing, 2016)

"I have often thought that the best of Christians are found in the worst of times. And I have thought again that one reason why we are no better, is because God purges us no more. Noah and Lot, who so holy as they in the time of their afflictions? And yet who so idle as they in the time of their prosperity?" (John Bunyan)

"The good old Puritans, I believe, never preached better than when in danger of being taken to prison as soon as they had finished their sermon. And however, the church may be at peace now, yet I am persuaded, unless you go forth with the same temper, you will never preach with the same demonstration of the Spirit and of power. Study, therefore, my brethren, I beseech you by the mercies of God in Christ Jesus, study your hearts as well as books; ask yourselves again and again whether you would preach for Christ, if you were sure to lay down your lives for so doing? "(George Whitefield)

"God is not looking for brilliant men, is not depending upon eloquent men, is not shut up to the use of talented men in sending His gospel out in the world. God is looking for broken men who have judged themselves in the light of the cross of Christ. When He wants anything done, He takes up men who have come to the end of themselves, whose confidence is not in themselves, but in God." - H.A. Ironside

"Contrary to what might be expected, I look back on experience that at the time seemed especially desolating and painful with particular satisfaction. Indeed, I can say with complete truthfulness that everything I have learned in my seventy-five years in this world, everything that has truly enhanced and enlightened my experience, has been through affliction and not through happiness, whether pursued or attained. In other words, if it were ever possible to eliminate affliction from our earthly existence by means of some drug or other medical mumbo jumbo... the result would make it too banal and trivial to be endurable. This, of course is what the cross signifies. And it is the Cross that has called me inexorably to Christ." —Malcolm Muggeridge

Finally, an inspirational poem from a suffering saint who knew the comfort of Christ in various trials.

My grace is sufficient.

"And he said unto me, <u>My grace is sufficient</u> for thee: for my strength is made perfect in weakness. Most gladly therefore will I rather glory in my infirmities, that the power of Christ may rest upon me. Therefore, I take pleasure in infirmities, in reproaches, in necessities, in persecutions, in distresses for Christ's sake: for when I am weak, then am I strong." (2 Cor 12:9-10)

> *"He giveth more grace when the burdens grow greater.*
> *He sendeth more strength when the labor's increased.*
> *To added affliction, He added His mercy.*
> *To multiplied trials, He multiplied peace.*
> *When we have exhausted our store of endurance . . .*
> *When our strength hath failed and the day is half done . . .*
> *When we reach the end of our resources,*
> *our Father's forgiving has only begun.*
> *His love has no limit.*
> *His grace has no measure.*
> *His power has no boundaries known unto men.*
> *For out of His infinite riches in Jesus,*
> *He giveth and giveth and giveth again."*

This poem was written by Annie Johnson Flint (1866–1932). She was orphaned, suffered blindness, cancer, and rheumatoid arthritis, yet had an inspiring perspective on life. http://www.homemakerscorner.com/annie.htm

Chapter 23
The Afterlife

Perhaps one of the most important subjects commonly ignored in today's pulpits is the proper teaching about *hell and the afterlife*. There is absolute certainty that all men will face judgment.

> **"Knowing, therefore, the terror of the Lord, we persuade men." (2 Cor 5:11) and "Our God is a consuming fire."**

(Heb 12:29) "For if we sin willfully after we have received the knowledge of the truth, there no longer remains a sacrifice for sins, but a certain fearful expectation of judgment, and fiery indignation which will devour the adversaries. Anyone who has rejected Moses' law dies without mercy on the testimony of two or three witnesses. Of how much worse punishment, do you suppose, will he be thought worthy who has trampled the Son of God underfoot, counted the blood of the covenant by which he was sanctified a common thing, and insulted the Spirit of grace? For we know Him who said, **"Vengeance is Mine, I will repay," says the Lord. And again, "The LORD will judge His people." It is a fearful thing to fall into the hands of the living God.***) (Heb 10:26–31)*

What will heaven be like? Scripture tells us that it will be a return to Eden. The first three chapters of the Bible in Genesis and the last three chapters in Revelation are the bookends of the Bible. The story begins with the Garden of Eden and its beauty, rivers, animals, and the tree of life. This vision is repeated in Revelation chapters 21 and 22. Some premillennial theologians believe the world will get so corrupted by sin that God will rapture his church before the return of the antichrist in order to save his church from demonic destruction and a final destruction of the earth. A deeper evaluation of this end-time eschatology reveals deep pessimism as the earth is caught up in the great deception of the antichrist and finally destroyed by fire by God. **Basically, the premillennial message is Satan wins!** The world, which God created and said was "very good," is lost! Satan wins; God's creation is destroyed! (Col 2:15)

The truth is that the earth will not be totally destroyed but simply purged by fire after the defeat of Satan and his demons, and then Eden will be restored on Holy unpolluted ground. Christ saved not only men by His sacrifice on the cross but the entirety of God's creation. "All things have been created through Him and for Him" (Col 1:16). It is a "new earth" (2 Peter 3:13; Rev 21:2; Isa 65:17) in that earth is restored and sanctified according to God's original plan. God is not defeated by Satan for God is always victorious. If Satan so desecrates the earth that God's plan for man is lost; then Satan has won the end time battle. However, Satan was defeated at the cross (Luke 10:18; Rev 12:7–12). The prophet Isaiah summarizes the character of the word "new" (from Hebrew *ḥādāš*) as (*New, new thing, renewed, repaired, fresh*[31]) earth and new heavens. The earth will be sanctified by fire as part of Jesus's victory over Satan. The garden of Eden will be restored, the lion shall lay with the lamb-Hallelujah! (Isa 11:6-10)

> *"For behold, I create new heavens and a new earth; And the former shall not be remembered or come to mind. But be glad and rejoice forever in what I create; For behold, I create Jerusalem as a rejoicing, And her people a joy. I will rejoice in Jerusalem, and joy in My people; The voice of weeping shall no longer be heard in her, Nor the voice of crying. "No more shall an infant from there live but a few days, Nor an old man who*

---

31   Weber, C. P. (1999). 613 חָדָשׁ. [[Comp: note Hebrew characters]] R. L. Harris, G. L. Archer Jr., & B. K. Waltke (Eds.), *Theological Wordbook of the Old Testament* (electronic ed., p. 266). Chicago: Moody Press.

has not fulfilled his days; For the child shall die one hundred years old, But the sinner being one hundred years old shall be accursed. They shall build houses and inhabit them; They shall plant vineyards and eat their fruit. They shall not build and another inhabit; They shall not plant and another eat; For as the days of a tree, so shall be the days of My people, And My elect shall long enjoy the work of their hands. They shall not labor in vain, Nor bring forth children for trouble; For they shall be the descendants of the blessed of the LORD, And their offspring with them. "It shall come to pass. That before they call, I will answer; And while they are still speaking, I will hear. The wolf and the lamb shall feed together, the lion shall eat straw like the ox, and dust shall be the serpent's food. They shall not hurt nor destroy in all My holy mountain," Says the LORD. (Isa 65:17–25)

Heaven is a place of beauty, love, and harmony beyond description—it is the Garden restored. Most Christians think that they will go immediately to heaven upon death because they are good people and avoid God's judgment. **Jesus spoke more about hell than heaven**. We are to fear the wrath of God. "And do not fear those who kill the body but cannot kill the soul. But rather fear Him who is able to destroy both soul and body in hell**." The "Almost a Christian" seeks heaven without giving up his life to the Lord. He has worldly desires yet seeks heaven**:

"Whoever desires to come after Me, let him deny himself, and take up his cross, and follow Me. For whoever desires to save his life will lose it, but whoever loses his life for My sake and the gospel's will save it. For what will it profit a man if he gains the whole world, and loses his own soul? Or what will a man give in exchange for his soul? For whoever is ashamed of Me and My words in this adulterous and sinful generation, of him the Son of Man also will be ashamed when He comes in the glory of His Father with the holy angels." (Matt 10:34–38)

Many evangelicals don't speak about hell, but they believe they are going to heaven. **To many, heaven is the Great Escape from life's problems, a well-deserved reward for being a good person. They deny the reality of hell.** Perhaps this is the reason that they are going there! Just believing in Christ saves no one. "You believe that there is one God. You do well. Even the demons believe—and tremble" (James 2:19)! True Christians bear spiritual fruit, fear God, and place no trust in their own righteousness, but trust entirely by faith in the righteousness of Christ alone.

Most Christians have heard very little about the characteristics of heaven and hell from the pulpit. Therefore, I will provide a short summary about the place of the departed. God is the central inhabitant of heaven, but not its only resident. The angels live there as well, as more than a dozen verses tell us and as Jacob's vision shows us with its imagery of angels ascending and descending the ladder to heaven (Gen 28:12). All believers will ultimately dwell in heaven in their resurrection bodies, which they will receive when the Lord comes for them from heaven (1 Thess 4:16, 17; Rev 19:1–4).

Jesus spoke to Martha about Lazarus that he "would rise again." Then Jesus said to her, "I am the resurrection and the life. He who believes in Me, though he may die, he shall live. And whoever lives and believes in Me shall never die. Do you believe this?" (John 11:25–26) The **Greek verb used for "believe or to have faith" used in this passage is pisteuo, which means complete trust in, reliance in, to believe in, to have full confidence in, to have faith in, and to be completely dependent on. It means to trust so fully and radically that all your hope is in Him to the point of death, as did the Christian martyrs. This is a saving faith that is supernatural, not intellectual, and cannot be manufactured by man since it is a supernatural gift of God.** Saving faith can be scary and desperate when we put all our hope and expectations in God, but God is faithful to His children.

What is heaven like? Jesus taught that there would be no marrying or giving in marriage in heaven (Luke 20:34–36). Scripture explains that Christian heaven is the believer's inheritance (1 Pet 1:4), an abode provided by God (2 Cor 5:1–5; John 14:2; Phil 3:20) as a reward for faithful service where believers will dwell eternally (Matt 5:12; 6:20; Col 1:5). In heaven, the blessedness of the righteous consists in the possession of "life everlasting," "an eternal weight of glory" (2 Co. 4:17), an exemption from all sufferings forever, a deliverance from all evils (2 Cor. 5:1, 2) and from the society of the wicked (2 Tim 4:18), and bliss without termination, the "fullness of joy" forever (Luke 20:36; 2 Cor. 4:16, 18; 1 Pet. 1:4; 5:10; 1 John 3:2).

The greatness of heaven is beyond our comprehension or description. It is portrayed in three different metaphorical prophet images in Revelation 21–22: the tabernacle (21:1–8), the city (21:9–27), and the garden (22:1–5). The believer's true citizenship is in heaven. Heaven is the goal of a quest and the reward for earthly toil, as in Paul's picture of himself as having "finished the race" and looking forward to "the crown of righteousness" (2 Tim 4:7–8). So too in Peter's vision of "the chief Shepherd" that confers "the unfading crown of glory" on those who have served faithfully (1 Pet 5:4). Heaven is also portrayed as a rest after labor; those who die in the Lord "rest from their labors, for their deeds follow them" (Rev 14:13 RSV). Similarly, "there remains a sabbath rest for the people of God," which believers "strive to enter" (Heb 4:9–11 RSV). Heaven is the place where the believer's inheritance is kept with care until the revelation of the Messiah (1 Pet 1:4). The days will come when heaven is no more (Job 14:12; Isa 51:6). As God once spread out the heavenly tent, so He will wrap up the heavens like a scroll (Isa 34:4). A new heaven and new earth will appear (Isa 65:17; 66:22). This is the place where man will rule and reign with God in a new heaven and earth, and man will receive his final inheritance.

Notice there is no mention in the Bible of golf courses, tennis courts, boats, cars, ocean beaches, and so forth. Many think of heaven as a sensual paradise of endless enjoyment, surrounded by friends, pets, and family. **Many will be disappointed to hear that heaven is not about earthly pleasures but about bowing down before our Lord and rejoicing in the magnificent beauty and the wondrous, holy presence of our glorious Lord. Fallen man is limited in appreciation of the magnificence of our Lord and His creation.** In heaven, we will have new bodies and minds so that we can see God in all His glory (Rev 4:1–11, 5:11–14). Heaven is about the throne and rule of God. He is the center of all things, not man. The experience with God will be other-worldly or beyond human comprehension. We will see Him in our resurrected bodies and be with Him forever. Our joy will be beyond earthly joy when we are in His presence. We will be born anew to the living hope in meeting our risen Lord (1 Pet 1:3; Isa 25:9). **Heaven is not about us but about our Lord, Savior, and King and the unbelievable joy of being in His presence.**

Most Christians are shocked about the concept of an intermediate or temporary state after death. And many of those who sleep in the dust of the earth shall awake, "Some to everlasting life, Some to shame and everlasting contempt" (Dan 12:2). They assume that they will go to heaven immediately after death. The resurrection of the dead was taught in the Old Testament (Job 19:25–26, Isa 26:19, 66:23–24; Dan 12:2), as well as the New Testament (Mark 9:18; 1 Thess 4:13–18; Rev 21:8). However, the resurrection of the dead does not occur until an extended period of time has been spent in an intermediate state of bliss or torment. The word hell is an English expression of the Hebrew word *Gehenna* or the notion of eternal punishment, especially by fire (Jer 7:31). Actually, the Greek word *Hades* or Hebrew word *Sheol* is sometimes, but misleadingly, translated "hell" in English versions of the NT. Another Greek word for hell or Gehenna is *Tartaros* is the classical word for the place of eternal punishment and is used only in 2 Peter 2:4.

Sheol (Hades) is the place of the departed or the place of the dead, the unseen world. It is described as a place where the souls of all dead reside but where the righteous and the wicked are separated. (Psalm 16:10; Matt 11:23; Acts 2:27). The word Sheol is used sixty-five times in the Old Testament and is translated in the King James translation of the Bible as "hell" thirty-one times, "The grave" thirty-one times or the "pit" three times. The King James Version has caused a lot of confusion in Christendom by mistranslating the word Sheol as hell. **Sheol/Hades refers to the place of the dead or *the place of the* departed, but not necessarily to a place of torment for the wicked dead.** God has temporarily entrusted the dead to the safekeeping of Hades/Sheol; at the resurrection, he will demand them back. Hades/Sheol then is the temporary abode of the dead, between death and the general resurrection at the end of the age. Some theologians call it the "intermediate state."

What about "soul sleep?" Soul sleep is not biblical and usually is described as a kind of temporary suspended animation of the soul between the moment of personal death and the time when our bodies will be resurrected. (1 Thess 4:15–17). When our bodies are raised from the dead, the soul is awakened to begin conscious personal continuity in heaven. Some theologians have thought incorrectly that, though centuries may pass between death and final resurrection, the "sleeping" soul will have no conscious awareness of the passing of time. Our transition from death to heaven will seem to be instantaneous if there is soul sleep. Jesus promised the thief on the cross that "today you will be with Me in Paradise" (Luke 23:43). Paul did not say, "My desire is to depart and be unconscious for a long period of time," but rather, "My desire is to depart and be with Christ" (Phil 1:23). This is consistent with other biblical evidence to the intermediate state where there is conscious bliss and conscious torment. (Phil 1:19–26; 2 Cor 5:1–10). In 1 Samuel, Saul calls upon the witch of Endor to bring up Samuel. The witch successfully calls up the spirit of Samuel who responds: "Why have you disturbed me by bringing me up?" (1 Sam 28:15), indicating that Samuel was resting in Paradise and not in soul sleep. **The promise to the thief was that he would be reunited with Christ in Paradise that very day and was meant to be understood literally. The intermediate state is one of continued spiritual blessing or suffering as described in Luke 16:19–31 about the "rich man" and Lazarus**. Jesus spoke to the spirits in prison, presumably when He descended into Hades/Sheol. (1 Pet 3:19) The place of the departed Hades/Sheol is real, and all those who have died remain with active consciousness in either paradise or torment until Christ returns. There is no such thing as soul sleep.

> *"For we know that if our earthly house, this tent, is destroyed, we have a building from God, a house not made with hands, eternal in the heavens. For in this we groan, earnestly desiring to be clothed with our habitation, which is from heaven, if indeed, having been clothed, we shall not be found naked. For we who are in this tent groan, being burdened, not because we want to be unclothed, but further clothed, that mortality may be swallowed up by life. Now He who has prepared us for this very thing is God, who also has given us the Spirit as a guarantee. So, we are always confident, knowing that while we are at home in the body, we are absent from the Lord. For we walk by faith, not by sight. We are confident, yes, well pleased rather to be absent from the body and to be present with the Lord." (2 Cor 5:1–8)*

Jesus explains the fate of the dead in this story of the rich man and the beggar Lazarus, which is about someone who is brought back temporarily from Hades in order to warn the living of the fate of the wicked (Luke 16:27–31). The fate of the dead was well understood by the Jewish community in the first century. This parable of the rich man and Lazarus is one of great irony. The rich man, supposedly blessed by God because of his riches, goes to hell or the place of torment, while the poor miserable beggar, seemingly cursed by God, goes to "Abraham's bosom," which was to the Jews a metaphor for paradise or heaven. There is a fixed gulf between Paradise and hell, indicating that both are permanent, fixed places. hell can be thought of the penitentiary of the wicked, ruled by tormenting spirits awaiting the final judgment. Paradise was the place of bliss of the righteous awaiting the final return of Christ for his church.

During the intertestament period, apocryphal prophets wrote about the Jewish understanding of Sheol and the state of the dead before Judgment. The Apocrypha is a collection of early writings and historical information collected during the intertestament period (400 BC–AD 1) that is not part of the Protestant Bible but was accepted as inspired by Catholics in 1546 at the Council of Trent. The Apocrypha was not accepted by Jerome who translated the Bible into Latin or the Vulgate around AD 400. Apocryphal writings are a class of documents rejected by many as not being worthy to properly be called Scripture, though, as with other Jewish writings, they may sometimes be referenced for support and historical information. The term apocryphal has often come to mean many Protestants something false, spurious, bad, or heretical. The ancient Jews and the authors of the Septuagint did accept the apocryphal writings as inspired. It was not included in the final authorized church cannon. However, it is quoted as an important historical document by many of the Church Fathers. The Anglican Communion has maintained that the apocryphal writings may be read for instruction about life, history, and manners but does not accept them to establish any doctrine. I have included the following passage to provide a historical presentation of ancient Jewish thought on the afterlife after death.

In 2 Esdras the author writes:

"I answered and said, "If I have found favor in your sight, O Lord, show this also to your servant: whether after death, as soon as everyone of us yields up the soul, we shall be kept in rest until those times come when you will renew the creation, or whether we shall be tormented at once?"(**This is called the intermediate state**) *He answered me and said, "I will show you that also, but do not include yourself with those who have shown scorn, or number yourself among those who are tormented. For you have a treasure of works stored up with the Most High, but it will not be shown to you until the last times. Now concerning death, the teaching is: When the decisive decree has gone out from the Most High that a person shall die, as the spirit leaves the body to return again to him who gave it, first of all it adores the glory of the Most High. If it is one of those who have shown scorn and have not kept the way of the Most High, who have despised his law and hated those who fear God—such spirits shall not enter into habitations, but shall immediately wander about in torments, always grieving and sad, in seven ways. (The first way, because they have scorned the law of the Most High. The second way, because they cannot now make a good repentance so that they may live. The third way, they shall see the reward laid up for those who have trusted the covenants of the Most High.* (2 Esdras 7:75–81)

The biblical view of human nature is that the eternal soul will be brought up from Hades or the intermediate state at the final return of Christ, the body raised from the grave, and then body and soul reunited and resurrected to be with Jesus. (Acts 2:27; 1 Thess 4:15–17) The blessed dead are in that part of Hades or Sheol called *Paradise.* (Luke 23:43) The blessed are also said to be in Abraham's bosom (Luke 16:22). The wicked are sent to *Gehenna,* (Hebrew "*Ge Hinnom*"), from which "*Gehenna* or the place of torment," which is a Hebrew word, derived from the name of the *Hinnom* valley south of Jerusalem, which traditionally was thought as a place of eternal fire. The Valley of Ben Hinnom is where idolatrous Israelites offered up child sacrifices to the gods Molech and Baal. (2 Chron 28:3; 33:6; Jer 7:31–32; 19:2–6; 32:35) Ironically, Western society has returned to the Valley of Hinnom through the return of child sacrifice to the gods of convenience and prosperity by abortion! Later in Jewish history, *Hinnom* became a garbage dump, hence the place of eternal fire. The name suggests the place of the final punishment of the wicked (Matt. 23:33). The bodies of God's enemies lay under God's continuing curse in Gehenna: "Their worm will not die, nor will their fire be quenched, and they will be loathsome to all mankind" (Isa 66:24). Jesus' depiction of hell in Mark 9:47-48 brings together these prophetic images. The fearful nature of the condition of the wicked is described in various figurative expressions (Matt. 8:12; 13:42; 22:13; 25:30; Luke 16:24). In Christian tradition, hell is associated with the notion of eternal punishment, especially by fire (Mt. 5:22, 29–30; 10:28; 18:9; 23:15, 33; Mk. 9:43, 45, 47; Lk. 12:5; Jas. 3:6, 2 Pet 3:7). The fire of hell is unquenchable (Mk. 9:43, Jude 7, Isa 66:24; Mt 3:12; 18:8–9; Heb 10:27; Rev 19:20), and eternal (Mt. 18:8). **The book of Revelation describes a lake that burns with fire and brimstone in which the wicked will be eternally punished** (Rev 19:20; 20:14–15; 21:8). Hell's eternal punishment is the converse of eternal life, peace, and joy with Christ our Lord and King (Mt. 25:46). The Apostle John warns us of the final judgment where Sheol or Hades will be no more after the final judgment of men at the Great White Throne of God.

> *"Then I saw a great white throne and the One Who was seated upon it, from Whose presence and from the sight of Whose face earth and sky fled away, and no place was found for them. I [also] saw the dead, great and small; they stood before the throne, and books were opened. Then another book was opened, which is [the Book] of Life. And the dead were judged (sentenced) by what they had done [their whole way of feeling and acting, their aims and endeavors] in accordance with what was recorded in the books. And the*

*sea delivered up the dead who were in it, death and Hades
(the state of death or disembodied existence) surrendered the
dead in them, and all were tried and their cases determined
by what they had done [according to their motives, aims,
and works]. Then death and Hades (the state of death or
disembodied existence) were thrown into the lake of fire. This
is the second death, the lake of fire. And if anyone's [name]
was not found recorded in the Book of Life, he was hurled
into the lake of fire."* AMP (Revelation 21:11–15)

**Most postmoderns don't believe in eternal punishment for the
wicked. Jesus speaks clearly about eternal punishment that is
part of, belonging to, the final order of things that follows the
end of this present age with the final judgment of all mankind.**
This is understood as an unending process (eternal) of punishment
consciously experienced by the wicked. "These will go away into
eternal punishment, but the righteous into eternal life" (Mt 25:46).
Jude, too, speaks of the judgment of eternal fire:

*"And angels who did not keep their own domain, but
abandoned their proper abode, He has kept in eternal bonds
under darkness for the judgment of the great day, just as
Sodom and Gomorrah and the cities around them, since
they in the same way as these indulged in gross immorality
and went after strange flesh, are exhibited as an example in
undergoing the punishment of eternal fire."* (Jude 7)

The Bible is clear that the wicked face eternal conscious fire in
hell (Luke 13:28–30; Matt 13:49–50; 25:46; Mark 9:47–48,
2 Pet 2:9–10). That there are degrees of punishment in God's
administration is evident from:

*"And that servant, who knew his Lord's will, and made not
ready, nor did according to his will, shall be beaten with
many stripes; but he that knew not, and did things worthy of
stripes, shall be beaten with few stripes."* (Luke 12:47, 48)

261

"After thy hardness and impenitent heart treasurest up for thyself wrath in the day of wrath and revelation of the righteous judgment of God; who will render to every man according to his works" (Rom 2:5, 6)

"For we must all be made manifest before the judgment-seat of Christ; that each one may receive the things done in the body, according to what he hath done, whether it be good or bad." (2 Cor 5:10)

Many who either don't believe in any life after death or are annihilationists chose largely to ignore the judgment of God. **Annihilationists believe that those who have sinned will be annihilated or instantly destroyed at death. The soul will be extinguished. This unbiblical perspective denies God's justice, which is part of the very character and righteousness of God** since all sin requires punishment. If God does not require severe punishment for sin, then He is not the God of the Bible. Psalm 73 reminds us that evil men may prosper, and people may *"find no fault in them,"* yet will be accountable for their sins upon death. The punishment of the wicked cannot cease, as Christ, heaven, hell, or the Holy Spirit cannot cease to live, to abide with believers; for all these are described using the same Greek word for **eternity (αἰώνιος)**, which is used sixty-six times in the New Testament (Matt 25:46).

If our bodies are destroyed after death why not eat, drink, and be merry for soon life will be over? The doctrine of annihilationism is simply an excuse for hedonism, since if we are annihilated at death, why not enjoy life and do what we please? If there is no life after death, then there is no moral compass, and every man becomes a law unto himself. It is the fear of eternal torment in hell that moderates human behavior. The fear of eternal damnation may not change religious attitudes but does change behavior. God is righteous, and

His righteousness that demands perfect justice. All sin will be punished now or later. All unrepented sins are eternal and therefore eventually must be punished. It is the understanding of the certainty of eternal torment in hell that protects society from disintegration.

If there is no hell, then there is no gospel. If there is no bodily resurrection, then Paul tells us that *"if the dead are not raised, we are a people most to be pitied."* For then we have believed a lie (1 Cor 15:19). Later, Paul again raised the critical importance not only of Christ's resurrection but our hope of resurrection and a new life in heaven with Him. Paul later reemphasizes: *"if the dead are not raised, then let us eat drink, for tomorrow we die"* or life has no meaning (1 Cor 15:32). Jesus came into this world to save us sinners from hell, and who by saving faith alone are justified alone by His saving work on the cross, where Jesus made substitutionary atonement for the sins of the saints and heaven possible (Rom 3:25–26; Gal 3:13; Col 2:13–14).

The Westminster Shorter Catechism Questions 37 and 38 confirm:

> "The souls of believers are at their death made perfect in holiness, (Heb. 12:23) and do immediately pass into glory; (2 Cor. 5:1,6,8, Phil. 1:23, Luke 23:43) and their bodies, being still united to Christ, (1 Thess. 4:14) do rest in their graves, (Isa. 57:2) till the resurrection. (Job 19:26–27)" and "At the resurrection, believers being raised up in glory, (1 Cor. 15:43) shall be openly acknowledged and acquitted in the day of judgment, (Matt. 25:23, Matt. 10:32) and made perfectly blessed in the full enjoying of God, (1 John 3:2, 1 Cor. 13:12) to all eternity." (1 Thess. 4:17–18)[32]

---

32   *The Westminster shorter catechism: with Scripture proofs.* (1996). (3rd edition.). Oak Harbor, WA: Logos Research Systems, Inc.

The "almost a Christian" may believe in divine punishment after death for sinners in a place of torment, followed after a period of time of reprieve by either annihilation or reunion with Christ after suffering a period of torment. **Catholics believe in purgatory which was adopted in Church Cannon Law at the Second Council of Lyon in 1274 AD. This was strongly opposed by the Eastern Orthodox church. Purgatory or disambiguation is the concept of a third or intermediate state between death and heaven where penance is accomplished.** Some ancients thought there was need for a necessary refinement of the sinner through trials and suffering during the period of the intermediate state in order to perfect the Catholic sinner prior to going to heaven. The Catholic is thought to remain in purgatory until he or she has performed enough penance to enter heaven. The Bible is clear there is no such thing as purgatory or a need of spiritual refinement and penance after death. We have only this life to live in a way that pleases God and after that the judgment. *There are no second chances after death.* Perhaps one of the scariest words in the bible for the lost is the word **eternity**. The phrase "eternal life" is used almost 50 times in the New Testament. The true believer has eternal life but the lost most tragically face eternal death and punishment. (Romans 6:23)

"For the wages of sin is death, but the free gift of God is eternal life in Christ Jesus our Lord."

Jesus makes it very clear that religion, good works, and spiritual anointing with works following do not save anyone. Salvation is not about being good enough since no one is good enough (Rom 3:10–12). Salvation is about knowing our redeemer relationally.

"Not everyone who says to Me, "Lord, Lord," shall enter the kingdom of heaven, but he who does the will of My Father in heaven. Many will say to Me in that day, "Lord, Lord, have

---

33   The Holy Bible: English Standard Version. (2016). (Ro 6:23–7:1). Wheaton, IL: Crossway Bibles.

we not prophesied in Your name, cast out demons in Your name, and done many wonders in Your name?" And then I will declare to them, "I never knew you; depart from Me, you who practice lawlessness!" (Matt 7:21–23)

The key verb in this passage is "*to know*," or in the Greek γινώσκειν or *ginoskein*, which was used by Jesus to connote sensual knowledge like a man knows his wife, not simple historical knowledge or intellectual understanding. It is knowledge derived from a personal intimate relationship of Jesus and the Father through the work of the Holy Spirit. It is knowledge of what is reality relationally. The implication of this Scripture is we can imagine Jesus standing at the gates of heaven saying *I know you, welcome*, or Jesus saying *who are you?* I don't *know you;* depart from me!

Many believe that ultimately there will be a way out of God's judgment. In actuality, there is no hope of repentance after death. The Bible is clear: **"Repent or Perish!"** Our destiny has already been determined at death. The Bible is very clear that sinners face eternal punishment with no chance of a way out unless they repent!

"The only way for us to escape that terrible judgment, is to be often passing a sentence of condemnation upon ourselves here. When the sound of the trumpet shall be heard, which shall summon the dead to appear before the tribunal of God, the righteous shall hasten out of their graves with joy to meet their Redeemer in the clouds; others shall call to the hills and mountains to fall upon them, to cover them from the sight of their Judge; let us therefore in time be posing ourselves which of the two we shall be.[34] (John Bunyan)

---

34   Bunyan, J. (2006). *Bunyan's Dying Sayings* (Vol. 1, p. 66). Bellingham, WA: Logos Bible Software.

"As the devil labours by all means to keep out other things that are good, so to keep out of the heart as much as in him lies, the thoughts of passing from this life into another world; for he knows if he can but keep them from the serious thoughts of death, he shall the more easily keep them in their sins. Nothing will make us more earnest in working out the work of our salvation, than a frequent meditation of mortality; nothing hath greater influence for the taking off our hearts from vanities, and for the begetting in us desires after holiness."[35] (John Bunyan)

In Summary, the Bible teaches clearly that:

1. Christians and unbelievers don't go immediately to heaven or hell after death, but to Hades/Sheol, which is the place of Paradise for Christians or the place of torment for unbelievers. This is also called the "place of the departed" or the "Intermediate State." Yet we immediately upon death go into the presence of the Lord (2 Cor 5:8) in paradise or to the place of eternal conscious torment (Phil 1:23), When Jesus returns, men will move from the place of the departed to heaven or the pit of hell after the final judgment.

2. The final state of the righteous is described as eternal life (Matt 25:46; John 10:10), glory (2 Cor 4:17), rest (Heb 4:9), knowledge (1 Cor 13:8–10), strength (Psalm 84:7), filled with the fullness of God (Eph 3:19), holiness (Rev 21:27), service (Rev 22:3), worship (Rev 19:1), fellowship with angels and men (Zech 8:4–5; Heb 12:22–23), communion with God (Rev 21:3), reward (1 Cor 3:14–15; Rev 3:12), and being reconciled to God (Col 2:20).

---

35   Bunyan, J. (2006). *Bunyan's Dying Sayings* (Vol. 1, p. 66). Bellingham, WA: Logos Bible Software.

3. There is no biblical basis for Purgatory or penance and the possible reduction in punishment or improvement in our position before the judgment seat of our Lord after death. Death is final and then the judgment. Jesus said, "It is finished or *Tetelestai*" (John 19:30). In the original Greek the word ***Tetelestai* is a legal term meaning the** complete finished discharge of debt. Nothing further can be added to our salvation such as man's works. Everything necessary for the salvation of man has been accomplished at the cross. Catholic doctrine reflects the medieval concept of sin that at death man dies as a sinner and still needs purification before entering the presence of a Holy God. Purgatory was thought to be a place of increasing holiness and purification. Of course, the concept of purgatory reflects an insufficient view of what Christ did on the cross in reconciling all believers as Holy, by His life of obedience, crucifixion, and assentation. (John 17:9-12) Indulgences are in the Roman Catholic Church as granted by the Pope for the remission of temporal punishment in purgatory still due for sins after absolution. Beginning with Martin Luther and the Protestant reformation, purgatory, indulgences and a treasury of merits were agreed to be without any biblical basis and heretical.

4. There is no such thing as reincarnation or a cycle of death (Karma) and rebirth that purges one's sin. This is a common pagan and Eastern religious belief. It directly opposes the Christian belief in only one death and then the resurrection and judgment. It trivializes death and hinders the motive of suffering

and negates responsibility and repentance. The belief in Karma is belief in an impersonal law that records good and evil deeds and then assigns a personal outcome in the next life, based on the good or evil life of the individual as a type of atonement and reward theology. It pretends to offer cosmic justice in a mythological world without absolute truth or an absolute moral standard. Our atonement is in the shed blood of our savior Jesus Christ. The Christian recognizes that none are righteous, and there is no hope of self-improvement without Christ (Rom 3:9–18, John 8:34). Jesus defeated death once and for all; life does not need to be repeated (Dan 12:2, Heb 2:14–15).

5. Death is gain for the believer. (2 Kings 22:20; Psalm 116:15; Luke 16:22, 23:43; John 14:2; Phil 1:21, 23; 2 Cor 5:8).

6. The final state of the righteous is described as eternal life (Matt 25:46; John 10:10), glory (2 Cor 4:17), rest (Heb 4:9), knowledge (1 Cor 13:8–10), strength (Psalm 84:7), filled with the fullness of God (Eph 3:19), holiness (Rev 21:27), service (Rev 22:3), worship (Rev 19:1), fellowship with angels and men (Zech 8:4–5; Heb. 12:22–23), communion with God (Rev 21:3), reward (1 Cor 3:14–15; Rev 3:12), and being reconciled to God (Col 1:20).

7. The final state of the wicked is described as being in eternal fire (Matt 8:12; 25:41; Rev 9:2–11), the pit of the abyss (Rev 9:2, 11), outer darkness (Matt 8:12), torment (Rev 14:10–11), eternal punishment (Matt 25:46), wrath of God (Rom 2:5), second death (Rev 21:8), a place where the

worm shall not die and the fire not quenched (Mark 9:48, Isaiah 66:24), eternal destruction from the face of the Lord (2 Thess 1:9), and eternal sin (Mark 3:29)

8. Heaven is largely a place of worship of our enthroned Lord and not a celestial playground (Rev 4; 5; 7:9–12)

9. There is *work* in heaven. We will rule and reign with Him in the new heaven and earth and not sit on a cloud, playing a harp (Isa 65:17; 66:22).

10. We have no assurance that we will meet our loved ones in heaven. The Bible is vague on details about the fellowship of the saints but very clear that heaven is about our fellowship with Jesus Christ, not others (Zech 8:4–8).

11. Eternity means *eternity* or forever and forever. The departed will be in either heaven or hell for eternity (Heb 9:27; John 3:18; Matt 25:41–46).

12. There is no biblical support for annihilation of the departed, or "*soul sleep,*" which is the belief that the soul sleeps until the day of resurrection. The bible is clear that at the moment of death we are in the presence of the Lord and will return with Him on the day of his return to earth. (I Corinthians 15:35-58) The Bible is crystal clear; the unbeliever faces immediate eternal, conscious torment. (Isa 66:23-24)

13. There is no support for praying for the dead. This is a false hope that the destinies of people might be changed after they die, something which Scripture nowhere encourages us to think.

14. There is no baptism for the dead. Some early Corinthian Christians practiced baptism by proxy. After they had been converted to Christianity, it is held, they desired to convey the benefits of their faith to their departed friends who had died in paganism, by having themselves baptized "in their behalf," perhaps on their graves. We have no evidence from history that such a practice prevailed in the early Christian churches Most interpretations of the phrase "baptized for the dead" is used only once in Scripture (I Cor 15:29). In Mark 10:38 and Luke 12:50, baptism is used as a metaphor for suffering or martyrdom. Some scholars, interpreting "baptism for the dead" as a metaphor for martyrdom, would translate it "being baptized with a view to death." Paul is arguing that if Jesus has not risen, then Christian faith, preaching, remission, hope, are all vain; so is "baptism for the dead." He cannot mean Christian baptism, for none of its conditions or benefits, as Paul expounds them, can be affirmed of the dead. Besides, the following phrase ("And as for us …And we ourselves …") dissociates Paul and his colleagues from the practice.

15. Remember: "Beloved, do not forget this one thing, that with the Lord one day is as a thousand years, and a thousand years as one day. The Lord is not slack concerning His promise, as some count slackness, but is longsuffering toward us, not willing that "ANY" (*i.e., none of those chosen before the beginning of this world who have already been born again and others still to be born again [Eph 1:4–6]*) "should perish but that all (His chosen or elect) should come to repentance. (2 Pet 3:8–9)

16. The major motive for the unbeliever to yield his life to the Lord has not been about the love and goodness of the Lord, but the fear of eternal conscious torment in hell. If there is no eternal consequence of sin why change? The message to the lost has always been: *Repent and believe or face the eternal fires of hell.*

17. Scripture invariably presents the judgment of God as proceeding on the accounting of this life, and it concentrates every ray of appeal into the present. For many, heaven is the hope of escape from this fallen world, and they neglect performing the works of God. "We must work the works of Him that sent me, while it is day: the night cometh when no man can work" (John 9:4). When night comes, there is no opportunity to secure salvation after death or a second probation.

18. Remember "the meek shall inherit the earth and shall delight themselves in the abundance of peace" (Psalm 37:11, Jeremiah 33:6).

19. Many people have written about a "life after death" vision of heaven. The issue of near-death experiences is complex, but I believe that after careful analysis, these metaphysical after-death experiences are not truly representative of a genuine biblical experience. Books like *Heaven Is for Real, 90 Minutes in Heaven,* and *The Boy who Came Back from Heaven* have sold over 100 million copies. This has been countered by Scott McKnight, a New Testament theologian, in his book *The Heaven Promise: Engaging the Bible's Truth about the Life to Come.* There is no specific

scriptural support for near-death experiences. Many people use 2 Corinthians 12:2–5 as a biblical proof text of near-death experiences. However, this is taking great liberty with interpretation and makes the assumption that Paul had actually died when he found himself in heaven. The passage nowhere states that Paul had died. It was a *vision* that God gave Paul of heaven, not a near-death experience.

20. Many delay their conversion until the last minute as did the Emperor Constantine. Bishop J. C. Ryle said: "One thief was saved, that no sinner might despair, but only one, that no sinner might presume."

21. "The happiness of heaven consists not only in contemplation and mere enjoyment, but consists very much in action, particularly serving and glorifying God" (Jonathan Edwards). Unfortunately, many have been distracted and had their eyes on the future heavenly life and are unprepared to wage the warfare that is very much present now. **We are called to wage that warfare today! We are called to be active and vigilant, to heal those who have spiritual and emotional needs, and to bring the gospel to a fallen world. The power of death is destroyed by the penetration of the gospel throughout the world. Let us go forth as Christian soldiers, carrying the cross before us.**

"Are there not millions of us who would rather go sleeping to hell; than sweating to heaven?" (Thomas Watson)

Chapter 24
Situational Eschatology

"I saw another ship approaching over the Horizon. It was a large imposing ship called 'The *Rapture*' from the Dispensational cruise line. The crew told me that the ship had representatives of all the major evangelical denominations on board. The ship looked like an aircraft carrier because it had a long flight deck crowded with people at ease sitting in lawn chairs, dressed in summer casual clothes sipping drinks, waiting for the return of Jesus. The people were not dressed for the coming storms because they felt Jesus would return for them and rapture them to heaven ahead of any storms, trials, or tribulations that lie ahead. They seemed very happy, and I was amazed at their confidence in the soon coming of Jesus. Whenever a large wave would rock the ship, everyone would look up to the sky. I asked the crewman to explain to me what the biblical foundation for their hope and beliefs was?" (Dorsett Smith MD, *The Merchandising of the Almighty in the American Church*)

Eschatology, from Greek *eschatos* or "last," is the study of the last things or end times. Much of the speculation about the return of Christ is based on one Bible verse: 1 Thessalonians 4:16–17. We are on very shaky ground when we use a single Bible verse to create a major theological position, but this is what many theologians have done! The word *millennium* means the number 1,000 literally. It is used in Revelation 20:6–7. The book of Revelation was written in the prophetic and apocalyptic genre and is not meant to be interpreted literally. **The debate among many Christians is about the millennial period. Does the**

millennium or 1,000-year period mentioned in Revelation chapter 20 mean a literal 1,000-year time period, or is this a metaphor for a spiritual period of time? For example, in Psalm 50:10, God says "For every beast of the forest is Mine, and the cattle on a thousand hills." There are millions of hills on earth, and the meaning of the word in the passage obviously was used in the prophetic Hebrew genre as an expression for an unlimited or very large undefined number.

It is the theological confusion over the interpretation of that one simple word that has brought division among end-time theologians. Christian theologians have had four major views of end-time events: amillennialism, postmillennialism, historic premillennialism, and dispensational premillennialism. **Dispensationalism is a recent popular Protestant evangelical tradition and theology based on a new biblical hermeneutic, or a literal system of interpretation, that sees a series of chronologically successive dispensations or periods in history in which God relates to human beings in different ways under different biblical covenants.** As a system, dispensationalism is rooted in the writings of John Nelson Darby (1800–1882) and the Brethren Movement beginning around 1830. The theology of dispensationalism consists of a distinctive eschatological end-times perspective, as all dispensationalists hold to premillennialism meaning "before the millennium" hope of the return of Christ and most hold to a "pre-tribulation rapture."

Basically, the dispensationalists believe that Jesus is going to return to establish a millennial kingdom on earth for 1,000 years after a period of great tribulation lasting seven years. They believe in two comings of Jesus. The first is called the rapture, at which time only the church will be removed. This could occur at any moment. They believe that the church is composed of those, and only those, who are saved between Pentecost and the rapture. After the rapture, the Jewish remnant will be God's agent on earth. Most dispensationalists think this rapture would occur before the seven-year period of the great tribulation. This is called pre-tribulation rapture. Some Christians believe in a mid-tribulation rapture, and others believe in a rapture of the church at the end of the tribulation period.

Dispensationalists believe there will be a second coming of Jesus with the saints at the time of the defeat of Satan at the end of the millennial period. In the meantime, after the church has been removed, the Jewish remnant will be empowered by the Holy Spirit for the conversion of the remaining unsaved Gentiles to begin the millennium. However, the concept of *two end-time comings of Christ* is not mentioned in Scripture!

Dispensationalists believe that the nation of Israel is distinct from the Church and that God will literally fulfill His promises to Israel. These promises include the land promises, a third temple, and Jewish worship promises, which in the future result in a millennial kingdom. Christ, upon His return, will rule the world from His throne in Jerusalem for 1,000 years. **Dispensationalists believe God has two distinct programs or covenants: one for Israel and one for the church. The church does not take over any of Israel's promises or purposes. The church age is thought of by dispensationalists as a *"parenthesis"* or *"intercalation,"* a period of time when God has temporarily suspended His primary purpose for Israel.** The church age began at Pentecost and will end at the pre-tribulation rapture of the church, according to dispensationalists. The Jewish saints such as Abraham, Joseph, Moses, and others will not be part of the rapture of the church! After the rapture of the church, God continues His promises to redeem Israel and the Jewish saints.

The suggestion that the church is just a "parenthesis" or "intercalation" conflicts with Scripture and was an entirely new concept unheard of prior to 1830. Paul makes it very clear in his epistles that the Old Testament points to the coming of Christ, whose sole purpose and ultimate goal is to build his church, Jews and Gentiles, which is now and ever more will be the temple of the Holy Spirit (Rom 9–11). **The church is not a replacement of the Jews (Replacement Theology, an unbiblical term used by premillennialists) but is grafted into the rootstock of the olive tree of Israel. (Eph 2:11-17) The saints in the Old Testament were saved by faith, not works, just like the saints in the New Testament (Gal 3:11).** Obedience to the law has always been an important sign only of a saving relationship with God (James 2:18). Only Joshua and Caleb made it to the Promised Land from their generation because of their faith in God's promises. The promises of God are inextricably intertwined together with Jew and Gentile (Rom 11:26). All the true Israel, (Gal 3:13–29), the promised seed of Abraham, those who believe by faith—Gentiles and Jews—will be saved.

> *"There is neither Jew nor Greek, there is neither slave nor free man, there is neither male nor female; for you are all one in Christ Jesus. And if you belong to Christ, then you are Abraham's descendants, heirs according to promise."* [36] (Galatians 3:28–29)

Jesus loves His church and gave his life for it. He loves those who now live and have lived by faith in ancient times equally.

> *"Do not marvel at this; for an hour is coming, in which all who are in the tombs will hear His voice and will come forth; those who did the good deeds to a resurrection of life, those who committed the evil deeds to a resurrection of judgment."* (John 5:28–29)

---

36   *New American Standard Bible: 1995 update.* (1995). (Ga 3:28–29). LaHabra, CA: The Lockman Foundation.

Jesus returns once for the righteous and unrighteous, and then the judgment for all will follow.

> *"And he put all things under his feet and gave him as head over all things to the church, which is his body, the fullness of him who fills all in all."* (Eph 1:22–23)

> *So that through the church the manifold wisdom of God might now be made known to the rulers and authorities in the heavenly places. This was according to the eternal purpose that he has realized in Christ Jesus our Lord, in whom we have boldness and access with confidence through our faith in him."* (Eph 3:10–12)

> *"Husbands, love your wives, as Christ loved the church and gave himself up for her, that he might sanctify her, having cleansed her by the washing of water with the word, so that he might present the church to himself in splendor, without spot or wrinkle or any such thing, that she might be holy and without blemish."* (Eph 5:25–27)

Dispensational premillennialism needs to be distinguished from Historic Premillennialism, which is also called Chiliasm (Greek, *chilioi* for one thousand) or Millenarianism (Latin *mille* for one thousand), which was often the view of many of the saints in the early church, particularly during periods of great persecution and the appearance of many antichrist-like world leaders. They looked forward to the soon return of Christ in their generation at the end of their present tribulation to establish His millennial kingdom on earth for 1,000 years. **This theological perspective did not include the rapture or a special dispensation for Israel or escape from tribulation prior to the return of Christ.** Examples are Hippolytus (170–236) and Sextus Julius Africanus (160–240), who taught the world would end around AD 500. The later fathers also stood firm in the conviction that there would be a final judgment at the end of the world. They spoke of this mostly, just as of other eschatological events, in a highly rhetorical fashion, without conveying any definite information. Augustine assumes that the scriptural representations of end times are figurative and spiritual and should not be interpreted literally. He expresses the conviction that Christ is coming again to judge the living and the dead. To Augustine, the millennium extends "from the first coming of Christ to the end of the world, when He shall come a second time." This view is called amillennialism, which means we are currently living in the millennium now. Both Luther and Calvin confirmed amillennialism and rejected premillennialism or what they called "chiliasts." The Anabaptists were considered rebels and were premillennialists.

The rise of Islam brought much speculation about the emergence of the antichrist and the soon return of Jesus. However, followers of Jan Hus thought that the return of Christ would come in 1420. Martin Luther (1483–1546) thought that the return of Christ would occur in the next hundred years. Cotton Mather (1663–1728) predicted the end of the age would be 1736. Jonathan Edwards (1703–1758) predicted the final return of Christ around the year 2000. William Miller predicted the return of Christ in 1843 then changed it to 1844 when Christ did not return as expected in 1843. More recently, Hal Lindsey and Edgar Whisenant predicted the return of Christ in 1988. Recently there was speculation about the return of Christ in 2012! It is best not to speculate about Christ's return in the future but live each day as though He would return tomorrow!

In other areas of theology, dispensationalists hold to a wide range of beliefs within the evangelical and fundamentalist spectrum. It is important to recognize that good Christians have argued among themselves for the last 2,000 years about the nature of the millennium. There has been no consensus among theologians about the millennium. There has been, however, a general consensus among Christian theologians for 1,800 years about the single return of Christ for all believers, whether Gentile or Jew, until Darby's speculation in 1830 of a pre-tribulation rapture of the church only, followed by a second coming of Christ at the end of the millennium for Israel and those converted during the millennial period.

The disagreement between various denominational and theological camps of the proper interpretation of the concept of a rapture is presented in 1 Thessalonians 4:17.

> *But we do not want you to be uninformed, brothers, about those who are asleep, that you may not grieve as others do who have no hope. For since we believe that Jesus died and rose again, even so, through Jesus, God will bring with him those who have fallen asleep. For this we declare to you by a word from the Lord that we who are alive, who are left until the coming of the Lord, will not precede those who have fallen asleep. For the Lord himself will descend from heaven with a cry of command, with the voice of an archangel, and with the sound of the trumpet of God. And the dead in Christ will rise first. Then we who are alive, who are left, will be caught up together with them in the clouds to meet the Lord in the air, and so we will always be with the Lord. Therefore encourage one another with these words.* (1 Thess 4:13–18)

How did this teaching of the apostle Paul ever come to be called "the Rapture?" The answer lies in the word translated "shall be caught up" (Greek *harpagésómetha* from verb *harparzo*). In Latin, this word is *rapere* or *rapio,* as used in the Latin Vulgate translation of the Bible, from which the English word *rapture* is derived. Free of any arcane or mysterious interpretation, **it simply means "to be caught up," "snatched," or "seized."**

Dispensationalists place their emphasis on the Greek word *harpazo* translated, "to be caught up" or raptured. **Other non-dispensationalists place their emphasis on the word "to meet or meeting" or "*apantesis*" from the Greek *apantáo* from *apó* = from + *antáo* = to come opposite to, to meet especially, to meet face to face.** It describes a meeting, especially a meeting of two who are coming from different directions. In Greek culture, the word had a technical meaning to describe the visits of dignitaries to cities where the citizens would formally meet an arriving dignitary. Typically, in Roman times, a deputation of dignitaries went out from the city to meet the arriving dignitary and would ceremonially escort him into the city of his destination (Acts 28:15). **The Greek word *apantesis* was often used to suggest the meeting of a dignitary, king, or famous person, and describing the people rushing to meet the one who was coming (1 Thess 4:17).**

In Hellenistic Greek, the expression had become a kind of technical term denoting "a ceremonial meeting with a person of position." In papyrus usage, it was used of an official delegation going forth to meet a newly appointed magistrate, or other dignitary, upon his arrival in their district. **Greek scholars Hogg and Vine have commented that, "Almost invariably the word *(apantesis)* suggests that those who go out to meet him intend to return to their starting place with the person met." In other words, the purpose of those Christians who meet Jesus in the air is not to be taken away with Him but to escort Him to His throne where He will rule and reign over the earth!**

The same Greek word *apantesis* is used in Acts 28 to describe the meeting of Paul with the saints in Rome. They came out of the city to meet Paul and they escorted him into the city of Rome. "And so we came to Rome. And the brothers there, when they heard about us, came as far as the Forum of Appius and Three Taverns to *meet* us. On seeing them, Paul thanked God and took courage" (Acts 28:14–15).

The concept of an *apantesis* today is still the correct protocol to bring a dignitary into a city. In the United States, a foreign dignitary is always met at Andrews Air Force Base by the State Department, White House dignitaries, and military officers and then escorted into Washington, DC. A Roman general returning from a conquest was made to wait outside of the city for three days so that the city could make appropriate preparations and then the city officials would come out and meet the dignitary and lead him into the city. **Jesus will meet his church in the air as victorious Lord and King for the sole purpose of having the Church take Him to His throne, where we will rule and reign with Him.**

The proper interpretation of 1 Thessalonians 4:16–17 is that at the end of time, Jesus is going to be seated on His throne on the New Earth or New Jerusalem with his Church to rule and reign forever. **Jesus returns only once to earth and not twice! He is coming, not to get His Church out of trouble or tribulation, but in His perfect time He returns as victorious to be enthroned with His Church to rule and reign forever. There is no secret rapture, but Christ openly displaces Himself.**

The dispensationalists' interpretation is that the rapture is about escape from tribulation and removing the church from a great time of Satan's anger, which has caused great tribulation and great persecution of the church. This coming worldwide chaos and woe implies that God is unable to protect His church during the time of tribulation and that Satan's power on earth is temporarily greater than Christ's who eventually becomes victorious. **Think about that! Scripture is very clear that the "Prince of this World" can do nothing that is not under God's control. Satan has already been defeated at the cross. The church through the work of Christ on the cross is victorious *now* as well as later! "He disarmed the rulers and authorities and put them to open shame, by triumphing over them in him" (Colossians 2:15).**

Why is this so important? Many want to escape troubles and trials. The concept of a rapture or deliverance out of a fallen world on the verge of collapse is very attractive to many. However, this results in an attitude of apathy, passivity, and laziness about the things of the Lord. Why improve or busy yourself about the Lord's business if He is coming soon and is going to get us out of our financial and relational troubles?

Basically, the belief in the rapture of the church from certain destruction produces apathy, escapism, and a weakened church. (See 2 Thess 3:6-12)

Dispensational thinking encourages many Christians to retreat from society rather than being salt and light to a fallen generation. Morale is critical for a victorious church. If Satan can convince many that the Antichrist is coming to rule and reign soon, then this produces spiritual paralysis, fear, and a weakened church. Victorious Christianity needs a positive eschatology to stand and fight in these difficult times. Christ has left great power to His church so that it may rule victoriously.

> *"Believe me that I am in the Father and the Father is in me, or else believe on account of the works themselves. "Truly, truly, I say to you, whoever believes in me will also do the works that I do; and greater works than these will he do, because I am going to the Father. Whatever you ask in my name, this I will do, that the Father may be glorified in the Son. If you ask me anything in my name, I will do it."* (John 14:11–14)

> *"For though we walk in the flesh, we are not waging war according to the flesh. For the weapons of our warfare are not of the flesh but have divine power to destroy strongholds. We destroy arguments and every lofty opinion raised against the knowledge of God, and take every thought captive to obey Christ, being ready to punish every disobedience, when your obedience is complete."* (2 Cor 10:3–6)

Proverbs 22:13 speaks to the issue of sloth and fear, which is epidemic in the church: *"The sluggard says, "There is a lion outside! I shall be killed in the streets*!" This can be paraphrased as: "Satan, the roaring lion, is outside in the streets, and so I am going to stay inside of my house (church) and wait for God to rapture me out of here." Instead, be a warrior, an overcomer, battling Satan in the streets and taking territory back from him, rather than like many who are hiding in their closets! How sad!

Some theologians have confused revelation and interpretation. *Revelation is what God said. Interpretation is what we think He meant by what he said.* It is not always easy to separate the literal from the symbolic or figurative—or the *precise* from the *allegorical*. Biblical books such as Ezekiel and Revelation are two examples. Eisegesis is the reading of one's own ideas into Scripture, from Greek eis "in, <u>into</u>" + ending from exegesis or to interpret <u>out of</u> Scripture allowing Scripture to interpret Scripture. The interpretation of a text (as of the Bible) by reading into it one's own ideas is a common error in premillennial end time bible interpretation. Bible scholars have improperly interpreted many plagues, wars, earthquakes, etc. as signs of the last days.

We need to remember the teaching that the Church would be raptured to heaven, leaving a Jewish remnant behind just prior to a time called the great tribulation was not known prior to the 1830s. Dispensationalists admit that this is a relatively new theology unknown to the ancients. Historical premillennial non dispensational eschatology was believed by some of the early church fathers that looked forward to the final coming (Greek *parousia*: coming or appearance) of Jesus to establish His eternal Kingdom. The historic premillennial worldview sees the Bible as a history of the Jews and the church from the beginning of time to the final coming of Christ. There is no special rapture of the church first and then later the Jews. Historic premillennialists believe that the Jews will be saved during end-time events and rise together with other Christians to meet the Lord. The traditional understanding was that there was only one coming of the Lord who would return for his church, Jew and Gentile, and then rule and reign for an indefinite millennial period with His church. The doctrinal statement in the Apostles Creed precludes a premillennial advent of Christ or two comings of the Lord, first for the church and the second for Israel.

Amillennialists believe that we are now living in the millennium, which began at Pentecost or immediately after Christ's resurrection. Postmillennialists believe in the gradual expansion of the Kingdom of God until a victorious Christ returns. The church was not to be removed from earth but would meet (*apantesis*) Jesus in the sky and escort Him to His throne to rule and reign with Him over a new earth. (Rev 21:1)

The traditional view of the mainline denominations and the view of the reformers since Augustine is amillennialism as mentioned earlier. The amillennial view holds that the 1,000 years mentioned in Revelation chapter 20:4–6 is a symbolic number, not a literal description, and that the millennium had already begun after the destruction of Jerusalem in AD 70 and is identical with the current church age, (or that it ended with the destruction of Jerusalem in AD 70, which is the view of preterists). Amillennialism holds that while Christ's reign during the millennium is spiritual in nature, at the end of the church age, Christ will return in final judgment and establish a permanent physical reign on earth. Revelation 20:4–6 is the chief and nearly the sole support of the doctrine of two corporeal resurrections. Remember, it is very dangerous to build a major church doctrine around one Bible verse. Consider that neither the phrase *second resurrection* nor the phrase *first death* is found in Scripture.

Dispensationalists believe that Christ comes twice: first for the church at the rapture, and again for the Jews after the millennium. The first and only resurrection occurred in the gospels. Christ finally returns again after the first resurrection for all the saints in Revelation 20:9–15. They are inferences from the phrases *first resurrection* and *second death,* the former in Revelation 20:5–7; the latter in 2:11; 20:6, 14; 21:8. One death and one resurrection are directly taught, and only one death and one resurrection followed by one final return of Christ are directly taught in Scripture.

The concept of a literal 1,000-year millennial period misinterprets a prophetic expression meant to express a long period of unknown duration. God doesn't think of things in the context of time because he exists outside of time.

He created the universe and the earth outside of time or before time began. Time didn't begin until God created the first twenty-four-hour day with light and darkness on the fourth day. (Genesis 1:14-19) God cannot be defined by time since He existed before time could be measured by the movement of the sun. Therefore, God is timeless or eternal. The age of the earth and creation is unknowable because it occurred before there was measurable time or a day/night 24-hour day. The concept of eternity means that it is a period not definable by the measure of time or a day/night cycle. (Rev 22:5) God has His plan, which cannot be defined by man's literal mechanistic concept of time but will be defined by God Himself.

It is inconceivable that the Church could have endured through the centuries without some voice being raised in support of the current premillennial dispensational doctrine if it does have any validity. Since no ancient voice spoke out in favor of this doctrine, the only conclusion possible is that the Church did not teach this in the beginning, and it should not be teaching it now. It is very dangerous to form a major doctrine on one verse or particularly one word in that verse!

More importantly, the dispensational pessimistic worldview that things are going to get worse and worse until Jesus raptures His church to save it from the great tribulation demeans God. It makes God appear to be powerless against His vanquished foe, Satan. Satan's war against the saints of God has become so effective that the only way God can save His church is to rapture it out of the clutches of Satan to heaven! Please, this is terribly pessimistic and unbiblical theology! We are called to be warriors and overcomers and to defeat our vanquished foe. We are called to be victors and not victims!

> *"Yours, O Lord, is the greatness and the power and the glory and the victory and the majesty, for all that is in the heavens and in the earth is yours. Yours is the kingdom, O Lord, and you are exalted as head above all."* (1 Chron 29:11)

> *"Beat your plowshares into swords, and your pruning hooks into spears; let the weak say, "I am a warrior."* (Joel 3:10)

> *"For everyone who has been born of God overcomes the world. And this is the victory that has overcome the world— our faith."* (1 John 5:4)

> *"Behold, I have given you authority to tread on serpents and scorpions, and over all the power of the enemy, and nothing shall hurt you."* (Luke 10:19)

> *"I have said these things to you, that in me you may have peace. In the world you will have tribulation. But take heart; I have overcome the world."* (John 16:33)

> *"I write to you, fathers, because you know him who is from the beginning. I write to you, young men, because you are strong, and the word of God abides in you, and you have overcome the evil one."* (1 John 2:14)

We are more than victors in Christ and need not fear man or Satan.

"No, in all these things we are more than conquerors through him who loved us. For I am sure that neither death nor life, nor angels nor rulers, nor things present nor things to come, nor powers, nor height nor depth, nor anything else in all creation, will be able to separate us from the love of God in Christ Jesus our Lord." (Rom 8:37–39)

Our eschatology (doctrine of end times) shapes our ecclesiology (doctrine of the Church) and our Christology (doctrine of Christ), as well as our Soteriology (doctrine of salvation). Sound doctrine produces a stable, growing, productive spiritual life. Defective doctrine produces weak Christians and a weak Church. The belief in a weak Christ with a weak helpless Church in an overwhelmingly strong, evil world system of Satan results in a completely distorted view of the victorious Christ and the victory we have through Him. Weak Christians live in fear of the coming antichrist and the tribulation rather than live in victory. Christians are called to expand the Kingdom of God, to raid the enemy's camp, and to take prisoners for Christ. **Those who live in fear and hide in their houses will be *left behind!* We are called to subdue and take dominion over the earth. "And God said to them, 'Be fruitful and multiply and fill the earth and subdue it and have dominion over the fish of the sea and over the birds of the heavens and over every living thing that moves on the earth'"** (Gen 1:28). Remember what Jesus did on the cross: "He disarmed the rulers and authorities and put them to open shame, by triumphing over them in him" (Col 2:15).

Those critics of my anti-dispensational worldview might think that I support radical "Dominion Theology," "Kingdom Now Theology," "Latter Rain Movement," "The New Apostolic Reformation," and "The New Paradigm" theologies, which purpose a progressive revelation of Christ, resulting in worldwide evangelism and perfection of His Bride, the church, through the release of end time anointing of a "new group" of apostles and prophets. Many of the current self-appointed apostolic leaders are very elitist and plan a global international movement to take over churches and nations.

These men appear to be more interested in fleecing the flock rather than equipping the saints as in Ephesians 4:11–12. The church needs men of vision and true leaders who are humble servants and not pride-filled, self-centered, narcissistic men or women who claim special revelation and anointing from God to manipulate the saints. These leaders believe Christ will then return to rule with his church only after the earthly rule has been established by these self-appointed apostles. Scripture warns us "But it is not the spiritual that is first but the natural, and then the spiritual" (1 Cor 15:46). The false precedes the true. Today's apostolic, prophetic ministry is but a shadow of the release of the Holy Spirit to come. God is raising up humble, anointed men to equip and edify the saints who will not draw men to themselves but focus men on Christ and the cross. (Eph 4:11–13)

Many postmillennialists hope that God's law will be the basis for all rule and behavior (theonomy). The Kingdom of God or a "Christian Republic" will be established on Earth through political and (in some cases) even military means as opposed to the work of the Holy Spirit. Postmillennialists see history culminating in worldwide victory for Christ as opposed to premillennialists who see history winding down to the return of the antichrist.

Some postmillennialists have adapted a type of social gospel focused on "social justice" and have focused on eradication of various vices such as slavery, alcoholism, child labor, prostitution, and other social evils and inequalities. Reconstructionists hope to renew society by demanding observance to God's moral law and seek to change society by applying biblical moral standards. Their focus is not only on personal discipleship and salvation, but the discipleship of nations through the transforming power of the Holy Spirit. Their motive is laudable, but there is a very fine line between the works of man and the work of the Holy Spirit!

Traditional postmillennialism of Jonathan Edwards, John Owen, and many of the Puritans visualized a less radical and more gradual world change as the gospel is spread throughout the world until the gospel is preached unto the ends of the earth (Matt 28:19). They visualized a "latter glory" prior to the return of Christ. The transformation of man is the end result of the work of the Holy Spirit and not the result of man's institutions or efforts. The Holy Spirit will bring the millennial return of Christ, who then will establish His rule on earth when and how He sees fit.

Postmillennialism is very positive and hopeful when it is the work of the Holy Spirit, but it has been distorted by some who believe that Jesus will not return until his earthly Kingdom has been established by these very dangerous self-appointed "apostles and prophets" who want control of the church for their own selfish purposes. This demonic doctrine of "A New Apostolic Reformation" is a work of man rather than a work of God and is not new. In contrast to postmillennialism, dispensational premillennialism is very negative. Its focus is on the return of the antichrist and a great worldwide tribulation.

Martin Luther said:

> "One must not make out of this the kind of kingdom or seek the sort of church that may be governed on earth by external secular power. The pope does this and praises it as the true church government. The Anabaptists and similar erring spirits dream that before the Last Day all the enemies of the church will be physically exterminated and a church assembled which shall consist of pious Christians only; they will govern in peace, without any opposition or attack. But this text clearly and powerfully says that there are to be enemies continuously as long as this Christ reigns on earth. And certain it is, too, that death will not be abolished until the Last Day, when all His enemies will be exterminated with one blow." (Luther's Works Vol. 13:263–264)

John Calvin expressed the view of many of the reformation scholars in his comments on 1 Thessalonians 4:17:

> "And so we shall be ever. To those who have been once gathered to Christ he promises eternal life with him, by which statements the reveries of Origen and of the Chiliasts are abundantly refuted. For the life of believers, when they have once been gathered into one kingdom, will have no end any more than Christ's. Now, to assign to Christ a thousand years, so that he would afterwards cease to reign, were too horrible to be made mention of. Those, however, fall into this absurdity who limit the life of believers to a thousand years, for they must live with Christ as long as Christ himself will exist. We must observe also what he says—we shall be, for he means that we profitably entertain a hope of eternal life, only when we hope that it has been expressly appointed for us." (Calvin's Commentaries on the Epistles of Paul; 1 Thessalonians 4:16–17).

The reformers understood that Christian hope could not be replaced by a hope in the return of Christ to set the world aright, (*Christ as savior*) rather than a hope in Him alone (*Christ as Lord*), a very subtle but important distinction.

Many Christians today hold an intermediate view, which I call *Situational Eschatology*, which means what one believes about end times is largely shaped by current world events and what he or she reads or sees on television or the Internet about the world situation. Our understanding of end times or eschatology is too often shaped largely by current events and despair about the world situation rather than the positive view of Scripture. This has been a problem in the church from the first century and the destruction of Jerusalem in AD 70. Evil rulers, such as Nero and other despots, the fall of nations such as the fall of Rome in AD 410, the rise of Islam and the fall of Constantinople in 1453, the plagues or black death (1342-1345) that killed as many as one-quarter to one-third of the European population in the Middle Ages. Wars such as the Hundred Years' War (1337-1453), and natural disasters such as the great earthquake that destroyed Lisbon in 1755, and signs in the sky such as comets and eclipses, all produced an outcry that this was certainly the end of the world. Many thought that with the appearance of Haley's comet in 989 that Christ would return in the year 1,000. The Taborites were radical followers of Jan Hus and predicted the return of Christ in 1420. Augustine and Martin Luther felt they were living in the last days. Cotton Mather, the great American Puritan pastor (1663–1728), thought Christ would return in 1697 and then later changed the date to 1736. Jonathan Edwards predicted the return of Christ in the year 2000! Hal Lindsey predicted the return of Christ in 1988. The re-establishment of the Nation of Israel in 1948 and capture of the temple mount in 1967 has further stoked end time speculations that Christ would return in that generation of forty years (1988 and 2007). This did not happen, so new speculations have followed concerning the year 2012! That didn't happen so now what?

Fear and pessimism saps the church of its vitality and ardor. We claim to believe Scripture that Jesus and the Kingdom of God will triumph but often feel overwhelmed by the seemingly great victory of evil in this wicked world. Unfortunately, at this time in church history, eschatological, or end time, teachings of the return of Christ are often far more important to the evangelical church than His ethical precepts!

The amillennial view, as well as the dispensational premillennial view, can be rather pessimistic when it focuses on the here and now rather than our blessed hope. Pessimism produces fear, fatalism, and what is even worse, immobilization! Amillennialists recognize the evil in this world system (1 John 5:19) but at the same time express hope in a total renewal of God's creation with the return of Christ (Isa 65:17–25). The amillennialist sees God at work in his Kingdom now and looks forward to its future consumption. **When we look at the world, we quickly forget that Satan has been defeated at the cross and is the vanquished foe. No matter how bad things look socially and politically, Christians are called to stand and fight for righteousness and societal transformation. We are the "*salt of the earth.*" We are victors and not victims.**

> *"Finally, be strong in the Lord and in the strength of his might. Put on the whole armor of God, that you may be able to stand against the schemes of the devil. For we do not wrestle against flesh and blood, but against the rulers, against the authorities, against the cosmic powers over this present darkness, against the spiritual forces of evil in the heavenly places".* (Eph 6:10–12)

Much of the confusion in Christendom today also relates to our understanding of our initial resting place before Christ returns from heaven to rule and reign. This is discussed in much greater detail in chapter 20, but for the purpose of this discussion, I have given a short review since each book chapter is designed to be a reasonably complete discussion of the subject matter by itself. Many of the saints now believe that Christians go directly to heaven, as did Darby and the early nineteenth century revivalists who popularized the concept that Christians go directly to heaven, bypassing the intermediate state.

For the first 1,900 or so years since the resurrection of Jesus, Christians have believed that the departed go to an intermediate place called Paradise, like the thief on the cross. (Paradise: a royal park or garden in Luke 23:43; 2 Cor12:4; Rev 2:7, as opposed to heaven, a transcendent kingdom where God and angels dwell and the final destination of the elect.)

Paradise is a state of conscious existence in the presence of our Lord and not "soul sleep." There we will await the final return of Christ in Paradise to rule and reign with Him forever (Psalm 16:10, 49:14–15, Eccl 12:7, Luke 16:22–43, Phil 1:23, 2 Cor 5:8, Rev 6:9–11, 14:13). I think of Paradise as a temporary place where we will be learning more about our Lord in preparation of His return to earth and our rule with Him. The ancients understood that death is just a transition from our mortal life to a new spiritual life where we will be transformed into the likeness of Christ. Jesus said, *"If anyone keeps my word, he will never see death."* (John 8:51; 5:24–25) **The biblical concept of death for the unbeliever is eternal separation from God, not cessation of bodily function. The best description for death for the Christian is *transition* or the passing from one life to another with the human intellect intact with the spirit. For the Christian there is no fear of death but a joyful anticipation of reunion with our Lord Jesus. There is no fear of death for those who have died to themselves and received a new life in Christ. We die once not twice! We live as dead men walking. Those who love God will never be separated from Him and in a spiritual sense never die!** We will be like Adam, and the earth will be restored. God's original plan for earth will be carried out under the rule of the Second Adam, Jesus Christ, Lord of Lords, King of Kings.

We are to remember that God doesn't change His plans, nor can He be defeated. The vision of His ultimate plan for the Garden of Eden and man is outlined in the first three chapters of Genesis and then repeated in the last three chapters of the book of Revelation. Here we see again the tree of life, the garden, and the river, the beginning of history and the end of history. The early church and the reformers understood that all spiritual life is about doing God's business. Heaven is not about sitting on a cloud, playing a harp. Kingdom work never ends even in eternity! We will rule and reign with Jesus forever and ever.

I thought about the postmodern church and its false concept of heaven as a place of just eternal bliss and rest where nothing will be required of the saints other than praise and a grateful heart! **Modern man is more concerned about a reunion with loved ones and having an endless party than Kingdom business. (Matt 22:23-30) Western prosperity has been a curse on the Western Church. Greek and Roman philosophers observed a leisure/affluence paradox. From Plato and Aristotle in Greece to Tacitus and Petronius in Rome societal commentators observed that affluence and leisure create a type of laxity that leads to societal and institutional disintegration.** *Western man has created a new image of God: A God of blessing and love that forgives sin without repentance, a hell without torment, and an eschatology of escapism.*

For many postmoderns, the fear of death and eternal punishment has been replaced by universalism, the hope that all men will be saved, or annihilationism, which is the hope that there is no eternal punishment for the wicked or that punishment will last for varying periods of time and then man will be extinguished or annihilated so that there is an end to the suffering of the wicked. Scripture makes it abundantly clear that there can be no separation in the justice of God: some will come to eternal bliss and others to eternal damnation and torment. Jesus spoke more of hell than heaven! There are twenty-one passages in the four gospels where Jesus warns unrepentant sinners about the eternal consequences of sin and eternal punishment in hell.

"Whoever believes in the Son has eternal life; whoever does not obey the Son shall not see life, but the wrath of God remains on him" (John 3:36).

It is the certainty of eternal judgment, pain, and suffering that is the motivating force of evangelism. The Bible teaches that the condition of the unconverted is as bad as it can possibly be for those who reject Christ. The battle over the doctrine of eternal punishment is a battle over a foundational issue that church creeds and confessions have confirmed as an essential church doctrine as in the book of Hebrews.

"Therefore, let us leave the elementary doctrine of Christ and go on to maturity, not laying again a foundation of repentance from dead works and of faith toward God, and of instruction about washings, the laying on of hands, the resurrection of the dead, and eternal judgment." (Heb 6:1–2)

"And just as it is appointed for man to die once, and after that comes judgment, so Christ, having been offered once to bear the sins of many, will appear a second time, not to deal with sin but to save those who are eagerly waiting for him." (Heb 9:27–28)

"And these will go away into eternal punishment, but the righteous into eternal life." (Matt 25:46)

Christ, who suffered for our salvation, descended to the world below, rose again from the dead, ascended into heaven, and sat down at the right hand of the Father to come from thence to judge the quick and the dead, at whose coming all men shall rise again with their bodies, and shall give account for their own deeds. ***And they that have done good will go into life eternal; they that have done evil into eternal fire.*** **(Athanasian Creed circa AD 293–373)**

"The rest of mankind God was pleased, according to the unsearchable counsel of His own will, whereby He extendeth or witholdeth mercy, as He pleaseth, for the glory of His sovereign power over His creatures, to pass by; and to ordain them to dishonour and wrath for their sin, to the praise of His glorious justice." (Matthew 11:25–26, Romans 9:17–18, 21–22, 2 Timothy 2:19–20, Jude 4, 1 Peter 2:8) (Westminster Confession of Faith 1643, Chap 3, #7)

"The end of God's appointing this day is for the manifestation of the glory of His mercy, in the eternal salvation of the elect; and of His justice, in the damnation of the reprobate, who are wicked and disobedient. For then shall the righteous go into everlasting life, and receive that fullness

*of joy and refreshing, which shall come from the presence of the Lord: but
the wicked, who know not God, and obey not the Gospel of Jesus Christ,
shall be cast into eternal torments, and be punished with everlasting
destruction from the presence of the Lord, and from the glory of His
power.*" (Matthew 25:31–46, Romans 2:5–6, Romans 9:22–23,
Matthew 25:21, Acts 3:19, 2 Thessalonians 1:7–10) (Westminster
Confession of Faith 1643, Chapter 33, #2)

**If there is no eternal punishment and eventually all will be
saved (Universalism) or extinguished (Annihilationism), then
eschatology is simply unimportant and merely an intellectual
mind game.** We cannot appreciate God's justice, great love,
mercy, and the glorious gift of eternal salvation without the
contrast of His eternal wrath on the wicked. Eternal punishment
motivates evangelism. Paul reminds us that, *"knowing the terror
of the Lord we persuade men."* (2 Cor 5:11 NKJV)

**Satan has always tried to minimize the consequences of sin
and the certainty of eternal damnation of the wicked. The
good news is that Satan was defeated at the cross; the bad
news is his eternal sentence has not yet been carried out, and
evil is still with us. God wants us to know heaven now, if we
don't know a little of heaven, (Kingdom of God) now, how
will we know it later?** We are new creatures in Christ and need
to assume our spiritual authority invading the secular world and
take back territory for the Lord. This is our eternal destiny. God's
plan never changes. **He expects us (new creatures in the Second
Adam) to take dominion now and forever.**

Unfortunately, many Western Christians have a defeatist worldview
that the world is evil, corrupt, and hopeless, which has its roots in
Gnosticism and Platonism, which in turn denies the goodness of
creation. Salvation then becomes an escape from the world to heaven
or the afterlife. When God created this world, animals, and man,
He said: *"It is good!"*

"The purpose of salvation is not to get a ticket out of this world or fire *insurance* from hell, but life *assurance* and hope through trials and troubles because of an ongoing living relationship with Jesus Christ our Lord, Prophet, Priest, and King over all things who will never leave us."

The proper focus is in "The Lord's Prayer": *let your kingdom come.* We are to pray for His Kingdom to be manifested now as well as in the future. Creation is not to be cursed but redeemed.

"Then God said, "Let us make man in our image, after our likeness. And ***let them have "dominion"*** over the fish of the sea and over the birds of the heavens and over the livestock and over all the earth and over every creeping thing that creeps on the earth. (The word rule or take dominion in Hebrew means *râdâh:* to tread down, *have dominion, prevail against, reign, [bear, make to] to rule over, take.)*

"And God blessed them. And God said to them, *'Be fruitful and multiply and fill the earth and subdue it and have "**dominion**" over the fish of the sea and over the birds of the heavens and over every living thing that moves on the earth'"* (Genesis 1:28). (The Hebrew word here is *kâbash:* to tread down; to tread under your feet, hence, to disregard; to conquer, subjugate, violate, bring into bondage, force, keep under, subdue, bring into subjection.)

Both of these Hebrew words speak of taking dominion or ruling over an enemy or that serpent Satan. The first Adam failed but the second Adam succeeded and crushed the enemy's head. God's plan is to prepare the saints to rule and reign with Him by conquering Satan now by living a holy life and taking dominion now over evil at every opportunity.

"Therefore, if anyone is in Christ, he is a new creation. The old has passed away; behold, the new has come. All this is from God, who through Christ reconciled us to himself and gave us the ministry of reconciliation; that is, in Christ God was reconciling the world to

himself, not counting their trespasses against them, and entrusting to us the message of reconciliation. Therefore, we are ambassadors for Christ, God making his appeal through us. We implore you on behalf of Christ, be reconciled to God. For our sake he made him to be sin who knew no sin, so that in him we might become the righteousness of God." (2 Cor 5:17–21)

"What then shall we say to these things? If God is for us, who can be against us? He who did not spare his own Son but gave him up for us all, how will he not also with him graciously give us all things?" (Rom 8:31–32)

"Therefore, as you received Christ Jesus the Lord, so walk in him, rooted and built up in him and established in the faith, just as you were taught, abounding in thanksgiving . . . for in him the whole fullness of deity dwells bodily, and you have been filled in him, who is the head of all rule and authority." (Col 2:6, 7–10)

Modern culture has lost its perspective of history. To the Greek, history is about a recurring cycle of events with no culmination and no perfection. To the Hebrew, history has a beginning and an end. It is about a progressive linear history of God's redemptive process, culminating in the return of Christ. Hebrew thinking brings meaning to history; since history is progressive, it brings hope and vision for the future. Self-centered Western Christians have seen the promises of Christ's return as an individual hope or privatized eschatology. This further encourages a withdrawal from society and a private piety. Christ is going to return to rule and reign and dramatically change the whole world. He is coming to judge the living and the dead. Justice and righteousness will be established. He is the consummation and the end of all things. The church is not the goal of history but the tool God is using to prepare and perfect His Bride to meet her Lord and Savior upon His return.

In summary, our Greek thinking, gnostic, narcissistic, and materialistic society has focused on a ***savior from* this world** (escapism, Platonism, gnosticism, dispensationalism) rather than a ***savior for* transforming this world** and building His kingdom on earth, where He will make us transforming agents to extend His rule and reign! There always will be some eschatological tension between the future and the now. ***Our focus need not be on end-time events but on being God's agents for societal transformation as salt and light now. Maranatha: Come Lord Jesus.***

"Today's church wants to be raptured from responsibility"
(Leonard Ravenhill)

Chapter 25
Christian Liberty

The question is *how a true Christian is to live*. A true Christian doesn't love this world but sees the world as it is: evil, corrupt, and immoral, men loving themselves and the deeds of the flesh, and many men who hate God and His people seem to prosper.

Peter gives us the proper context of the Christian's life:

*"Beloved, I implore you as aliens and strangers and exiles [in this world] to abstain from the sensual urges (the evil desires, the passions of the flesh, your lower nature) that wage war against the soul. Conduct yourselves properly (honorably, righteously) among the Gentiles, so that, although they may slander you as evildoers, [yet] they may by witnessing your good deeds [come to] glorify God in the day of inspection [when God shall look upon you wanderers as a pastor or shepherd looks over his flock]. Be submissive to every human institution and authority for the sake of the Lord, whether it be to the emperor as supreme, or to governors as sent by him to bring vengeance (punishment, justice) to those who do wrong and to encourage those who do good service. For it is God's will and intention that by doing right [your good and honest lives] should silence (muzzle, gag) the ignorant charges and ill-informed criticisms of foolish persons. **[Live] as free people, [yet] without employing your freedom as a pretext for wickedness; but [live at all times] as servants of God."** (*1 Pet 2:11–16, AMP)*

What a wonderful revelation of the Holy Spirit given to Peter to share with his persecuted church. Peter speaks about the *freedom of the believer*. Perhaps the words liberty and freedom are one of the most misunderstood word pictures for Christians.

Jesus said, "*He has sent me to proclaim release to the captives and recovering of sight to the blind, to set at liberty those who are oppressed*" (Luke 4:18; Isa 61:1–2). Biblical freedom is from self-servitude, satanic oppression, sin, death, and Old Testament legal requirements. So also, in John 8:31–32, Jesus said, *"If you continue in my word, you are truly my disciples, and you will know the truth, and **the truth will make you free**."* And again, *"Everyone who commits sin is a slave to sin. So, if the Son makes you free, you will be free indeed"* (John 8:34, 36).

"For freedom Christ has set us free," writes Paul; "stand fast therefore, and do not submit again to a yoke of slavery" (Gal 5:1). Christ was "born under the law, to redeem those who were under the law" (Gal 4:4–5). To "rely on works of the law" for salvation is to be "under a curse" (Gal 3:10). Similarly, to place oneself under the Old Testament law is "slavery," while choosing "the Jerusalem above is free" (Gal 4:24–25). **The Christian, Jew or Gentile, Paul maintained, is free from all need to perform works of law for acceptance, for as a believer in Christ he is fully accepted already (Gal. 3:28), as the gift of the Spirit to him proves.** (Gal. 3:2, 14; 4:6; 5:18).

The biblical idea of liberty (freedom) has as its background the thought of imprisonment or slavery so common in the Roman world. Jesus had come, He said, to overthrow the prince of this world, the strong man, and to release his prisoners (Jn. 12:31; Mk. 3:27; Lk. 10:17) Man's response to the divine gift of liberty (Greek: *eleutheria*), and indeed the very means of his receiving it, is a free acceptance of bondservice (Greek: *douleia*) to God (Rom 6:17–22), to Christ (1 Cor 7:22), to righteousness (Rom 6:18), and to all men for the sake of the gospel (1 Cor 9:19–23) and of the Saviour (2 Cor 4:5).

There is no reason why a Gentile convert should burden himself with Mosaic ceremonies (circumcision, the Jewish festal calendar; Gal. 4:10), which in any case belonged to the pre-Christian era. **The redeeming work of Christ has freed him completely from the need to seek salvation through law (Gal 3:13; 4:5; 5:1). His task now is, first, to guard his God-given liberty against any who would tell him that faith in Christ alone is not enough to save him** (Gal. 5:1) and second, to put his liberty to the best use by letting the Spirit lead him into responsible fulfillment of the law of love (Gal 5:13).

Christian liberty is neither an abolishing of responsibility nor a sanctioning of license.

"Any concept of grace that makes us feel more comfortable sinning is not biblical grace. God's grace never encourages us to live in sin, on the contrary, it empowers us to say no to sin and yes to truth" (Randy Alcorn).

Martin Luther explained the liberty produced by Christ's sacrifice on the cross that while:

> "He permitted the law to accuse Him, sin to damn Him, and death to devour Him; He abrogated the law, damned sin, destroyed death, and justified and saved me. Thus, Christ is a poison against the law. Sin, and death, and simultaneously a remedy to regain liberty, righteousness, and eternal life." (What Luther Says, a Practical In-Home Anthology for the Active Christian, Concordia Publishing House, St Louis, MO. 1959)

The Christian is no longer "under law" (Rom 6:14) for salvation but under grace, but he is not therefore "without law toward God" (1 Cor 9:21). Christians are thus "under the law of Christ" (1 Cor 9:21). The "law of Christ" (Gal 6:2) or James' "law of liberty" (James 1:25; 2:12) is the law of love (Gal 5:13; Mark

12:28; John 13:34), the principle of voluntary and unstinting self-sacrifice for the good of men (1 Cor 9:1–23; 10:23–33), and the glory of God. (1 Cor 10:31) When Christ becomes Lord or Master in an individual's life, the believer feels compelled to please his Lord by actions and spiritual fruit.

"You are slaves of the one whom you obey," and to obey sin "leads to death" (**Rom 6:16;** see also Rom 6:20; 7:14; John 8:34; and 2 Pet 2:19,) which asserts: "you are a slave to whatever has mastered you"). The trouble is that no one can make a clean break with sin without Christ. Jesus says plainly that people are really free only when the Son sets them free (John 8:36). **Correspondingly, a Christian can give "thanks . . . to God that you who were once slaves of sin have . . . been set free from sin" (Rom 6:17–18). Our freedom in Christ is to serve Him, not serve ourselves. All men are in bondage; some to sin and some to righteousness. What are you?** Jesus reminds us: *"If the righteous is scarcely saved, what will become of the ungodly and the sinner?"* (1 Pet 4:18).

Finally, many Christians are in despair. They have been looking for a charismatic, godly man to restore our nation to its prior glory. Their hope has been in man and government leaders to provide solutions to society ills, but things continually get worse. Most Christians do not know who they are in Christ. Peter calls us: "aliens and strangers" (1 Pet 2:11). Paul reminds us in Ephesians 2.19: "So then you are no longer strangers and aliens, but you are fellow citizens with the saints, and are of God's household." The author of Hebrews encourages the suffering saints by the promise of a better country

All these died in faith, without receiving the promises, but having seen them and having welcomed them from a distance, and having confessed that they were strangers and exiles on the earth. For those who say such things make

303

it clear that they are seeking a country of their own. And indeed, if they had been thinking of that country from which they went out, they would have had the opportunity to return. But as it is, they desire a better country, that is, a heavenly one. Therefore, God is not ashamed to be called their God; for He has prepared a city for them. (Hebrews 11:13–16)

David cries out to God in Psalm 39:12, *"Hear my prayer, O LORD, and give ear to my cry; Do not be silent at my tears; For I am a stranger with You, A sojourner like all my fathers."* The Lord reminded Israel that the land promise was temporary in that the land was God's and they were to occupy the land, remembering that they were temporary residents in Leviticus 25:23: *"The land, moreover, shall not be sold permanently, for the land is Mine; for you are but aliens and sojourners with Me."* **The postmodern world will collapse because it puts its hope in man rather than in God. Those who are looking for worldly solutions will be terribly disappointed. Scripture reminds us that God is the absolute sovereign over all world events. Daniel 4:17 reminds us that God appoints all those in authority, even the most wicked of men.** God orders all events and is sovereign over all the nations of this earth. God is the one who determines the rise and fall of nations and those who will advance and those who will decline. His sovereign choices are absolutely perfect.

What wonderful peace and joy for the saints who trust in God. The world system cannot defeat us since *we are not of this world but sojourners, aliens, and strangers.* Our hope is in the Kingdom to come, not in this world, but a better country, a city prepared by God for us.

Chapter 26
Worship

Christian worship involves honor, homage, and praise to our Lord. A great deal of emphasis has always been placed on the forms of communal worship varying from singing psalms acapella to a modern praise band. One of the most common criticisms for leaving a church has been "We liked the pastor but didn't like the worship music!"

What distinguishes worship music from simple praise music is a combination of melody and theology. Style is not as important as content. Good worship music includes the timeless classics from the past as well as excerpts from scripture (e.g., Psalms)**. What is most important is good, solid theology and the focus of the music should be on God and not man. Worship is vertical not horizontal**. New and novel isn't always better. One's worship expresses, teaches, and governs the doctrinal beliefs of that church community. According to this view, alterations in the patterns and content of worship would necessarily reflect a change in the confessional faith itself. When a heresy arose in the Church, it was ofttimes be accompanied by a shift in worship of the heretical group. Orthodoxy in faith is directly reflected to orthodoxy in worship, and vice versa. For example, the following is an example of good melody and timeless doctrine.

"What can wash away my sin? Nothing but the blood of Jesus; What can make me whole again? Nothing but the blood of Jesus.". —Robert Lowry

Current Christian communal worship practices are diverse, with a range of customs and theological views. Some elements are universal, but style and content vary greatly due to the history and differing emphases of the various branches of Christianity. Many modern worship songs don't even actually name Jesus. We sing praises to "God" or "Lord" or "Him", but often do not name Jesus Christ by name. We must remember that there are many gods in this world demanding worship, like the gods of wealth, health, power, and preeminence. The only one true God is Jesus Christ. Some modern praise music is not truly focused on Jesus Christ and contains no doctrine. **In Isaiah 58, the prophet talks about true and false worship. At the heart of** <u>false worship</u> **is that it is all about us, all about what God can do for us, a warm feeling of self-satisfaction. However, true worship has an outcome that is good for all: the imprisoned and oppressed are set free, the hungry are fed, and the naked are clothed. Most of our worship does not see any of this happen.**

*"I appeal to you therefore, brothers, by the mercies of God, to present your bodies as a living sacrifice, holy and acceptable to God, which is **your spiritual worship**. Do not be conformed to this world, but be transformed by **the renewal of your mind**, that by testing **you may discern what is the will of God, what is good and acceptable and perfect.** "*(Romans 12:1-2)

What does it mean to worship? Christian worship requires not only an emotional response, but an intellectual understanding obtained through the study of scripture to discern the perfect will and character of God including, His wonder, His grace, His goodness, His kindness, His compassion, His mercy, His love, His perfection, His forgiveness, His creation, His sacrifice at the cross, and His mystery. Think about these things! **We can only worship God in reverence, adoration, and ardor through understanding Him by the renewal of our minds by the Holy Spirit and scripture.**

When we love our God with all our heart and soul (Matt 22:37-39); we are also loving God with our minds. To love God properly requires an understanding of our self-centerness and sin as well as our debased mind. (Rom 1:18, 28) Our inherited human nature does not love God but is in hostility to Him. We can't love God without being born again or regenerated. It is the work of the Holy Spirit that transforms the natural unregenerated man into a true worshiper. True worshipers understand their sin and God's grace. We bow before Him in humility and contrition as unworthy sinners not deserving His love but saved only by Grace, not our works. (Eph 2)

It is most helpful to examine the Hebrew and Greek etymology of the words for worship. (Heb. *shachah*; Gk. *proskynéō*; Anglo-Saxon *weorthscipe* "worthship") or to pay homage to or, literally, to ascribe worth to some person or thing, hence, worship embraces the whole of the reverent life, including piety, submission, obedience, and liturgy. In Hebrew worship (Ps. 99:5) *shachah* (shah-*chah*); *means* to bow, to stoop; to bow down before someone as an act of submission or reverence; to worship; to fall or bow down when paying homage to God. The primary meaning is "to make oneself low." In the present reference, *shachah* is used in contrast to exaltation: exalt the Lord (lift Him up high) and worship (bow yourselves down low before Him) at the place of His feet. Also, the Greek word *proskuneo* (pros-koo-*neh*-oh); from *pros*, "toward," and *kuneo*, "to kiss;" means to prostrate oneself, bow down, do obeisance, show reverence, do homage, worship, adore. (Rev. 4:10) In the New Testament the word especially denotes homage rendered to God and the ascended Christ. All believers have a one-dimensional worship, to the only Lord and Savior Jesus Christ. We do not worship angels, saints, shrines, relics, or religious or political personages.

To the ancient Jew the liturgical calendar consisted primarily in the celebration of three major agricultural feasts: Passover and the Feast' of Unleavened Bread, Weeks or Pentecost, and the Feast of Booths or Ingathering. Worship was rich and diverse, and included instrumental and vocal music, solos, anthems, shouting or chanting, dancing, processions with instruments, incense, offerings, tithes, a form of preaching, oracles, recitation of sacred stories, petitions, prayers, vows, vigils, promises, creeds, confessions, sacred meals, washings, and even periods of silence.[37]

Early Christians drew liturgical practices primarily from Jewish sources, though there was some Gentile influence, to form worship as rich and multifaceted as its Old Testament counterpart. Included were public prayer, reading of psalms, Scripture, teaching and preaching, and private devotions. As many of the early Christian followers and leaders were Jewish, early Christian worship draws heavily from its Jewish roots. At first Christians worshipped in the temple, and to that added communal meals (Acts 2:46; 5:42). Soon, however, a rift developed between Jews and Christians, with Christians being denied access to the temple. Christians quickly developed independence from the temple and synagogue.

Despite heavy borrowing from Jewish worship practices, Christian liturgy underwent a radical transformation. Most importantly, the sacrificial practices of the temple were abandoned since Christians regarded such as having been fulfilled in the cross (cf. Hebrews). In part an extension and reinterpretation of the Passover meal, the Lord's Supper both recalled and, in a sense, enacted symbolically Christ's death upon the cross (1 Cor. 11:26). Such elements as Scripture reading, preaching, psalmody, and public prayer were also taken over from Jewish worship.

The New Testament does not instruct worshipers in a specific procedure to follow in their gatherings, but several elements appear to be component parts of the worship in the early church: seem to show a combination of participation by the leaders and laity alike. (Psalms, 1 Corinthians 14:26, Philippians 2:6-11, 1 Timothy 4:13, and 2 Timothy 3:10-4:5, Rev 15:3-4)

---

37   Myers, A. C. (1987). In *The Eerdmans Bible dictionary* (p. 1067). Grand Rapids, MI: Eerdmans.

Of course, other basics are revealed for corporate worship:

1. 1. Prayer had a leading place in Christian worship. The letters of Paul regularly open with references to prayer for fellow Christians who are instructed to "pray without ceasing" (1 Thess. 5:17).

2. 2. Praise, either by individuals or in hymns sung in common, reflects the frequent use of psalms in the synagogue. Also, possible fragments of Christian hymns appear scattered through the New Testament (Acts 4:24-30; Eph. 5:14; 1 Tim. 3:16; Rev. 4:8; 5:9-10, 12-13).

3. 3. Lessons from the Bible to be read, taught, and studied were another part of the worship procedure of the New Testament church. Remember, the Old Testament (LXX or Septuagint) was their "Bible" at first, and emphasis was probably given to the messianic prophecies which had been fulfilled in Jesus Christ, as well as practical lessons from the rest of the Scriptures (1 Cor. 10:6; Rom. 15:4). Jesus' teachings also received a primary place.

4. 4. The Lord's Table was practiced (1 Cor. 11:10-34); prophecies and other gifts of the Spirit in manifestation (1 Cor. 12, 14); contributions were received (1 Cor. 16:2); and the sick were prayed for (James 5:13-16).

Despite difficulties posed by the nature of the apocalyptic genre, the book of Revelation provides some insight into the nature of Christian worship toward the close of the first century. There appear to be liturgical influences upon the visions (esp. Rev chaps. 4–6). Some elements of worship may bear similarity to practices recorded by Justin Martyr (100-165 AD) in the second century; combined with evidence preserved in a letter from Pliny, governor of Bithynia, to

Trajan (113 AD), a clearer picture begins to emerge. Christians of Bithynia appear to have observed two separate services, one before dawn that included antiphonal hymnody and a recitation of the Decalog. The early service may have arisen in response to persecution or to accommodate the slaves who made up a large portion of early Christians. Later in the day a communal meal was held (later abandoned when outlawed by the *Lex Julia* or Roman common law). It remains unclear as to whether this meal was the Lord's Supper or simply the communal meal or agape meal. By the time of Justin Martyr, the service opened with the reading of Scripture (both the Septuagint and the Gospels), perhaps involving the use of a lectionary. Following the readings, the bishop delivered a sermon seated in his chair (a customary manner of ancient teaching). The congregation then rose for prayers, praying in the Jewish manner with outstretched arms, perhaps using a litany that included the deacons, with individual requests and a concluding collect by the bishop. Such prayers were intoned or chanted (spoken prayer developed in medieval times) and concluded with the affirmation of ("Amen", which means it is truth) by the congregation expressing their assurance in fulfillment (2 Cor. 1:20). The worshippers shared the kiss of peace, followed by the offertory, which consisted in food rather than money (perhaps developed from the practice of the communal meal); the deacons then arranged these elements on the table before the bishop, who offered a prayer of consecration. The service concluded with communion, portions of which were later taken to those absent because of sickness or other reasons. No benediction was offered. There were no church buildings to support until late in the 2nd century AD and few survived Roman persecution until Constantine in the 4th century AD. Tithes were largely directly distributed to the needy in the form of food.

The laying on of hands was also part of the ordination rite during the church service that the early Church continued from Judaism, whereby select persons were installed in various offices and duties

(Acts 6:1–6; cf. Num. 11:24–25). Early practices also included healings and exorcisms through various means of prayer (e.g., Mark 9:29), anointing (Jas. 5:14), baptisms, and laying on of hands (Mark 16:18; Acts 9:17), prophesy and tongues (I Cor:13-25) The Church also practiced discipline and, in the case of recalcitrant offenders, ex-communication (Matt. 18:17; 1 Cor. 5:3–6).[38]

Both the Old and New Testament share the notion that acceptable worship involves more than simply prescribed rites, namely a correct attitude and concomitant moral rectitude. The prophet Samuel rebukes King Saul with the harsh words: *"Behold, to obey is better than sacrifice ..."* (1 Sam. 15:22). Among the wisdom sayings one finds: *"The sacrifice of the wicked is an abomination to the Lord, but the prayer of the upright is his delight"* (Prov. 15:8, 21:3, 27; Mal. 2:10.). Ps. 2 proclaims, *"Serve the Lord with fear (reverence)"* (Ps 2: 11), and throughout Ps. 51 the psalmist offers eloquent voice to the notion of appropriate living and attitude: ***"The sacrifice acceptable to God is a broken spirit; a broken and contrite heart, O God, thou wilt not despise"*** (Ps 51:17; cf. 1 Sam. 15:22). Such an attitude is echoed in the New Testament in the forceful words of Jesus ***"God is spirit, and those who worship him must worship in spirit and truth"*** (**John 4:24**).

This rejection of Israel's worship by God in the seventh and eighth centuries BC was echoed by Jesus in his dealings with the Pharisees of his own day. Indeed, he quoted Isaiah 29:13 as a 'prophecy', by which he meant not simply that this verse foretold the hypocrisy of the Pharisees, but that it expressed a divinely revealed principle which was equally applicable to them.

> "You hypocrites! Isaiah (29:13) was right when he prophesied about you": said Jesus in Matthew 15:8.
> 'These people honour me with their lips,
> but their hearts are far from me.
> They worship me in vain.
> their teaching as doctrines the commandments of men."

38   Myers, A. C. (1987). In *The Eerdmans Bible dictionary* (pp. 1068–1069). Grand Rapids, MI: Eerdmans.

There are two assumptions here—assumptions shared by Christ and the Pharisees—which those taking part in the modern debates about worship are likely to have in common too.

The first is that worship is a *good* thing. Quoting Isaiah, Jesus said, 'These people *honour me*' God's problem with the inhabitants of Jerusalem, and Christ's problem with the Pharisees, was not that **they honoured God but that they did so in the wrong way. Everyone should honour God by offering to him the honour and glory which he deserves. Indeed, this is the meaning of worship. The very word implies it. For 'worship' is an abbreviation of 'worthship'.** It indicates that God is worthy to be praised, that worship is the appropriate recognition of his absolute worth. In worship we come to him—as creatures to honour him as our Creator, as sinners to honour him as our Saviour, as children to honour him as our Father, as servants to honour him as our Lord. Worship is not, therefore, an optional activity which may be added to life's timetable by those who enjoy that sort of thing and ignored by those who do not. It is a daily obligation because it is the acknowledgment of plain facts that we serve a God that deserves daily worship.

The second assumption which underlies the words of Isaiah and of Christ is that worship is something to be done with others in public: '*These people* honour me …' There is of course a place for private worship, the adoration of God by individuals on their own (e.g., '*when you pray, go into your room, close the door and pray to your Father, who is unseen*' Matt 6:6). But the worship referred to here is public, the worship of God by His people when they meet together. Jesus took it for granted that they would assemble for public worship. It is safe to say that he never had in mind just private or 'religionless or worthshipless Christianity'.

In this further controversy with the Pharisees, then, Jesus is not finding fault with the practice of worship itself, nor with its public and corporate nature. What he is against is its external quality, its formalism, its hypocrisy: 'You *hypocrites*! Isaiah was right when he prophesied about you …' **They were not true worshippers at all, but merely actors**. The honour they gave to God was all pretence rather than reality. And the essential distinction here is between the worship of the lips and of the heart. Worship is expressed through the lips, but it does not consist just of words. What is acceptable to God is worship with the heart rather than just the head and the hands, so the **worship acceptable to God is lived out by humble adoring devotion of the heart accompanied by continued repentance, confession, and obedience, rather than what is said to him by the lips. Pharisaic worship is lip-worship; Christian worship is heart-worship.**

Worship is also about giving to others because God has given so much to us, most of all His Son, who in turn gave everything for us. God doesn't want to be second to that which we worship more than Him, such as our wealth, heath, social position, happiness, etc.! He demands to be first as Jesus taught the rich young ruler. (Matt 19:16-21) After all, all that we have belongs to Him anyway. We are only stewards of His wealth. We, including all our wealth, are called to be a living sacrifice to our Lord.

"From the days of your fathers you have turned aside from my statutes and have not kept them. Return to me, and I will return to you, says the LORD *of hosts. But you say, 'How shall we return?' Will man rob God? Yet you are robbing me. But you say, 'How have we robbed you?' In your tithes and contributions. You are cursed with a curse, for you are robbing me, the whole nation of you. Bring the full tithe into the storehouse, that there may be food in my house. And thereby put me to the test, says the* LORD *of hosts, if I will not open the windows of heaven for you and pour down for you a blessing until there is no more need. I will rebuke the devourer for you, so that it will not destroy the fruits of your soil, and your vine in the field shall not fail to bear, says the* LORD *of hosts. Then all nations will call you blessed, for you will be a land of delight, says the* LORD *of hosts".* (Malachi 3:7-12)

What, then, are the characteristics of true heart-worship?

The first characteristic of heart-worship is that it is based on reason; the mind is fully involved in it. In the Bible the 'heart' is not simply equivalent to the emotions, as it usually is in today's language. In biblical thought the 'heart' is the centre of the human personality and is often used in a way that emphasizes the intellect more than the emotions. Thus, the plea in Proverbs 23:26, '*My son, give me your heart,*' has often been understood as an appeal for our love and devotion. But it is a command to listen, to pay attention, to sit up and take notice, an appeal more for concentration than for consecration. This is particularly clear in the book of Proverbs, where we read that the heart should pay attention to 'understanding' and be 'wise' and not disparage knowledge of the Holy One for He will be "**refreshment**" from the Hebrew word that means "tranquility." It implies the absence of strife, war, or trouble on the one hand, and worry or anxiety on the other. It may also imply the absence of a pressing obligation, or again, of some disturbing element that mars a relationship between individuals[39]. In worship we find the peace of God.

> Then they will call upon me, but I will not answer;
> they will seek me diligently but will not find me.
>> Because they hated knowledge
> and did not choose the fear of the LORD,
>> would have none of my counsel
> and despised all my reproof,
>> therefore, they shall eat the fruit of their way,
> and have their fill of their own devices. Prov 1:28-31

---

39   Austel, H. J. (1999). 2453 שָׁקַט. R. L. Harris, G. L. Archer Jr., & B. K. Waltke (Eds.), *Theological Wordbook of the Old Testament* (electronic ed., p. 953). Chicago: Moody Press.

BUT for those are repentant and humble.

> Trust in the Lord with all your heart,
>
> and do not lean on your own understanding.
>
> In all your ways acknowledge him,
>
> and he will make straight your paths.
>
> Be not wise in your own eyes.
>
> fear the LORD AND turn away from evil.
>
> It will be healing to your flesh
>
> and **refreshment** to your bones. (Prov 3:5-8)

Passages in which the 'heart' means above all the 'mind' may be quoted from the New Testament too. Take, for example, the conversion of Lydia, the seller of purple goods who traded in Philippi. Here is how Luke describes her: 'The Lord opened her heart to respond to Paul's message.' In other words, he opened her understanding to grasp and receive the gospel. Of course, the heart includes more than the mind. But it does not include less. So, heart-worship is rational worship. To love God with all our heart involves loving him with all our mind as well.

This leads us to state the first basic principle of Christian worship, which is that we must know God before we can worship him. It is true that Paul found an altar in Athens which was inscribed 'to an unknown God'. But he recognized it as a contradiction in terms. It is impossible to worship an unknown god, since, if he is himself unknown, the kind of worship he desires will be equally unknown. That is why Paul told the philosophers that they were *'ignorant of the very thing you worship—and this is what I am going to proclaim to you."* (Acts 17:22-30)

The same principle emerges clearly in Christ's conversation with the Samaritan woman at Jacob's well. (John 4:7-26) For more than 700 years the Samaritans and the Jews had developed their religious life independently. This separate development had a political origin, in that the Samaritans were a mixed race descended partly from Israelites and partly from Mesopotamian foreigners who had been settled there in the eighth century BC. But spiritually it was due to their reliance on different Scriptures. The Samaritans accepted the Pentateuch but rejected the later revelation which God had given of himself through the prophets. Having the law without the prophets, the Samaritans' knowledge of God was incomplete. This is what Jesus referred to in his conversation with the woman by the well: 'You Samaritans worship what you do not know; we [the Jews] worship what we do know, for salvation [the promised Messiah] is from the Jews.' Jesus continued: 'Yet a time is coming and has now come when the true worshippers will worship the Father in … truth.' So 'true worship' is 'worship in truth'. (John 4:22-24) It is worship of God the Father as he has been fully and finally revealed in Jesus Christ, His Son through the word of God by the Holy Spirit. "And behold, I am coming soon. Blessed is the one who keeps the words of the prophecy of this book." (Rev 22:7)

If the worshippers whom God is seeking are those who draw near to him with their heart and worship him in truth, we must be careful, when we go to church, not to leave our minds behind. We must beware of all forms of worship, both communal and personal, which appeal to the senses and the emotions, but which do not fully engage the mind, especially those which even claim that they are superior forms of worship. **No, the only worship that pleases God is heart-worship, and heart-worship is worship based on reason. It is the worship of a rational God who has made us rational beings and given us a rational revelation so that we may worship him rationally 'with all our mind'.**

This is why the only perfect worship which is offered to God is in heaven, not on earth, because it is only in heaven that God is clearly seen and fully known: 'His servants will serve him, they will see his face, and **His Name** will be on their foreheads.' Rev 14:1, 22:4. His Name is the Branch (Zech. 3:8, 6:12, Isa 11:1), Shepherd of the flock (Zech 11:4), the Lord our righteousness (Jer. 23:6), Wonderful Counsellor, Mighty God, Everlasting Father, Prince of Peace (Isa. 9:6), His name is the Word of God (Rev. 19:13), King of Kings and

Lord of Lords (Rev 19:16), "I am the root and the descendant of David, the bright Morning Star." (Rev 22:16)

Because here on earth we see Him only as a vague reflection as in a smoky mirror (1 Cor 13:12), even our best worship is bound to be imperfect. But when we see him face to face in heaven, we shall be able to worship Him as He is. As the hymn writer of "Amazing Grace," John Newton put it:

> Weak is the effort of my heart,
> And cold my warmest thought,
> But when I see Thee as Thou art,
> I'll praise Thee as I ought.[40]

Worship must be sincere and requires honesty, confession, humility, repentance, and an open heart to receive correction before God. In Hebrew one of the common words for praise is the Hebrew word *Yada* which means both praise, confession, and openness demonstrated by raising our arms with an open hand as an invitation of exposure of our inner man. We are to be open handed, meaning our lives are to be exposed before God as He sees our unclean hands. We can't worship God with our hands in our pockets. This open-handed confession of our sinfulness is what it means to worship God in Truth!

To worship God properly we must understand the central claim of the gospel is that all truth is found in God through His word. The word truth (אֱמֶת, *emeth*; αιεθήλὰ, *alētheia*), means that factuality, faithfulness, firmness, reality, and reliability are inherent in understanding *truth*. The English. *amēn*, is the transliteration of Heb. *nemā᾽*, and *sōhtēla* which is the Greek translation of the same word (both most often rendered "truly" or "verily"), are frequently used in the New Testament, particularly to introduce words of Jesus

---

40   Stott, J. (2013). <u>"But I Say to You …": Christ the Controversialist</u> (pp. 158–159). Nottingham: Inter-Varsity Press.

(e.g., Luke 21:3; John 3:3). This introduction emphasizes that the statement which follows is beyond doubt. Similar affirmations are made to characterize the Christian witness as "true" (John 5:31–32; 8:13–14; Titus 1:13). The gospel itself is the preaching of truth (Gal. 2:5; Col. 1:5–6; 2 Tim. 2:15; Jas. 1:18), which must therefore be obeyed (Gal. 5:7).

In the Gospel of John, the concept of truth is more prominent than in the other Gospels. John uses 'truth' to refer to genuineness, the opposite of falsehood, but also to the revelation of God in Jesus Christ, which can be understood only by disciples through faith. It is God who reveals Christ to an individual, and Christ is both the gospel message itself and the messenger. In the prologue to John's Gospel Christ is said to be 'full of grace and truth' (John 1:17) Jesus is the true vine (John 15:1), Jesus is the true light (John 1:9), Jesus is the truth (John 14:6.) The word generally used means 'constant, permanent, faithful, reliable.' God above all is true, that is, real and reliable (Isa. 65:16; Jer. 10:10); people are to seek God's truth (Ps. 25:5; 51:6; 86:11). Christ shares in God's truth, He is himself full of grace and truth (John 1:14, 17). Indeed, He is 'the way, and the truth, and the life' (John 14:6); He is the true light and the true vine (John 1:9; 15:1). Christ sends the Counselor or Holy Spirit as the Spirit of truth (John 15:26). The believer is guided into truth (John 16:13), to worship God in spirit and truth. (John 4:23–24) Obeying Christ's word enables one to know the truth and so be free (John 8:32). This Christian freedom is not due to possession of correct knowledge but rather comes from a relationship with that which is truly real, namely, God Himself. Jesus is "the true light" (John 1:9), "the true bread" (6:32), and "the true vine" (15:1), i.e., the source of the life that comes through God's redemption of mankind. For John, Jesus is more than the proclaimer of truth, though he is that (John 8:40; 18:37) but **He is the truth itself** (John 1:14, 17; 14:6). Pilate's question "What is truth?" (John 18:38), which he probably conceived in abstract terms, had an ironic ring because Pilate was facing truth itself!

God's law is to be delighted in (Ps. 119:142–143), but at the same time it is a lamp and a light (Ps 119:105), it shows the true way in practice. God may be relied upon because of his faithfulness, and his word is truth in that it is real and has integrity: his sayings are consistent with his doings.

For the Apostle John, discussing the triune God, the Father, is the truth. Jesus teaches only what the Father has given to him (John 3:33; 8:40; 18:37), and the Father is true (John 7:28; 8:26; 17:3). Jesus said to Philip: "Whoever has seen me has seen the Father. How can you say, 'Show us the Father'? Do you not believe that I am in the Father and the Father is in me?" (John 14:9-10) To understand His truth, it is necessary to have faith in Jesus as the one who has come down from heaven and is the way to God (John 14:6). To worship the Father in truth, it is necessary to perceive Him as He is revealed in His son Jesus Christ (John 4:23–24). To perceive truth as opposed to falsehood, light as opposed to darkness, one need only look to God the Father as revealed though the Son and His Word by the Holy Spirit. (John 5:24; 8:31–32, 42–47).

"And around the throne, on each side of the throne, are four living creatures, full of eyes in front and behind: [7] *the first living creature like a lion, the second living creature like an ox, the third living creature with the face of a man, and the fourth living creature like an eagle in flight. And the four living creatures, each of them with six wings, are full of eyes all around and within, and day and night they never cease to say,*

"Holy, holy, holy, is the Lord God Almighty,
who was and is and is to come!"

And whenever the living creatures give glory and honor and thanks to him who is seated on the throne, who lives forever and ever, the twenty-four elders fall down before him who is seated on the throne and worship him who lives forever and ever. They cast their crowns before the throne, saying,

"Worthy are you, our Lord and God,
to receive glory and honor and power,
for you created all things,
and by your will they existed and were created." (Rev 4:6-11)

"Worthy are you to take the scroll and to open its seals,
for you were slain, and by your blood you ransomed people for God
from every tribe and language and people and nation,
and you have made them a kingdom and priests to our God,
and they shall reign on the earth."

Then I looked, and I heard around the throne and the living creatures
and the elders the voice   of many angels, numbering myriads of
myriads and thousands of thousands, saying with a loud voice,

"Worthy is the Lamb who was slain,
to receive power and wealth and wisdom and might
and honor and glory and blessing!"

And I heard every creature in heaven and on earth and under the
earth and in the sea, and all that is in them, saying,

"To him who sits on the throne and to the Lamb
be blessing and honor and glory and might forever and ever!"

And the four living creatures said, "Amen!" and **the elders fell down**
and worshiped.
(Rev 5:9-14)

What is worship about? It is about Jesus and giving Him the
proper honor and glory as deserved by His humble unworthy
servants with thanksgiving. When we forget about ourselves,
flow with the Holy Spirit, and focus our thoughts on Him alone,
confess our sins, obey Him, and serve others. That is worship.
Worship may use a combination of melody and doctrine in
communal worship or silence in personal worship. A spirit of
praise and thanksgiving is meant to fill our hearts continually

that we might: "*Rejoice always, pray without ceasing, give thanks in all circumstances; for this is the will of God in Christ Jesus for you.*" (I Thes 5:16-18)

" ***So, worship is all about Him: giving Him praise, giving Him our hearts, listening to Him speak to us through the Scriptures, singing to Him. So, that vertical dimension prioritizes what worship is essentially about.***

"*So, we don't make it up, but God has given us certain principles—rules, if you like. This is how you worship God. You, you read Scripture, you interpret Scripture in preaching, you sing Scripture, you pray Scripture back to Him. You see Scripture visibly in the sacraments.* "Dr Derek Thomas Table talk Magazine November 2023

Chapter 27

The Fear of God

This last chapter is largely copied from my last chapter of my book, *The Merchandising of the Holy in the American Church,* on "The Fear of God." **Many "almost Christians' ' trust they have reached the Promised Land or have entered the Kingdom of God and are excited about God but never learn His ways. They are more interested in obtaining the "milk and honey" of the Promised Land than the Lord of the land. They assume that once they have entered the race, they will finish it.** They seem unaware of the many who trip and fall and never complete the race. Some churches teach, "Once saved always saved," or eternal security. I certainly believe that those chosen by God before the foundation of this world to be His children will be saved, and none will be lost. There will be perseverance of the saints chosen by God (Eph 1:4–14) however, many of us think we are saved, and we are not! In the United States of America, surveys have suggested that less than one out of ten people claiming to be born-again Christians actually have a living, saving faith. God will never lose any of His children (John 6:37; 10:27–30), but there are a great many who have false assurance and will be lost. Each believer needs to be periodically challenged to reevaluate his relationship with God. **Pastors, led by compassion, often try to encourage believers with assurance of salvation while the great men of the past such as George Whitfield and Jonathan Edwards emphasized mankind's self-deception and lack of true repentance and regeneration. These men emphasized the wrath of God and certainty of eternal damnation in hell, a**

message heard too infrequently today. We are all human and hence very vulnerable to self-deception. *"The heart is deceitful above all things and desperately wicked. Who can know it?"* (Jeremiah 17:9). It is the trials, troubles, and tribulations of life that help us see our true position with our Lord.

I often think of Apostle John's disappointment with members of his own church when he said, *"They went out from us, but they were not of us; for if they had been of us, they would have continued with us. But they went out, that it might become plain that they all are not of us"* (I John 2:19). Even the Apostle John with all of his discernment and anointing had church members who were presumably saved or converted until there was a moment of accountability, and they left the fellowship.

There are many false finishes along the racecourse of life. When man gets comfortable and has his needs met, he thinks he has God's approval. He then gets comfortable with his position with God and puts his feet up and rests from the race and has lost the fear of the Lord. What do I mean by "they have lost their fear of God?" Those who fear God know Him as their loving Father, who also is to be feared and who will discipline His children. Luther called this "filial fear" or the type of fear a son has for his father. This is the fear of discipline and not the fear of losing one's salvation. If you are not disciplined, it is because you are not His child. The fear of the Lord is not only about fearing His chastisement and rebuke; it mainly is about disappointing our loving Father; but not fearing His rejection of us as being a child of God.

> *"If you endure chastening, God deals with you as with sons; for what son is there whom a father does not chasten? But if you are without chastening, of which all have become partakers, then you are illegitimate and not sons. Furthermore, we have had human fathers who corrected us, and we paid them respect. Shall we not much more*

readily be in subjection to the Father of spirits and live? For they indeed for a few days chastened us as seemed best to them, but He for our profit, that we may be partakers of His holiness. Now no chastening seems to be joyful for the present, but painful; nevertheless, afterward it yields the peaceable fruit of righteousness to those who have been trained by it." (Hebrews 12:5–11)

With all his wisdom, Solomon repeatedly speaks of the fear of the Lord in the Book of Proverbs beginning with:

"The fear of the Lord *is the beginning of knowledge."* (Proverbs 1:7)

"Then they will call upon me, but I will not answer; they will seek me diligently but will not find me. Because they hated knowledge and did not choose the fear of the Lord*".* (Proverbs 1:28)

"Then you will understand the fear of the Lord *and find the knowledge of God."* (Proverbs 2:5)

"Be not wise in your own eyes; fear the LORD *AND turn away from evil. It will be healing to your flesh and refreshment to your bones".* (Proverbs 3:7)

"The fear of the Lord *is hatred of evil. Pride and arrogance and the way of evil and perverted speech I hate."* (Proverbs 8:13)

If the fear of the Lord is to hate evil, then this fear must lead to personal holiness and hatred of all those things that are unclean before the Lord.

"The fear of the Lord *is the beginning of wisdom, and the knowledge of the Holy One is insight."* (Proverbs 9:10)

"The fear of the Lord *prolongs life, but the years of the wicked will be short."* (Proverbs 10:27)

"In the fear of the LORD one has strong confidence, and his children will have a refuge. The fear of the LORD is a fountain of life, that one may turn away from the snares of death". (Proverbs 14:26–27)

"Better is a little with the fear of the LORD than great treasure and trouble with it. "(Proverbs 15:16)

"The fear of the LORD is instruction in wisdom, and humility comes before honor." (Proverbs 15:33)

"The fear of the LORD leads to life and whoever has it rests satisfied,

he will not be visited by harm." (Proverbs 19:23)

"The reward for humility and fear of the LORD is riches and honor and life."(Proverbs 22:4)

"My son, fear the LORD and the king, and do not join with those who do otherwise, for disaster will arise suddenly from them, and who knows the ruin that will come from them both?"(Proverbs 24:21)

"Blessed is the one who fears the LORD always, but whoever hardens his heart will fall into calamity (Proverbs 28:14)

"Charm is deceitful, and beauty is vain, but a woman who fears the LORD is to be praised."(Proverbs 31:30)

Finally, at the end of the Book of Ecclesiastes, Solomon concludes his teaching and advises with: *"The end of the matter; all has been heard.* **Fear God** *and keep his commandments, for this is the whole duty of man. For God will bring every deed into judgment, with every secret thing, whether good or evil"* (Eccl 12:13).

The Hebrew word *yare* or fear is translated as "fear" 188 times, "afraid" 78 times, "terrible" 23 times, "terrible thing" 6 times, "dreadful" 5 times, "reverence" 3 times, "fearful" 2 times, and the word *fear* is used for a total of 314 times in the King James Version. This can be a term of reverence, an emotional reaction of terror, or a dread of God's vengeance. The twentieth-century church usually downplays the word *fear* and substitutes the word *reverence*, which is a much weaker word. People revere or reverence their favorite sports figure or movie star. **The concept of actually being afraid of God conflicts with the modern understanding of God as a loving, nonjudgmental, feminine mother God. God is very masculine. He tells us that He is a jealous God, full of wrath against the wicked. He is coming to judge and destroy this world by fire. The wicked face eternal judgment in hell. He is to be feared!**

The fear of the Lord is to hate evil, yet modern man can't understand how a loving God can hate evil (Prov 8:13). This is because we don't understand God's holiness. A Holy God hates or loathes that which is unholy. Light hates darkness and the two can coexist with each other. We think that God doesn't see our own personal sin and the evil of this fallen world. If we are to have fellowship with God, we must learn to see the world as He sees it. We are not to hate our fellow man but to hate the sin that entraps us all and the corruption in this world as God does.

It was the fear of the Lord that caused men to cry out at Pentecost: *"Men and brethren what shall we do?"* (Acts 2:37) and the Philippian jailer to cry: *"Sirs, what must I do to be saved?"* (Acts 16:30).

I can remember misbehaving as a small boy and my mother warning me that if I didn't stop misbehaving, she would tell my father when he got home about my bad behavior. I loved and respected my father and didn't want to disappoint him, so I was careful not to offend him and I did what was necessary to please him. My father never abused me but was a large man who would rarely exhibit righteous anger. To me, the whole world shook when he was angry. I had more than reverence for my father. I had genuine fear, particularly when I deserved a spanking. I was just like Adam, who had intimate fellowship with Father God. After Adam sinned in the Garden of Eden, he said, "*I was afraid, because I was naked, and I hid myself*" (Gen 3:10). If there was any man created by God who had a very intimate love relationship with God, it was Adam. **Yet Adam feared God because he knew that his loving Father was also a God of justice and holiness, who demanded righteousness. Adam knew that God would exact severe consequences for disobedience to His spoken word.**

I knew that my earthly father loved me, as God loved Adam, and God could never reject Adam or me as his son, but most of all I was afraid of losing my earthly and heavenly Father's respect. If we love God, we want to please Him and not offend Him, therefore we try our best to obey Him like we would our earthly father. **The fear of God is being afraid of displeasing our heavenly Father because we love Him. It is also about knowing that sin has painful consequences.** Our Father God mourns at our sin, and our sin hurts our righteous Father. Jesus wept over Jerusalem. God also should be feared because He is holy and righteous and will punish sin because He is a righteous, good, and holy Father. We should tremble at His Word and the thought of hurting our Father. In this life, the believer will get away with no sin. All sin will be judged and punished in this life if we are true disciples that we might enjoy the fruit of our righteousness through Christ in the heavenly life to come. The unrighteous may escape judgment in this life but will face the wrath of God after death (Psalm 73). God is the perfect Father who will discipline and train us like sons that we might be partakers of His Holiness.

"You have not yet resisted to bloodshed, striving against sin. And you have forgotten the exhortation, which speaks to you as to sons: "My son, do not despise the chastening of the LORD, Nor be discouraged when you are rebuked by Him; For whom the LORD loves He chastens, and scourges every son whom He receives. "If you endure chastening,

God deals with you as with sons; for what son is there whom a father does not chasten? **But if you are without chastening, of which all have become partakers, then you are illegitimate and not sons.** *Furthermore, we have had human fathers who corrected us, and we paid them respect. Shall we not much more readily be in subjection to the Father of spirits and live? For they indeed for a few days chastened us as seemed best to them, but He for our profit, that we may be partakers of His holiness. Now no chastening seems to be joyful for the present, but painful; nevertheless, afterward it yields the peaceable fruit of righteousness to those who have been trained by it.* " (Hebrews 12:4–11)

> **Vengeance is mine; I will repay." And again, "*The Lord will judge his people.*" It is a fearful thing to fall into the hands of the living God.** (Hebrews 10:30–31)

> *"Let us offer to God acceptable worship, with reverence and awe (or fear), for our God is a consuming fire.* (Hebrews 12:28–29)

Notice that reverence and fear or awe are separated and not inclusive. Some define the fear of the Lord as only reverence and do not include the word *fear* because they do not have a holy dread, awe, or fear of God. If we ignore the truth of God's wrath, we compromise the gospel message. If God is not full of just wrath, then there is no need for the cross, nor fear of the judgment to come or fear of eternal punishment. ***The Holy Wrath of a Just God is central to the gospel message.*** The holy wrath of a just God is a missing message in the church today. Jesus came to satisfy the wrath of God. It is His righteousness that protects us from the eternal punishment that we all deserve. **If God is a loving God and not a God of wrath, then there is no reason to fear or obey God. Jesus would have died in vain, if man is basically good and loved by God, and man will not face eternal punishment!** The Gospel begins with the fall of man and God's wrath at man's sin. God sent his son to be the propitiation for our sin since no man is righteous. *"Flesh and blood cannot inherit the kingdom of God; nor does corruption inherit incorruption"* (1 Cor 15:50). Jesus fulfilled God's demand for perfect righteousness and thus satisfied His wrath. *"The first Adam became a living being and the second Adam a life-giving spirit"* (1 Cor 15:45). Jesus was crucified and arose triumphantly on the third day, having purchased for His elect resurrection life now and forever. *"Jesus will reign until He has put all enemies under His foot. The last enemy to be destroyed is death"* (1 Cor 15: 20–26, 45, 50).

Paul concludes 1 Corinthians 15 with words of encouragement. **If we fear God, we need not fear death.**

> *"For the trumpet will sound, and the dead will be raised imperishable, and we shall be changed. For this perishable body must put on the imperishable, and this mortal body must put on immortality. When the perishable puts on the imperishable, and the mortal puts on immortality, then shall come to pass the saying that is written: "Death is swallowed up in victory." "O death, where is your victory? O death, where is your sting?" The sting of death is sin, and the power of sin is the law. But thanks be to God, who gives us the victory through our Lord Jesus Christ. Therefore, my beloved brothers, be steadfast, immovable, always abounding in the work of the Lord, knowing that in the Lord your labor is not in vain."* (1 Cor 15:52–58)

The fear of God is a gift of God. Jeremiah 32:40 says, "I will put My fear in their hearts, that they shall not depart from me," and 32:39, "Then I will give them one heart and one way that they may fear me forever for the good of them and their children after them." It is one of God's treasures. Isaiah 33:6 says, "The fear of the Lord is His treasure." We need to all pray for more of that treasure—the holy fear of the Lord." "*But on this* *one I will look on him who is poor and of a contrite spirit, and who trembles at my word."*Verse 5 repeats the same admonition to give it more emphasis: "Hear the word of the Lord, *you who tremble at His word."* (Isaiah 66:2, 5)

> *"For the Lord spoke thus to me with his strong hand upon me and warned me not to walk in the way of this people, saying: "Do not call conspiracy all that this people call conspiracy, and do not fear what they fear, nor be in dread. But the Lord of hosts, Him you shall honor as holy. **Let Him be your fear and let Him be your dread**. And He will become a sanctuary and a stone of offense and a rock of stumbling to both houses of Israel, a trap and a snare to the inhabitants of Jerusalem. And many shall stumble on it. They shall fall and be broken; they shall be snared and taken."* (Isaiah 8:11–15)

We live in a time of great fear about the future, and there is much talk about various conspiracy plans among world leaders. God is in control, and we are not to live in fear of what man can do. *When we fear God, we will have perfect peace and not stumble.*

Finally, ***the fear of the Lord means obedience***! Abraham waited until he was 100 years old to have a son. His hope for future generations was upon Isaac, but suddenly God spoke to Abraham and said, *"Take your son, your only son Isaac, whom you love, and go to the land of Moriah, and offer him there as a burnt offering on one of the mountains of which I shall tell you"* (Gen 22:2). Abraham obeyed and told his servants, *"Stay here with the donkey; I and the boy will go over there and worship and come again to you"* (Gen 22:5). This is the first mention of worship in the Bible and is an example of obedience and the fear of God.

Abraham obeyed God and placed Isaac on the altar and was prepared to kill him when God spoke again and said:

*"Do not lay your hand on the boy or do anything to him, for now **I know that you fear God, seeing you have not withheld your son, your only son, from me** . . . and in your offspring shall **all the nations of the earth be blessed, because you have obeyed my voice**."* (Gen 22:12, 18)

There is no sin so prevalent, so insidious, and so deep as the sin of fearing people more than we fear God. (Kevin DeYoung)

The remarkable thing about God is that when you fear God, you fear nothing else, whereas if you do not fear God, you fear everything else. (Oswald Chambers)

The person who fears God seeks to live all of life to the glory of God . . . All the activities of life should be pursued with the aim of glorifying God. (Jerry Bridges)

We fear men so much because we fear God so little. (William Gurnal)

John Bunyan reminds us that: "Fear of God flows from …a sound impression that the word of God makes on our souls; for without any impression of the Word there's no fear of God. Hence, it is said that **God gave to Israel good laws, statues, and judgments, that they may learn them, and in learning them learn to fear the Lord their God**…. For us as to the extent a man drinks good doctrine into his soul, so to that extent he fears God. If he drinks in much, he fears him greatly; if he drinks in but a little, he fears Him but little; if he drinks it (the word) not at all; he fears Him not at all."

What we men often worship is that which is more important to us than God Himself, such as our dreams, homes, jobs, position, sports, physical fitness, health, wealth, loved ones, beauty, friendships, children, and so forth. To know God and to fear

Him is to obey Him and place everything we love on the altar. ***What we withhold from God is that which we worship and is what defines our relationship with God!*** Worship or *worship* is proportional to the value we place on God above everything else. The understanding of the Greek word for worship used in Romans 12:1 is λατρεία or (latreia) means "the service of worship and veneration," which Christians are to offer, consists in the fashioning of our inner lives and outward physical conduct in a way that plainly distinguishes us from the world and corresponds to the will of God.

"If any man loves the world, the love of the Father is not in him," (I John 2:15)

Our worship is also proportional to our obedience to Him (John 14:15). **True worship is extravagantly focused love and adoration, based on who He is and what He has done for us, displayed by extreme submission, humility, and obedience.**

> *"I appeal to you therefore, brothers, by the mercies of God, to present your bodies as a living sacrifice, holy and acceptable to God, which is your spiritual worship. Do not be conformed to this world but be transformed by the renewal of your mind, that by testing you may discern what is the will of God, what is good and acceptable and perfect."* (Rom 12:1–2)

It is this Fear of God that encourages us to press on through difficulties and not get complacent. **It is this desire to please and obey Him that will get us *Home at Last!***

Chapter 28
Christian Idolatry

Christians fall into idolatry frequently because of fear of coming world catastrophe, financial collapse, health problems, family problems, and many other issues. Some are embarrassed by sin and fear God's judgment. We subtlety trust man's institutions more than God such as government, political, religious, and military leaders. Americans place hope in the constitution and democratic process often more than hope in God. **Christian faith is, essentially, trust in the person and character of God ALONE!** We are to trust in God not men or demons which is idolatry. (Ps. 25:2; Ps. 31:6; Ps. 31:14; Ps. 55:23; Acts 27:25)

The Jews were God's Chosen People (Romans 11:1-36), the custodians of God's revelation (Rom 3:2), and the people through whom Christ came (Rom 9:5), they have a preference of privilege expressed historically in a chronological priority. As the Lord Jesus stated it, "Salvation is from the Jews" (John 4:22). **Idolatry is the worship of an Idol or image, being a picture, a statue, or a person in place of God. In Judaism, Christianity and Islam, idolatry means worshiping something that is not God. The worship of a material or person, political party, candidate for political office, or representation of any deity is forbidden**. The Old Testament bans the worship of any images or idols (Exod 20:4–6, 23; 34:17; Lev 19:4; 26:1; Deut 4:15–19, 25; 5:8–10). Despite repeated prohibitions against making idols, the people of Israel worshiped idols throughout the Old Testament. In the Old Testament, several words in Hebrew were used for idolatry: "statue" (צֶלֶם, *tselem*), "image" (סֵמֶל, *semel*), "molten image" (מַסֵּכָה, *massekhah*), and "likeness" (תַּבְנִית, *tavnith*) functioned as synonyms for "idol." The term *idolatry* comes from the <u>Ancient Greek</u> word *eidololatria*(εἰδωλολατρία), which itself is a compound of two words: *eidolon* (εἴδωλον"image/idol") and *latreia* (λατρεία «worship», related to λάτρις). The word *eidololatria* thus means "worship of idols", which in Latin appears first as *idololatria*, then in Vulgar Latin as *idolatria*, therefrom it appears in 12th century Old French as *idolatrie*, which for the first time in mid 13th century English appears as "idolatry".

<u>Moses</u> told the people not to make any image or statue since "you saw no form when the Lord spoke to you at Horeb out of the fire" (<u>Deut 4:15</u> NRSV). God was not seen; therefore, no idol could be made. Most ancient Near Eastern peoples were polytheists who believed the power of each deity waxed and waned. Such views meant that Jews living in this environment often thought other gods could help them when Yahweh could not. Isaiah would have none of this. When God told Israel to have no other gods before Him (Ex. 20:3), He meant that Israel owed Him **exclusive devotion and that He was the only God**, the Lord of all creation. Yahweh's ability to foresee the future reveals Him to be the one true God, and **if He is Lord of all, He alone can save (Isa. 44:6–8).**

A church may become idolatrous in a heartbeat because of fear of man, wars, and financial collapse. So, we cannot set our worship on autopilot. We cannot mistake the appearance of busy religiosity for worship in spirit and truth. We see in Exodus 32:5 that even the worshipers of the golden calf ascribed their worship to the covenant Lord Yahweh.

The parodies of idol making suggest that Israel banned idols because they were lifeless, human-made objects (<u>Pss 115:1–8</u>; <u>135:15–18</u>; <u>Jer 10:1–16</u>; <u>Isa 44:9–20</u>). These parodies focus on the human role in the idol making process: selecting the wood for the idol, carving the wood into the right shape or more recently cutting down a fir tree and decorating it to celebrate the pagan holiday of Christmas.

Jer 10:3-10

For the customs of the peoples are vanity. *A tree from the forest is cut down. and worked with an axe by the hands of a craftsman. They decorate it with silver and gold, they fasten it with hammer and nails so that it cannot move. Their idols are like scarecrows in a cucumber field, and they cannot speak; they have to be carried, for they cannot walk.*

Do not be afraid of them, for they cannot do evil, neither is it in them to do good." There is none like you, O LORD; you are great, and your name is great in might.

Who would not fear you, O King of the nations? For this is your due; for among all the wise ones of the nations and in all their kingdoms there is none like you. They are both stupid and foolish. The instruction of idols is but wood! Beaten silver is brought from Tarshish, and gold from Uphaz. They are the work of the craftsman and of the hands of the goldsmith. Their clothing is violet and purple; they are all the work of skilled men.

But the LORD is the true God; he is the living God and the everlasting King.

At his wrath the earth quakes, and the nations cannot endure his indignation.

Ex 20:3–6

"You shall have no other gods before me. *"You shall not make for yourself a carved image, or any likeness of anything that is in heaven above, or that is in the earth beneath, or that is in the water under the earth. You shall not bow down to them or serve them, for I the Lord your God…*

Judges 17:5–6

And the man Micah had a shrine, and he made an ephod and household gods, and ordained one of his sons, who became his priest. ***In those days there was no king in Israel. Everyone did what was right in his own eyes.*** When God is not worshiped in truth idolatry and false worship follow. In the post-Christian Western World paganism, rebellion, sexual sin, ungodliness, and unrighteousness have replaced God's law. (Romans 1:18-32)

Ps 115:4–8

Their idols are silver and gold, the work of human hands. They have mouths, but do not speak; eyes, but do not see. They have ears, but do not hear; noses, but do not smell. They have hands, but do not feel; feet, but do not walk; and they do not make a sound in their...

Acts 17:24–29

The God who made the world and everything in it, being Lord of heaven and earth, does not live in temples made by man, nor is he served by human hands, as though he needed anything, since he himself gives to all mankind life and breath and everything. And he made from one man...

1 Cor 10:14-22

Therefore, my beloved, flee from idolatry. *I speak as to sensible people; judge for yourselves what I say. The cup of blessing that we bless, is it not a participation in the blood of Christ? The bread that we break, is it not a participation in the body of Christ? Because there is one bread, we who are many are one body, for we all partake of the one bread. Consider the people of Israel: are not those who eat the sacrifices participants in the altar? What do I imply then? That food offered to idols is anything, or that an idol is anything?* ***No, I imply that what pagans sacrifice they offer to demons and not to God. I do not want you to be participants with demons.*** *You cannot drink the cup of the Lord and the cup of demons. You cannot partake of the table of the Lord and the table of demons. Shall we provoke the Lord to jealousy? Are we stronger than he?*

Col 3:5

Anything that comes ahead of God is an Idol!

Put to death therefore what is earthly in you: sexual immorality, impurity, passion, evil desire, and covetousness, which is idolatry.

Rev 13:4

And they worshiped the dragon, for he had given his authority to the beast, and they worshiped the beast, saying, "Who is like the beast, and who can fight against it?"

II Thes 2:9-12

*The coming of the lawless one is by the activity of Satan with all power and false signs and wonders, and with all wicked deception for those who are perishing, because they refused to love the truth and so be saved. Therefore, God sends them **a strong delusion**, so that they may believe what is false, in order that all may be condemned who did not believe the truth but had pleasure in unrighteousness... 2 Thes 3:**3 But the Lord is faithful**. He will establish you and guard you against the evil one.*

2 Tim 3:1-7

But understand this, that in the last days there will come times of difficulty. [2] For people will be **lovers of self,** lovers of money, proud, arrogant, abusive, disobedient to their parents, ungrateful, unholy, [3] heartless, unappeasable, slanderous, without self-control, brutal, not loving good, [4] treacherous, reckless, swollen with conceit, lovers of pleasure rather than lovers of God, [5] having the appearance of godliness, but denying its power. Avoid such people. [6] For among them are those who creep into households and capture weak women, burdened with sins and led astray by various passions, [7] always learning and never able to arrive at a knowledge of the truth.

In these last days the world has become increasingly evil with internet pornography, pedophilia, political lying, fraud, bribery, treachery, deception, and many other sins. Christians have become increasingly worried and fearful as they see society deteriorating with criminals becoming increasingly violent and lawless while simultaneously subtly encouraged in crime by politicians promoting no bail policy and free drugs etc. Many frustrated Christians have placed there hope in political candidates or political parties. Other place their hope in survivalism with guns, fresh water, food, solar power, and mountain cabins.

Idolatry is a condition of the heart or a place of trust and hope! Our hope must be in Jesus Christ alone, not in men, demons, or man's institutions! In these last days man increasingly depend on government leaders, armaments such as guns, rockets, atomic bombs, technology, political parties, and their own resources to protect them in a very uncertain world.

Tim Keller elaborates: "So Luther says that even after you are converted by the gospel your heart will go back to operating on other principles unless you deliberately, repeatedly set it to gospel-mode."

Idolatry is a condition of the heart or a place of trust and hope! Our hope must be in Jesus Christ alone, not in men, demons, or man's institutions!

The Bible encourages us to examine ourselves regarding our finances, since GREED is one of the most powerful seducing spirits of Satan. Tickets to certain sporting events, Super Bowls, World Series, and various high-end singers may cost more than $2000. It's amazing how much money we can spend on our hobbies such as boating, golf, hunting, Country Club dues etc. We must check our Credit card bills and checkbook to understand what we really worship!

(Malachi 3: 7-12)

Return to me, and I will return to you, says the LORD of hosts. But you say, 'How shall we return?' [8] **Will man rob God?** Yet you are robbing me. But you say, 'How have we robbed you?' In your tithes and contributions. [9] **You are cursed with a curse, for you are robbing me**, the whole nation of you. [10] Bring the full tithe into the storehouse, that there may be food in my house. And thereby put me to the test, says the LORD of hosts, if I will not open the windows of heaven for you and pour down for you a blessing until there is no more need. [11] I will rebuke the devourer for you, so that it will not destroy the fruits of your soil, and your vine in the field shall not fail to bear, says the LORD of hosts. [12] Then all nations will call you blessed, for you will be a land of delight, says the LORD of hosts.

The more uncertain the world becomes we naturally become frightened and vulnerable to deception and can place our hope in spiritual leaders and man's institutions rather than in Jesus Christ and the true promises in scripture. We are to *walk after the Spirit, and not after the flesh*

1 Tim 4:19

For to this end we toil and strive, **because we have our hope set on the living God,** who is the Savior of all people, especially of those who believe.

Hebrews 6:17

So ,when God desired to show more convincingly to the heirs of the promise the unchangeable character of his purpose, he guaranteed it with an oath, [18] so that by two unchangeable things, in which it is impossible for God to lie, we who have fled for refuge might have strong encouragement to hold fast to the hope set before us. [19] **We have this as a sure and steadfast anchor of the soul, a hope that enters into the inner place behind the curtain,** [20] **where Jesus has gone as a forerunner on our behalf, having become a high priest forever after the order of Melchizedek**

"**Hope means more than a vague wish that something will happen. It is a sure and confident expectation in God's future faithfulness and presence**. The horizon of **Christian hope** extends beyond death into an eternity prepared by God himself, the reality of which is guaranteed by Jesus Christ." **God is our hope, not men, nor world leaders, or mans institutions.**

Rom 8:37-39 No, **in all these things we are more than conquerors through him who loved us.** [38] **For I am sure that neither death nor life, nor angels nor rulers, nor things present nor things to come, nor powers,** [39] **nor height nor depth, nor anything else in all creation, will be able to separate us from the love of God in Christ Jesus our Lord.**

Chapter 29
Conclusion

At the conclusion of this book, I now return to my professional role as a practicing physician and diagnostician, researcher, and Clinical Professor of Medicine. I trained in internal medicine, infectious diseases, and pulmonary diseases at Johns Hopkins Hospital and School of Medicine. I have been asked to give my best assessment of what is the final diagnosis of **the illness of the American Church**. There are still some fine, healthy churches in America remaining, which have not fallen ill. However, there are many more that have been infected with a fatal illness but are not aware of their condition. I have carefully listed many of the symptoms of this fatal illness, including greed, lust, covetousness, selfishness, self-righteousness, pride, arrogance, lack of humility, narcissism, deception, and a religious spirit. I have performed a careful examination of the patient and performed appropriate testing. My conclusion is that this is a severe, **near fatal, case of national narcissism or "*Self Pox*"!**

We live in the age of entitlement. This is due to the independent, proud, self-confident, self-reliant, self-focused, narcissistic American Spirit. It is a fatal illness if not treated. The treatment is often very painful, and many have suffered for decades with frequent relapses. The treatment is self-evaluation followed by humility, faith, confession, and repentance. This illness is highly contagious and is epidemic in America. It has already been spread through too much of the world. It is too late to be quarantined. Fortunately, there is a vaccine available. It is the Cross of Christ! We have all eaten of the poisoned fruit of "the tree of knowledge of good and evil." *There is a divine antidote, and it is the blood and cross of Jesus acquired only through humility, faith, and repentance* (Gal 2:20, 5:24, Phil 3:8). Those who return and who are humbled, cling to the message of the cross, repent, and fear God will be protected from this insidious illness. Perhaps then, the Lord will show mercy and bring revival to America.

And now, Church of America, *"What does the LORD your God require of you, but to fear the LORD your God, to walk in all his ways, to love him, to serve the LORD your God with all your heart and with all your soul, and to keep the commandments and statutes of the LORD"?*
(Deuteronomy 10:12)

This book wouldn't be complete without a sober warning to the "Almost a Christian." Hopefully, we can champion again the manifesto of the Reformers: **Sola Fide** (by faith alone); **Sola Gratia** (by grace alone); **Sola Scriptura** (on the Word alone); **Solus Christus** (because of Christ alone); and **Soli Deo Gloria** (to the glory of God alone)? All of us will someday stand before a righteous Holy God who on Judgment Day will say **"I know you or I know you not"** to those who will stand before Him. **There will be no "almost good enough" men and women in heaven. Good people go to Hell, and only sinners go to Heaven.** If you don't know Christ as your only hope and personal savior that has resulted in a radically transformed life *now*, it is unlikely you will find Him much later in life. *Surrender your life to Christ now*, while there is still time. Time is short when compared to an eternity in hell or heaven!

"Enter by the narrow gate; for wide is the gate and broad is the way that leads to destruction, and there are many who go in by it. Because narrow is the gate and difficult is the way which leads to life, and there are few who find it!" (Matt 7:13–14)

THE END

Chapter 30
Further Reading

I recommend to all believers *The Almost Christian Discovered* by Matthew Mead (1629–1699), who was an English Puritan who preached in London in the seventeenth century. *The Almost Christian Discovered* was first printed in 1661 and reprinted in 1989 by Soli Deo Gloria Publications. This book is truly a Christian classic and is recommended to all Christian leaders, particularly those who struggle with the shallowness and flippancy that characterizes today's Christianity. Mead reminds us that as **"many go to heaven by the very gates of hell, so more go to hell by the gates of heaven, and that number those who profess Christ is greater than the number of those who are truly close with Christ."**

I would also recommend: the following books as foundational for understanding the content of each book chapter. I have chosen a collection of older and recent publications. God's truth never changes and often the older tested references offer refreshing clarity. A simple book that perhaps is the best discussion of the difference between Law and Gospel was written in 1585 by

Petrus Dathenus and called *The Pearl of Christian Comfort* and republished by Reformation Heritage Brooks, 1997
The Almost Christian Discovered, by Matthew Mead 1661, Soli Deo Gloria Publications, 1989
Real Christianity, by William Wilberforce 1797, Multnomah Press, 1982
How Saved are We, by Michael L. Brown, Destiny Image Publisher, 1990
Stop Asking Jesus into your Heart, by J. D. Greear, B&H Publishing 2013

The True Believer, The Marks and Benefits of True Faith, by Jonathan Edwards, Soli Deo Gloria Pub 2001.

Concise Theology, by J.I. Packer Tyndale House 1993

Knowing God by J.I. Packer IVP Connect 1975

Things Unseen: A Systematic Introduction to the Christian Faith and Reformed Theology, by J. Gresham Machen, Westminster Seminary Press 1935, 2020

The Heavenly Man, by Brother Yun. Monarch Books, 1988

The Holiness of God, by R.C. Sproul, Tyndale House, 1985

Impossible People: Christian Courage and the Struggle for the Soul of Civilization, by Os Guinness, IVP, 2016

Secrets of the Early Church, by Andrew Strom, 2004

The Sovereignty of God, by A. W. Pink, The Banner of Truth Trust, 1928

The Mystery of Providence, by John Flavel 1678, The Banner of Truth Trust, 1963

The Essentials of the Christian Faith, by R.C. Sproul, Tyndale, 1992

Spiritual Refining, The Anatomy of True and False Conversion, Anthony Burgess,1652, International Outreach Inc., Ames, Iowa, 1996

Desiring God by John Piper, Multnomah 1986

Providence by John Piper, Crossway, 2020

The Justification of God: An Exegetical and Theological Study of Romans 9:1-23 by John Piper, Baker Academic 1993

Evangelism and the Sovereignty of God, by J, I, Packer, InterVarsity Press,1961

Gospel Witness, Defending & Extending the Kingdom of God, by Joseph Boot, Ezra Press, Toronto, 2017

The Gospel According to Jesus: What Is Authentic Faith? by John MacArthur, Zondervan, 1988

The Gospel's Power and Message by Paul Washer. Reformation Heritage Books, 2012

The Christian View of Man, by Gresham Machen, Banner of Truth Trust, 1937

The Merchandising of the Almighty in the American Church, by Dorsett D Smith MD, Vesuvius Press, 2012

Christian Culture, by P. Andrew Sandlin, Center for Cultural Leadership, 2013

Original Sin

No Place for Truth or Whatever Happened to Evangelical Theology, by David F. Wells Eerdmans, 1993
Original Sin, General Defence of that Great Important Doctrine, by Jonathan Edwards, Reformed Church Publications 2009
The Mortification of Sin: Dealing with sin in your life. by John Owen 1656, Christian Focus Publications 2006
Mere Christianity, by C. S. Lewis, New York: McMillian 1943, Eerdmans, 1993.
The Bondage of the Will, By Martin Luther 1537, Fleming H. Revell, 1957
The Freedom of the Will, by Jonathan Edwards 1758, Soli Deo Gloria Pub, 1996
A God Entranced Vision of All Things: The Legacy of Jonathan Edwards, by John Piper (Editor)_Justin Taylor (Editor), Crossway 2004

What about the Blood?
Covenant Theology

Introducing Covenant Theology by Michael Horton, Baker Books 2009
Kingdom Through Covenant by Peter J. Gentry and Stephen J. Wellum, Crossway 2012
The Christ of the Covenants by O. Palmer Robertson, Presbyterian and Reformed Publishing 1980
Covenants Made Simple, by Jonty Rhodes, P&R Publishing 2013

Self-Righteousness

Preaching the Cross, by Mark Dever and several others, Crossway Books, 2007.
The Cross of Christ, by John W. Stott, IVP Books 1986, 2006.
The Cross, by Martyn Lloyd-Jones, Crossway, 1986
The Religious Affections, by Jonathan Edwards, Banner of Truth Trust, 1746, 1961
Grace Abounding to the Chief of Sinners, by John Bunyan 1666

Biblical Conversion

Mere Christianity, by C. S. Lewis, New York: McMillian 1943, 1972

The True Believer by Jonathan Edwards, Soli Deo Gloria Publications 2001

Pilgrims Progress, by John Bunyan, Brown Chair Books 1678, 2020

Regeneration, by J.C. Ryle, Christian Heritage, 2003

What the Bible Teaches about Being Born Again, by Gary Brady, Evangelical Press, 2008

The Puritans on Conversion, by Samuel Bolton, Nathaniel Vincent, Thomas Watson, Soli Deo Gloria, 1990

Out of the Depths, Restoring Fellowship with God, by D. Martyn Lloyd-Jones, Crossway Books, 1995.

Not a Fan, by Kyle Ideleman, Zondervan 2011.

God in the Whirlwind, by David F. Wells, Crossway, 2014.

Christianity and Liberalism, by J. Gresham Machen Eerdmans 1923, reprinted 1994.

Impossible People: Christian Courage and the Struggle for the Soul of Civilization, Os Guinness IVP 2016.

Spiritual Refining: The Anatomy of True and False Conversion, by Anthony Burgess 1652, International Outreach, 1996

God Centered Evangelism, by R. B. Kuiper, The Banner of Truth Trust, 1966

Today's Evangelism, by Ernest C. Reisinger, Craig Press, 1982

The Gospel Driven Life, by Michael Horton, Baker Books, 2009

The Religious Affections, by Jonathan Edwards, Banner of Truth Trust, 1746, 1961

The Normal Christian Life, by Watchman Nee, Tyndale House,1957

The Mystery of Providence, by John Flavel, Banner of Truth, 1678, 1963

Puritan Theology, by Michael Horton, Zondervan, 2011

What is the Gospel? By Greg Gilbert, Crossway 2010

It Will Cost You Everything, by Steven J. Lawson, Christian Focus 2021

Repentance

Repentance: The First Word of the Gospel, by Richard Owen Roberts, Crossway Books, 2002.

The Doctrine of Repentance, by Thomas Watson 1668, (Puritan Paperbacks) The Banner of Truth Trust, 1988.

Repent or Perish, by John Gerstner. Soli Deo Gloria, 1990

Repentance, Its Nature, Necessity, and Encouragement. J C Ryle 1878

True Repentance, by Thomas Boston (1676 -1732), Vintage Puritan Series 1849

Pride

The *Merchandising of the Almighty in the American Church, by* Dorsett Smith MD, Vesuvius Press, 2012.

The Cost of Discipleship, by Dietrich Bonhoeffer, Simon and Shuster, New York, 1959.

A Practical View of Christianity, by William Wilberforce, 1797, Hendrickson Publishers, 1996

Bondservice and Submission

Christless Christianity, by Michael Horton, Baker Books ,2008.

The Great Divorce, by C. S. Lewis, New York: HarperOne, 2015.

The Bondage of the Will, by Martin Luther 1521, Fleming H. Revell, 1957

The Freedom of the Will, by Jonathan Edwards 1758, Soli Deo Gloria Pub, 1996

Postmodernism and Personal Freedom

Christianity and Liberalism, by J. Gresham Machen Eerdmans 1923, reprinted Eerdmans,1997

The Arrogance of the Modern, by David Hall, The Calvin Institute, 1997

Dining with the Devil, The Megachurch Movement Flirts with Modernity, by Os Guinness, Baker Books, 1993.

God in the Whirlwind, by David F. Wells, Crossway 2014.

The Great Evangelical Disaster, by Francis A. Schaeffer, Crossway 1984

Above All Earthly Powers, Christ in a Postmodern World, by David F. Wells, Eerdmans, 2005.

Predators in Our Pulpits, by Phillip Keller, Harvest House Publishers, 1988.

Christ and Culture, by D.A. Carson, Eerdmans, 2008

A Christian Manifesto, by Francis A. Schaeffer, Crossway 1981

The Best of A.W. Tozer, Baker Books, 1978

The Crook in the Lot, by Thomas Boston, Banner of Truth, 1737, 2017

No Reason to Hide /Standing for Christ in a collapsing culture, by Erwin W. Lutzer, Harvest House 2022

The Rise and Triumph of the Modern Self, by Carl R. Truman, Crossway 2020

Live not by Lies: A Manual for Christian Dissident, by Rod Dreher, Sentinel 2022

Nineteen Eighty-Four, by George Orwell, Signet Classics 1949, 1977

Brave New World Revisited by Aldous Huxley, Bantam Book 1958

Failed Church, Restoring Vision of Ecclesial Victory, P. Andrew Sandlin Editor, Center for Cultural Leadership 2022

Entitlement Mentality

A Practical View of Christianity, by William Wilberforce 1797, Hendrickson, 1996

The First Will be Last, A Biblical Perspective on Narcissism, D.C. Robertson, Davidson Trust Publishing, 2020

The Rare Jewel of Christian Contentment, by Jeremiah Burroughs 1648, Banner of Truth Trust, 1979

The Narcissism Epidemic, Living in the age of Entitlement by Jean Twenge PhD and W. Keith Campbell PhD, Atria Paperback, 2009

Waiting *For Heaven: Freedom from the Incurable Addiction to Self,* by Larry Crabb, Larger Story Press 2020

The Gnostic Empire Strikes Back, by Peter Jones, P&R Publishing 1992

No Reason to Hide by Erwin W, Lutzer, Harvest House 2022

The Rise and Triumph of the Modern Self, by Carl R. Truman, Crossway 2020

Live not by Lies: A Manual for Christian Dissident, by Rod Dreher, Sentinel 2020

Confession and Contrition

The Bruised Reed, by Richard Sibbes 1630, The Banner of Truth
Trust 2011.
Christianity: The True Humanism, by J. I. Packer and Thomas
Howard, Word Books 1985

The Holy Spirit

The Person and Work of the Holy Spirit, by Benjamin B. Warfield,
Solid Ground Christian Books, 2010
The Holy Spirit, by Sinclair B. Ferguson, IVP 1996
Rediscovering the Holy Spirit, by Michael Horton, Zondervan 2017
The Doctrine of the Holy Spirit, by H, Berkhof, Epworth 1965
The Work of the Holy Spirit, by Abraham Kuyper, Funk &
Wagnalls 1900
Growing in God's Spirit, by Jonathan Edwards 1733, P&R
Publishing 2003
The Release of the Spirit, by Watchman Nee, Sure Foundation 1965
The Charismatic Gifts in the Early Church by Ronald A. N. Kydd,
Hendrickson 2014
What the Bible says about the Holy Spirit by Stanley M. Horton,
Gospel Publishing House 2005
The Doctrine of the Holy Spirit by George Smeaton, The Banner of
Truth Trust 1882, 1974

The Holy Spirit as Revealer of Mystery (The Trinity)

Delighting in the Trinity, by Michael Reeves, IVP Academic, 2012
Delighting in the Trinity, by Tim Chester, The Good Book, 2005
The Trinitarian Devotion of John Owen, by Sinclair Ferguson,
Reformation Trust, 2014
The Forgotten Trinity, by James R. White, Bethany House, 1998
The Holy Trinity, by Robert Letham, R&R Pub, 2004
The Mysteries of Christianity, by T.J. Crawford, Banner of Truth
Trust 1874

Gifts of the Spirit

Showing the Spirit, by D. A. Carson, Baker Books 1987
Preaching and Preachers, by Martyn Lloyd Jones, Hodder & Stroughton 1972
The Art of Prophesying by William Perkins 1592, The Banner of Truth Trust, 1996
Revival God's Way, by Leonard Ravenhill, Bethany House, 1983
Revival & Revivalism, Ian H. Murray, The Banner of Truth Trust, 1994
Pentecost-Today? By Ian H. Murray, The Banner of Truth Trust, 1998
True and False Revival, By Andrew Strom, Revival School, 2008
The Latent Power of the Soul, by Watchman Nee, Christian Fellowship Publishers, 1972
War on the Saints, by Jessie Penn Lewis, Thomas E. Lowe LTD. New York, 1973

The Holy Spirit as Healer

Healing and Spiritual Abuse, by Ken Blue, IVP, 1993
Forgiveness, by John MacArthur, Crossway,1998
Forgive by Timothy Keller, Viking 2022
Healing, by Francis MacNutt, Ava Maria Press 1974, revised 1999
Deliverance from Evil Spirits, by Francis MacNutt, Chosen Books ,1995
Blessing or Curse, by Derek Prince, Chosen Books,1990
Healing and the Scriptures, by D. Martin Lloyd-Jones, Thomas Nelson, 1982
A Theology of Christian Counseling, Jay E. Adams, Zondervan, 1979
Biblical Eldership, by Alexander Strauch, Lewis and Roth, 1995
The Torch of the Testimony, by John Kennedy, Christian Books 1965

Listen and Obey

The Mystery of Providence, by John Flavel 1678, Puritan Paperbacks, Banner of Truth Trust,1963
Absolute Surrender, by Andrew Murray, Bridge-Logos, 2005
What Shall This Man Do? by Watchman Nee, Tyndale, 1981

Love of God

The Love of God, by Martyn Lloyd Jones, Crossway, 1994
How can a God of Love Send People to Hell? By John Benton,
Evangelical Press, 1985
Love Not the World, By Watchman Nee, Tyndale House, 1968
The Four Loves, by C.S. Lewis, Harcourt, 1960
The Puritans on Loving One Another, Edited by Don Kistler, Soli
Deo Gloria, 1997
Charity and its Fruits, by Jonathan Edwards, 1738, The Banner of
Truth Trust,1969

The Wrath of God

The Wrath of Almighty God by Jonathan Edwards, Soli Deo Gloria
Pub, 1996
But What About God's Wrath? The Compelling Love Story of
Divine Anger, by Kevin Kinghorn and Stephen Travis, IVP 2019

Suffering and Persecution

Suffering & Sovereignty, by Brian H. Crosby, Reformation
Heritage Books, 2012
Suffering and the Sovereignty of God, by John Piper and Justin
Taylor, Crossway, 2006
The Bruised Reed, by Richard Sibbes, The Banner of Truth Trust
1630, 2011.
*In the Shadow of the Cross, A Biblical theology of persecution &
Discipleship,* by Glenn M. Penner, Living Sacrifice Books, 2004
Tortured for Christ, by Richard Wurmbrand, David C. Cook, 1967
Live not by Lies, A Manual for Christen Dissidents by Rod Dreher,
Sentinel 2020

The Afterlife

Fear Not, Death and the Afterlife from a Christian Perspective, by
Ligon Duncan, Christian Focus, 2008.
The Resurrection of the Dead, by William Milligan, Edinburgh
1894, Forgotten Books, 2015.

The *Resurrection of the Dead and Eternal Judgment,* John Bunyan 1688, Scriptura Press, New York, 2015.

Heaven, by Randy Alcorn, Wheaton: Tyndale, 2004.

Heaven and Hell, By Edward Donnelly, Banner of Truth, 2001

The Fear of Hell, Restrains Men from Sin, by Solomon Stoddard, Soli Deo Gloria, *1713*

Journey to Hell, by John Bunyan, (1671?) Whitaker House 1999

Situational Eschatology

Triumph of the Lamb, A Commentary on the Book of Revelation, by Dennis E. Johnson, P&R Publishing, 2001.

The Last Days According to Jesus, by R.C. Sproul, Baker Books, 1998.

Before Jerusalem Fell, by Kenneth L. Gentry, American Vision, 1998.

The Book of Revelation Made Easy, by Kenneth L. Gentry Jr., American Vision, 2008

Four Views on the Book of Revelation, by Kenneth L. Gentry, Sam Hamstra, C. Marvin Pate, Robert L. Thomas, Zondervan, 1998

These Last Days, A Christian View of History Alistair Begg, D.A. Carson et al., Edited by Richard Phillips, Gabriel N.E. Fluhrer P&R Publishing 2011

Three Views on the Millennium and Beyond, by Darrell L. Bock ed, Zondervan,1999

Wrongly Dividing the Word of Truth, by John H. Gerstner, Soli Deo Gloria, 1991

The Apocalypse Code, by Hank Hanegraaff, Thomas Nelson, 2007

The Apocalypse Conspiracy, by John Noe, Wolgemuth & Hyatt, 1991

Kingdom Come, The Amillennial Alternative, by Sam Storms, Mentor 2013

A Case for Amillenniasm, Understanding the End Times, Kim Riddlebarger, Baker Books 2003

Christian Liberty

The Arrogance of the Modern, by David Hall, The Calvin Institute 1997.

Christless Christianity, by Michael Horton, Baker Books, 2008.

The Fear of God

The Fear of the Lord, by John Bevere, Charisma House, 1997
The Fear of the Lord, by John Bunyan, Updated 1679, Good News Publishers, 2016
The Joy of Fearing God, by Jerry Bridges, Waterbrook, 1997
The Wrath of Almighty God, by Jonathan Edwards Soli Deo Gloria Publications 1996
Recovering Our Sanity, How the fear of God Conquers the Fears that Divide us, by Michael Horton, Zondervan 2022

For those who desire a deeper systematic approach to Christian Theology I recommend:

Anselm of Canterbury, (1033-1109), The Major Works, Ed. Brian Davies and G.R. Evans, Oxford Univ. Press,1998
Systematic Theology: An introduction to Bible Doctrine, by Wayne Grudem, IVP Press,1994, 2020
Systematic Theology, by Charles Hodge, 3 volumes, Wm. B. Eerdmans, 1995
Systematic Theology, by Robert Letham, Crossway, 2019
Systematic Theology, by Louis Berkhof, Wm. B. Eerdmans, 1941
A Summary of Christian Doctrine, by Louis Berkhof, Wm. B. Eerdmans, 1938
The Christian Faith a Systematic Theology for Pilgrims on the Way, by Michael Horton, Zondervan, 2011
Pilgrim Theology, by Michael Horton, Zondervan 2011
Evidence That Demands a Verdict by Josh McDowell and Sean McDowell, HarperCollins 2017
Grace Defined and Defended by Kevin DeYoung, Crossway 2019
Biblical Theology, by John Owen, Soli Deo Gloria, 1661, 1996
Institutes of Elenctic Theology, by Francis Turretin, (3 Volumes) 1679–1685, P&R Publishing, 1992.
History of Western Philosophy and Theology, by John M. Frame, P&R Press, 2015,
Christianity for Modern Pagans-"Pascal's Pensees"- by Peter Kreeft,

Ignatius Press, San Francisco, 1993

Institutes of the Christian Religion, by John Calvin, Pantianos Classics, Pub in Latin then French 1539, and translated into English 1581, 2017

Calvin's Commentaries by John Calvin, (23 volumes), Baker Books, 2009

What Luther Says, a Practical In-Home Anthology for the Active Christian, Concordia Publishing House, St Louis, MO. 1959

Mere Christianity, by C.S. Lewis, Harper Collins New York, 1952

Christianity and Liberalism, by J. Gresham Machen, Eerdmans, Grand Rapids, 1923

The Cost of Discipleship, by Dietrich Bonhoeffer, Simon and Schuster, New York, 1937

Evangelism and the Sovereignty of God, by J.I. Packer InterVarsity Press, Downers Grove, Illinois, 1961

The Reformed Pastor, by Richard Baxter, Banner of Truth Trust, 1656, 1974

The Pearl of Christian Comfort by Petrus Dathenus 1585, Reformation Heritage Brooks, 1997

Christless Christianity, by Michael Horton, Baker Books Grand Rapids, 2008

The Theology of Augustine, by Matthew Levering, Baker Academic, 2013

Matthew Henry's Commentary, by Matthew Henry, who died 1714, (6 volumes) Hendrickson, Published 1828 & 1991

Truths we Confess, a Systematic Exposition of the Westminster Confession of Faith by R.C. Sproul, Reformation Trust, 2019

What is Reformed Theology, by R.C. Sproul, Baker Books 1997

The Valley of Vision, A Collection of Puritan Prayers and Devotions, Arthur Bennett Editor, Banner of Truth Trust, 1975

Above All Earthly Power, by David F. Wells, Wm. B. Eerdmans, 2005

Practical Christianity, by Arthur W. Pink, Baker Books 1974

The Westminster Confession A Commentary by A.A. Hodge, The Banner of Truth Trust 1869, 2002

We Believe; Creeds, Catechisms, and Confessions of Faith, from Apostles Creed (Second Century) to Second London Baptist Confession of Faith (1689), Ligonier Ministries 2023